WEEKE...
CITIES

Short breaks in 8 popular European cities

WEEKEND CITIES

Short breaks in 8 popular European cities

James Bentley

GEORGE
PHILIP

This book is copyrighted under the Berne
Convention. All rights reserved. Apart from any fair
dealing for the purpose of private study, research,
criticism or review, as permitted under the Copyright
Act, 1956, no part of this publication may be
reproduced, stored in a retrieval system, or
transmitted in any form or by any means, electronic,
electrical, chemical, mechanical, optical, photocopying,
recording, or otherwise, without prior written
permission. All enquiries should be addressed to the
Publishers.

British Library Cataloguing in Publication Data
Bentley, James, *1937–*
  Weekend cities.
  1. Cities and towns—Europe   2. Europe—
  Description and travel—1971– —Guide-
  books
  I. Title
  914'.04558   D909
ISBN 0–540–01167–3

Text © James Bentley 1988
Maps © George Philip 1988

First published by George Philip,
27A Floral Street, London WC2E 9DP

Maps by John Gilkes
Line drawings by Julia Bikham
Typeset by Tameside Filmsetting Limited
Lancashire
Printed in Great Britain by
Butler and Tanner Ltd, Frome and London

Contents

Acknowledgements

I would like to thank the following for their invaluable contribution to this book:

I could not have written my chapter on Amsterdam without the help of Mr Marcel Baltus, Press and PR Officer of the Netherlands Board of Tourism, 25–28 Buckingham Gate, London SW1E 6LD (tel. 01-630 0451), Mrs Els Wamsteeker, PR co-ordinator of VVV Amsterdam Tourist Office, Rokin 9-15, 1012 KK Amsterdam, and the manager and staff of the Amsterdam Ascot Hotel.

For help with my chapter on Barcelona I am grateful to Mrs Paloma Notario and Gill Mindham, respectively Deputy Director and PR Director of the Spanish National Tourist Office, 57 St. James's Street, London SW1A 1LD (tel. 01-499 0901/6).

In Berlin I was given much help by my friend Frau Sabine Zerzau (even to the extent of being offered warm water to bathe my blistered feet), and I must also here much thank Mrs Marion Rowlands-Hempel of the German travel specialists GTF Tours, 182–186 Kensington Church Street, London W8 (tel. 01-229 2474), as well as Mr Bernhard Heidemann, Deputy Director of the German National Tourist Office, 61 Conduit Street, London W1R 0EN (tel. 01-734 5853).

In writing about Florence I was greatly helped by the management and staff of the Hotel Kraft, Florence; by Jennie Paton of The Magic of Italy, 47 Shepherds Bush Green, London W12 8PS (tel. 01-743 9900) and by The Magic of Italy's representative in Florence, Margriet Wassing. In addition I was given much useful advice and help by Mrs Pauline Young, PR Director of *Citalia*, Marco Polo House, 3/5 Landsdowne Road, Croydon, CR9 1LL (tel. 01-686 5533), and by Signora Federica Bellici, Press Officer of the Italian National Tourist Office at no. 1 Princes Street, London W1R 8AY (tel. 01-408 1254).

I would like to express my thanks here for the help I was given by Mrs Pauline Hallam of the French government tourist office in

Acknowledgements

London, and by the staff of the Bibliothèque of the Institut Français du Royaume-Uni, Queensbury Place, London SW7 2DT.

My work on Vienna was considerably eased by the kindness of Miss Audrey Chessell, PR Director of Austrian Airlines in London, and by the ever-available generosity of Herr Karl-Heinz and Frau Inge Bensberg.

Finally I must thank the editor of this book, Lydia Greeves, who suggested that I write it and then persistently and patiently improved it.

Introduction

What do you do on a weekend in one of the world's great cities?

Some people find themselves spending a weekend in one by accident, on the way somewhere else, but more and more of us are simply taking time off, and flying abroad for an inexpensive short break. The question is how to spend your time when you get to your destination, and what to select from all the sights on offer.

My eight weekend cities are Amsterdam, Barcelona, Berlin, Florence, London, Paris, Venice and Vienna. Each has a peculiar charm and flavour of its own. Whereas London seems to turn its back on its great river to entice you into its mysterious alleyways, Paris insists that you stroll along the Seine and admire the way its heart is an island. Florence too nestles around the Arno; but its chief attraction is its cultural richness. Vienna, equally ancient, reeks of decadence, baroque decadence and *fin de siècle* decadence, both irresistible. Berlin speaks to me about the tragedy of an overweening will for power, of its own downfall, and of a city rising from ashes. As for Venice, for me the city combines serenity with hints of the sophisticated wickedness which Thomas Mann perceived over eighty years ago. By contrast the wickedness of Amsterdam, though real enough, is more superficial; Amsterdam is essentially Dutch commerce combined with the Dutch genius for having your cake and eating it. And Barcelona is wildly, insanely creative, above all in the architecture of the crazed and irreplaceable Antonio Gaudí.

People tend to throng to these cities when they are packed with other tourists. My advice is to go out of season. No one who has been in Venice in winter, when the skies are clear and the air is fresh, would want to experience again the humidity and heat of July and August.

This book is aimed to help anyone with two or three days in one of these cities, but I think even those who are staying for a week or more will find it helpful. First I try to sum up what to me is the essence of the city. And then I suggest a tour, on foot (with occasional lifts by public transport), to savour the major sights – the cathedrals, the sumptuous palaces, the back streets and medieval enclaves, the markets, the great parks. In every city except London and Paris these tours begin and end in the same place. I do not necessarily expect you to walk them at one go though you could do so in a day. You can hop on and off a tour at will. I have walked them all until I was weary, yet always they delighted me anew.

No walking tour can include every superb feature of a great city. Because of this, after each tour I have added a section of 'Further delights'. Do I think each item is a 'must'? I am glad to know them all. But you can choose according to your needs. In Barcelona, for example, no one accepting my recommendations would miss the Sagrada Familia. But if you take children you might prefer to spend a whole afternoon at the fun-fair on Montjuïc.

Some weekenders may like to leave the bustle and noise for a time. One of the pleasures of visiting the cities in this book is that you can use them as a base for an excursion to places outside – royal palaces, unspoilt villages, exquisite resorts and ancient castles. For each I have suggested a day's outing, by train or by hired car (if you are planning to hire a car, it is wise to carry an international driving licence).

And of course you must eat. In all my years of travelling and writing about travel I have never ceased to marvel that the moment you cross a border you cross a culinary divide. Parisian food and Viennese food could not be more different, even though Parisian chefs have always thrived in Vienna. Even Florence and Venice offer different Italian delights. If the food differs, the wine varies even more. My 'Food and drink' section tells you what to expect.

What do you do at night? Theatre, casinos, cabarets, ballet, flamenco dancers and floor shows are on hand in every major city – but in variable degrees. My sections on 'Night life' try to deal with the variety.

Lastly, the second time I ever reached Italy, I arrived on 15 August. Every bank was closed for three days. I had not a single lira in my pockets. My hope is that after reading this book no one will be found in the same predicament, for I offer much information (essential information) on banking hours, as well as on transport and on when everything will close for a public holiday, oblivious to the needs of the weekend tourist.

Amsterdam

*The shops richly furnished and from their neatness, and the
brightness of the window-panes, not to mention the propriety of the
figures within, in many respects surpassing most in London, and far
those of every other city, not excepting Paris. The Dutch, by planting
trees wherever water ran, have given a cheerful charm to a Morass.
Canals they love to a madness — they make them where they don't find
them — along the side of every road — round every villa — every one
has a canal of his own and builds as near the public canal as he can.*

Samuel Rogers, 1815

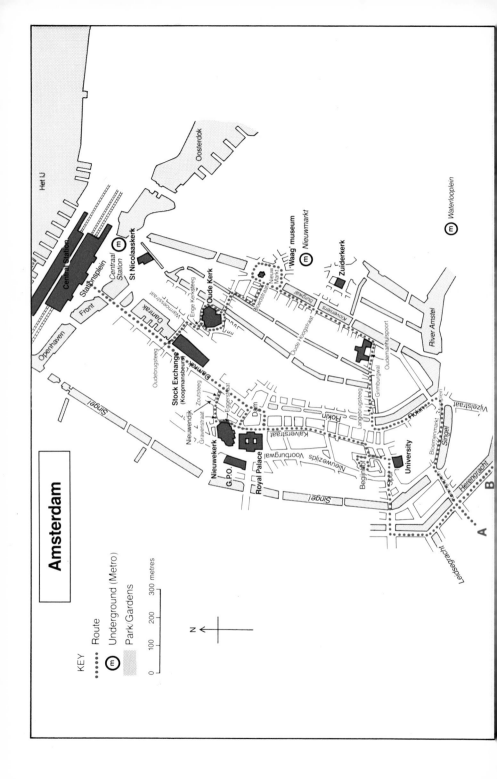

Amsterdam

KEY

●●● Route

Ⓜ Underground (Metro)

Park/Gardens

0   100   200   300 metres

N

Het IJ

Openhaven

Central Station

Stationsplein

Front

Centraal Station

Ⓜ

St Nicolaaskerk

Oosterdok

Damrak

Warmoesstraat

Enge Kerksteg

Oude Kerk

Oudebrugsteeg

Stock Exchange
(Koopmansbeurs)

Damrak

Koopmansbeurs

Zoutsteeg

Eggertstraat

Gravenstraat

Nieuwendijk

Singel

Nieuwekerk

G.P.O.

Royal Palace

Dam

Kalverstraat

Voorburgwal

Nieuwezijds

Singel

Nieuw
Markt

Bloedstraat

Ⓜ Nieuwmarkt

Waag museum

Zuiderkerk

Warmoesstraat

Oude Hoogstraat

Oudezijds

Kloveniers

burgwal

Oudemanhuispoort

Grimburgwal

Langebrugsteeg

Rokin

Rokin

River Amstel

Vijzelstraat

Bloemenmarkt

Singel

University

Spui

Begijnhof

Herengracht

Ⓜ Waterlooplein

A

B

Leidsegracht

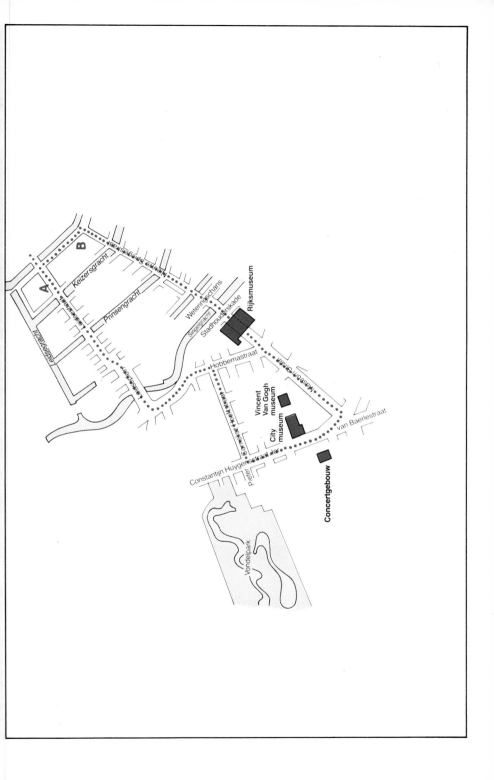

Samuel Rogers wrote of his delight in the city of Amsterdam in his journal for 28 April 1815. The Dutch still love their canals, crossed by some 1280 bridges, and so does every visitor. The shops of Amsterdam are still elegant, sometimes expensive and always beautifully set out. The city's cheerful charm is spontaneous. As the novelist Nicolas Freeling, creator of the Dutch detective Van der Valk, has written, 'I know of no city where the outsider can so spontaneously be taken to heart.' Although he concedes that the Dutch are a commercial and business-like people, Freeling rightly insists that none the less 'Amsterdammers remain open, of a southern quickness and warmth'.

The city of Amsterdam is famed for its tolerance, spiritual, intellectual and moral. In the past it welcomed persecuted Jews and French Huguenots, both of whom enriched it artistically and intellectually; but today this tolerance has its price. Drug addicts and drop-outs profit from the spirit of live-and-let-live, as well as those who might legitimately feel persecuted elsewhere.

In the seventeenth century the great French philosopher René Descartes spent about twenty years living in Holland, and he wrote his *Principles of Philosophy* and his *Passions of the Soul* in an Amsterdam already known for its willingness to accept and tolerate new, perhaps provocative ideas. 'Where else could one enjoy such complete liberty, and sleep at nights without the slightest anxiety!' Descartes exclaimed. I accept the first half of his eulogy but not the second. In Amsterdam you should, for example, certainly sleep anxiously unless your car is safely locked away in a garage. Otherwise some vandal is likely to break off a windscreen-wiper or break in to steal the car radio. Yet this obverse side of the city's famed openness and tolerance is a price that Amsterdammers are willing to pay.

They live in an entrancingly unique city. In 1270 or so, settlers dammed the River Amstel to protect their homes from flooding and so the place became known as Amstel Dam. Their successors built more and more dams and dug more and more canals. Since then Amsterdam has developed into the city we know today, with 575,000 bicycles, a royal palace, around 1500 cafés, a floating flower market, hundreds of ducks, several public parks, 700,000 inhabitants and 7 million happy tourists a year. It is the city of Rembrandt and Van Gogh, a place of high gabled houses, of narrow streets, of canal boats gliding under elegant bridges, of 'brown' bars (so-called because of their characteristic colour, a legacy of the smoke from countless cigars, pipes and cigarettes), Indonesian food and fine beers.

A city tour

The tour begins and ends at Amsterdam's splendid gothic central station, which you could easily mistake for the city's famous Rijksmuseum, since both were designed by Pieter Cuypers in the nineteenth century. Finished in 1889, the station is covered with carvings representing trade, navigation, Amsterdam's history and the brotherhood of man. The Japanese were so impressed by it that they copied the design for their own main station in Tokyo.

Built on three islands, Amsterdam central station is virtually surrounded by water, to the north-east a harbour packed with craft, to the south-west canal boats offering trips on the city waters. A wide bridge on this side leads to the glamorous, bustling Damrak, which a century ago was not a street at all but part of the River Amstel. To the left is the triple-domed Catholic church of St Nicholas, built in 1875. The Dutch helped to invent Father Christmas, taking him to New Amsterdam, now New York, as 'Sinter Claes' (from where the lore spread to the rest of the USA and then back to Europe). Fittingly, on the third Sunday in November this patron saint of sailors and children — as well as pawnbrokers — is honoured in a pageant centred on this church. St Nicholas arrives here by sea, as if from Spain, accompanied by his black servant (a Moor), and then tours the city on a white horse.

Further on along Damrak on the left is another architectural symbol of a Dutch tradition — this time a reminder of their business acumen. The avant-garde design of the remarkable Stock Exchange, built by Hendrik Pieter Berlage between 1899 and 1903, caused considerable controversy in his day.

Damrak is packed with details illustrating the playfulness of the Dutch. On the other side of the street from the Stock Exchange stands a delightful office block on which 4 baboons and 24 owls are carved, the work of the sculptor J. Mendes da Costa in 1905. He also decorated this façade with improving women, representing vigilance (she walks with a dog), the vicissitudes of life (note her hourglass and chameleon), womanly wisdom subduing evil, thrift (she carries a money box) and 'the love that protects'. A wheel of fortune crowns the entrance, topped by a bronze widow. The sculptures were paid for as an advertisement by the life assurance company that once owned the building!

Amsterdammers love sculpture, and this fashionable street of shops and bars, hotels and boutiques, bureaux de change and travel agents excellently displays the fact. Near the life assurance office block is the statue of a man with a newspaper. In this city of businessmen he is naturally carrying the Dutch Financial Times, which gave the statue to the city. He is known as the 'little Stock Exchange man' ('t Beursmannetje), and was sculpted by Pieter d'Hont in 1966. The fine art nouveau (Jugendstil) shop at nos.37/38 was put up in 1903. Decorated with Mercury on the Damrak façade, there are monkeys breaking open a coconut round the corner.

Across the stock exchange square (which is graced by Nic Jonk's 1977 sculpture Jonah and the Whale) is Amsterdam's largest department store, the Bijenkorf. Inside it is very spacious and extremely well-ordered, boasting a fine bookshop and a restaurant, as well as virtually everything else a person needs. And beyond the Bijenkorf is the city's most celebrated square: the massive, extremely lively Dam. Flanked by the royal palace and the New Church, and containing Holland's national monument to the dead of World War II, this was once Amsterdam's market-place.

The young sit happily drinking and hugging each other and smoking heaven know's what around the steps of this 22-metre obelisk, with its aggressive male figures representing war, suffering and resistance (the work of J. J. Oud and John Rädecker). A woman holding a child while a dove flutters above is sculpted in the middle of the obelisk, all three symbolizing peace. The monument also incorporates twelve urns containing earth from the eleven Dutch regions and from the former Dutch colony, Indonesia.

Opposite stands the monumental Dutch royal palace, built as

Amsterdam's town hall between 1648 and 1655. Jacob van Campen designed it, and 13,659 piles had to be sunk into the swampy ground to provide adequate foundations. Then Artus Quellijn the Younger decorated the palace with sculptures glorifying Amsterdam. Curiously enough, one of these statues, called *Peace striding ahead* (she carries an olive branch and Mercury's staff), looks directly across the Dam at Rädecker's woman of peace. Above these sculptures is an octagonal tower topped by a graceful cupola.

Napoleon Bonaparte's brother Louis transformed this town hall into his palace when he was created King of Holland in 1808. On his abdication two years later he left a splendid collection of Empire style furniture, and the palace was also sumptuously decorated by some of Rembrandt's pupils. (There is a 1-hour guided tour of the palace every day, except Saturdays, from 10.00 to 12.00 and 13.00 to 16.00 during the months of July and August.)

On the right of the royal palace is Amsterdam's flamboyant gothic new church – described as 'new' because the 'old' church was already 200 years old when the 'new' was built in the fifteenth century. Its steeple was added 450 years later.

If you want to enjoy just one of Amsterdam's fine churches, try this one. The new church was built in the place of one razed by a disastrous fire in 1452 which destroyed two-thirds of Amsterdam. The superb treasures inside include a late seventeenth-century organ case by Jacob van Campen, lovely baroque carvings, and the tombs of great Dutch heroes. The most famous tomb is that designed by Rombout Verhulst for Admiral de Ruyter, who died in 1679 and lies beside the high altar.

The church pulpit is stunning, with six carved angels and another six statues representing perseverance, hope, love, faith, justice and truth. As if this were not enough, the pulpit also bears the carved figures of mercy and the four evangelists. This astounding pulpit, which Albert Vinckenbrinck took thirteen years to create, finishing it in 1649, is borne by a pillar which itself is embellished by splendid woodcarvings of the Last Judgment and of Jesus's parables of the talents and the wise and foolish virgins.

The aisles and fourteen chapels of the church are lit by seventy-five gleaming windows. The finest of these, in the north transept, is also the oldest, made by Johannes Gerritz Bronkhorst in 1650. You can visit Amsterdam's new church from Tuesday to Saturday from 11.00 to 16.00 and on Sundays from 12.00 to 15.00.

Vying with both the royal palace and the new church, across the Nieuwe zijds Voorburgwal, stands Amsterdam's main post and telegraph office. This utterly arrogant example of nineteenth-century confidence was built in the Dutch renaissance style and nicknamed the 'Perenburg' by Amsterdammers because of its pear-shaped towers.

Leave the Dam by Eggerstraat which leads round the east end of the new church. Among other shops, the church shelters the two smallest in Amsterdam (scarcely 8 metres square). Here, a few metres from imposing Dam square, is Amsterdam at its most intimate, a complete and charming antithesis. Turn right into Gravenstraat to enjoy one of the city's tiny alleyways, crammed with fascinating shops and 'brown' bars. No.18, for instance, is a typical old Dutch pub, The Three Little Bottles (*De Drie Fleschjes*), with a seventeenth-century interior; no.15 is The Three Little Counts (*Die Drie Graefjes*); no.4 is The Three Candles (*De Drie Kaarsjes*), with three candles alight inside; no.2 is the café *De Wenteltrap*, a cooking pot surmounting its gothic signpost. Cross Nieuwendijk into Zoutsteeg. Today it houses shops and little restaurants, but when the Damrak was a river, this was the quay where ships unloaded salt (*zout* in Dutch, hence the name Zoutsteeg).

Zoutsteeg leads back into Damrak. Walk right across the Dam and into Holland's most flourishing and packed shopping street, the pedestrianized Kalverstraat. In the Middle Ages this was a cattle market (hence its name, Calves' Street). Cattle have been replaced by the most elegant shops, as well as sex establishments and restaurants. At no.156 is a wax museum (Madame Tussauds, open daily from 10.00 to 18.00, staying open till 20.00 in July and August). More fascinating than the wax museum is Amsterdam's first orphanage (now the city's historical museum), designed by Aldo van Eyck in 1581. Its entrance is at no.92 Kalverstraat, and in the courtyard you can see little cubicles let into the walls where the orphans stored their few tools on their days off.

The famous Begijnhof off Kalverstraat to the right is a complete contrast, a sudden oasis of peace and tranquillity. The deliciously quiet square is surrounded by houses dating from the fifteenth and sixteenth centuries, though their façades frequently date from the seventeenth. No.34, the oldest house in Amsterdam, happily retains its plain, clapperboard fourteenth-century façade (and a gable of 1475). Since 1346 Begijnhof has been the home of pious women (and fishermen's widows), devoted to teaching and good works. Today it is still lived in by women – elderly citizens of Amsterdam.

The so-called 'English' church here was built in 1392 and given for the use of English Presbyterians in 1607. Here the Pilgrim Fathers would worship before setting off for the New World. In 1665 it was enlarged, and restored in 1975. Over the pulpit is written 'Make me a clean heart, O God.' The elaborate Catholic chapel of 1665 opposite is a direct contrast to its spartan beauty. Once Catholicism was officially proscribed in Holland, but even then the city was tolerant, turning a blind eye to the law and allowing Catholics to worship clandestinely, as they did here. Inside, a stained-glass window depicts a turning-point in Amsterdam's history, the moment when a wafer of the Holy Communion, which a sick man had failed to swallow, was thrown on the fire and failed to burn. The miraculous wafer was preserved, bringing countless pilgrims to adore it and (as tourists) to enrich the chrysalis city.

In spite of this tolerance, religious passion could occasionally run high. One devout member of the Begijnhof named Cornelia Arens begged to be buried here in a gutter, in shame for the members of her family who had converted from Catholicism to Protestantism. On 2 May each year after her death, other members of the community would gather around the grave and cover it with flowers. To the left of the Catholic church are a couple of houses (one of them dated 1744) with hooks hanging from beams on their gables. These were used to drag grain sacks to the upper storeys.

The alley between houses no.37 and no.38 in the Begijnhof leads to the Spui, on the other side of which is the chief building of the university of Amsterdam. To the right is one of the city's most delightful modern statues (though, alas, frequently defaced): a street urchin of 1960 by Carel Kneulman, his hand on his hips, his cap set rakishly, his stockings untidily rolled down.

One of Amsterdam's greatest delights is its patrician houses. To see some of the finest, continue right, cross over the bridge spanning the Singel and continue straight on over the Herengracht. The street to the left along the canal is filled with lovely Amsterdam gables, some of them sculpted with splendid statues and carvings, many of them equipped with hooks to haul sacks and provisions to their upper storeys.

But the best houses line the celebrated 'golden bend' of the Herengracht, across the Leidsegracht. Here you can see one of the finest sets of late seventeenth-century houses in Amsterdam. A little further on you turn right into a clean, charming pedestrianized street crammed with antique shops: Nieuwe Spiegelstraat. Many of these antique shops open on Sundays, selling prints, clocks, cherubs, pottery, silver and broken-off stone carvings from medieval cloisters. Gables overhang the street. Restaurants offer crêpes. One shop sells apothecaries' wares, another chinoiserie. Some of their contents are too precious to allow people to wander in at will, so a sign tells you to ring to be let in (*Gelieve te bellen*).

Ahead across Weteringschans stands the Rijksmuseum, which the architect Cuypers finished four years before he completed the central railway station. The Rijksmuseum opens on Tuesdays to Saturdays from 10.00 to 17.00 and on Sundays and holidays from 13.00 to 17.00. Over 260 rooms are filled with masterpieces that (in my view) equal Rembrandt van Rijn's *Night Watch*, some of them by Rembrandt himself; but no one should miss the *Night Watch*. Its name is completely misleading. Only its unhappy darkening in the eighteenth century, the result of oxidization, misled spectators into supposing that the scene depicted took place at night. Rembrandt was really illustrating the events preceding the ceremonial entry of Marie de' Medici into Amsterdam in 1642. The company of Captain Franz Cocq and Lieutenant Willem van Ruytenburch are waiting to join the triumphal cortège. A dog barks; children play; each figure is depicted as an unforgettable individual.

Rembrandt's *Night Watch* has been beautifully restored after it was slashed in 1975. Matching it, in my opinion, are his extraordinary *Anatomy Lesson of Dr Dreijman* and his striking *Jewish Bride*. Here too are entrancing works by Franz Hals and Jan Vermeer van Delft, as well as Rubens (in room 226). Fascinating terracotta models of the sculptures by Artus Quellijnus which now decorate Amsterdam's royal palace are in room 258.

When you walk underneath the great central arch of the

Rijksmuseum, look back at the lovely ceramics and sculpted pseudo-medieval masons on the south façade. There is further sculpture in the park beyond: a *Squatting Woman* of 1917 by Auguste Renoir; and Jean Tinguely's *Fountain* of 1968. The most moving, if not the finest, is a memorial on the right dedicated to the women of Ravensbrück concentration camp. The memorial, seemingly chimneys of the gas chambers, turns out to be an Aeolian harp which plays in the wind. In addition it emits the sound of a beating heart.

To the right are the Vincent Van Gogh museum and the City Museum, and at the end of this square is Amsterdam's celebrated concert hall, the Concertgebouw. A. van Gendt designed this hall in the 1880s after Johannes Brahms had chastised the Amsterdammers for their lack of musical understanding. At the same time Willem Kes was commissioned to recruit a group of musicians whose successors became today's world-famous Concertgebouw Orchestra. So decisively did it reclaim Amsterdam's musical reputation that Richard Strauss dedicated his *Heldenleben* to its resident conductor, Willem Mengelberg. The concert hall, topped by a gilded lyre, was finished in 1888.

Turn right here along van Baerlestraat. On the right are a group of modernistic statues, including Henry Moore's *Reclining Figure* of 1957, Wessel Couzijin's *Africa Awakes* of 1961 and a stainless steel cubic construction of 1970 by André Voltan. The only image here which I really like is Rik Wouters' statue of an overworked housewife, called *Domestic Concerns* and sculpted in 1913.

If you love parks, Amsterdam's Vondelpark is laid out ahead. Named after Holland's most famous poet, it houses a statue by no less a master than Picasso, as well as a mid nineteenth-century idealization of Vondel by L. Royer. The poet in question, Joost van den Vondel, was in fact born not in Amsterdam but in Cologne in 1587. His parents came from Antwerp and were Baptists. Vondel was soon totally absorbed by and in love with Amsterdam. From the start he was deeply anti-Calvinist and he ended his life a convert to Catholicism. But his conversion by no means made Vondel a friend of Amsterdam's chief enemy at this time, Catholic Spain. When Jacob van Campen had finished building the royal palace, Vondel wrote a poem in his honour suffused with confidence in the independence of his own people and their ability to beat the

Spanish. Religion was no match for patriotism.

Vondel's art displays the proud nationalism that has kept the tiny Dutch nation intact over the centuries. His dramatic genius could mingle a deep Christian faith with an equal warmth for his adopted city. For instance, the new Classical Theatre which opened in Amsterdam in 1683 was inaugurated by a performance of his tragedy *Gisbreght von Amstel*, in which a group of medieval Amsterdam traitors are compared with those who murdered the innocents on behalf of King Herod. The deliverance of Amsterdam after a long siege is compared with the long-awaited deliverance brought by the birth of Jesus himself.

If you prefer shopping and Dutch elegance to wandering in the Vondelpark, continue along van Baerlestraat and turn right into Amsterdam's best shopping street, Pieter Cornelisz Hooftstraat. Initially the street does not seem prepossessing, but then art shops, diamond merchants, chocolate emporia, restaurants and coffee houses appear. Here you can buy prints, clothing, shoes, carpets from Nepal, perfumes, toys, jewellery − and also fish, vegetables and cheese.

This is a part of Amsterdam packed with wickedness, culture, charm and unexpectedness. Turn left at the end of P. C. Hooftstraat along Hobbemastraat which leads to Stadhouderskade. Here you walk left again until you reach the bridge across the Singelgracht, the first of the great canals thrown around the city. Once the city boundary, the Singel was essential to Amsterdam's defences − not as a canal but as a moat, further defended by a wall. Beyond were vegetable gardens and meadows, always ready to be abandoned for the safety of the walled city should enemies appear. When Amsterdam expanded the moat and wall were no longer needed; the wall was replaced by houses; the moat became the Singelgracht.

Across the bridge is the Leidseplein, sporting some of the most extraordinary strip-clubs imaginable at night. On the left is the national theatre of 1894. The initials SPQA above the façade are the Latin acronym for 'Senate and People of the City of Amsterdam'. Opposite the theatre are sculpted two of Amsterdam's favourite Thespians of yesteryear, Wim Can and Corry Vonk. If you relish *Jugendstil* architecture, buy a drink at the American Hotel and admire its tableaux, as well as the frolicking fishes in the fountain fronting its terrace.

Leidseplein continues into Leidsestraat, a delicious treat of fine shops and façades, which also takes you over three canal bridges. As a reminder that long ago peasants and farmers could have their horses and carts cared for at Leidseplein when they came to market in the city, no.54 Leidsestraat is sculpted with a plougher, a sower and a reaper.

At the end of the street you arrive at Koningsplein, the stretch of water known as the Singel, and a romantic, living reminder of Amsterdam's former flower gardens. Between Koningsplein and Vijzelstraat the Singel has become an extraordinary floating flower market (closed only on Sundays). Floating glasshouses sell not only tulips, daffodils and chrysanthemums in season but also flower pots, delicate delftware, dried plants, Bonsai, ferns and yukka plants, not to speak of the pottery frogs and rabbits that adorn suburban gardens. Beside the market are several dark, cool 'brown' bars, where you can relax over a wine or beer, and choose from the snacks chalked up on boards: a paté, a beefsteak, a couple of herrings on bread, or even an entrecôte.

Walk along by the floating flower market and you reach Muntplein. This is the square of the old mint, whose tower, with a clock and bells, dates back to 1620 and was once part of the city walls. This graceful structure is a perfect display of the brilliance of its designer, Amsterdam's greatest city architect, Hendrik de Keyser, who died the following year. Hendrik loved experimenting with renaissance towers. Alas, many of his masterpieces were wantonly pulled down in the nineteenth century, and only this, the Mint tower, and the tower of the Zuiderkerk (which we shall shortly see) show what has been lost.

Muntplein is not really a square but in truth a 68-metre wide bridge across the River Amstel. Cross over and walk under the arch of the Mint tower into one of Amsterdam's most fashionable streets, the Rokin, which runs beside water until the statue of Queen Wilhelmina (1880–1962), sitting side-saddle on her horse, very dignified and wearing a boater. You can take a candlelit canal cruise in the evening from this spot. It starts at 21.00, lasts two hours and is accompanied with cheese and wine. You need to book in advance, at the jetty over the steps behind the queen.

Turn right where the canal ends along Langebrugsteeg, a street of cafés and theatres, and once the home of countless convents (as the name of an alleyway, Gebed Zonder End or 'Prayer without End', indicates). Now walk along the Grimburgwal. Diagonally across a little square is a lovely doorway that once was the entrance to a hospital, and next to it an archway leading to one of the quaintest spots in the city. Here was once a home for old men, hence the name of the passageway, Oudemanhuispoort. The building is still there on the left, a fine classical affair of 1642, but the old men are gone and the university administrators now work here. In consequence there is a bust of Minerva, the goddess of wisdom, in the courtyard. And all along the cool, arcaded alleyway are bookstalls, spilling out of the shops into the passageway, selling forgotten books of yesterday, old postcards, and tattered sheets of music.

As you leave Oudemanhuispoort through the classical arch at the other end, turn back to admire its symbolic carvings, representing withered old people protected by Charity. The old ones look suitably upset and haggard, not to say harrowed. I am surprised that the university administrators have not removed them, just as the old codgers have been removed. Across the water (Kloveniersburgwal) you can see the Poppenhuis (no.92), with its swags and Corinthian columns, named after Johannes Poppen who endowed and paid for the old men's home.

Turn left along Kloveniersburgwal from where there is an entrancing view to the right of Hendrik de Keyser's second remaining masterpiece, the graceful white tower and open carillon on the Zuiderkerk, a church which he completed in 1614. You can see the date, picked out in gold on red, above the clock. If you want to visit the lovely interior of this church (where Rembrandt's first three children lie buried), you can do so only on Fridays from 11.00 to 14.00 and on Saturdays from 11.00 to 16.00.

Amsterdam made money from the East Indies, and to the left of Kloveniersburgwal is a little street called Oude Hoogstraat in which stands the Oost Indisch Huis of 1606 with a fine courtyard. Having explored it, come back to the waterside and continue left into the new market square (Nieuw Markt), which in spite of its name happens to be the oldest in the city. In the middle of this large space, which today houses a rather pathetic market of books and junk, rises another powerful vestige of the city walls, the massive fifteenth-century St Anthony's gate. Everyone in Amsterdam calls it the

'Waag', since it became the public weigh-house in 1617. The five towers possess a sturdy elegance, though the original purpose of the Waag — to keep out unwelcome visitors — is still obvious. Amongst the guilds who decided to occupy the upper floors were blacksmiths, masons and surgeons, and here Rembrandt painted his *Anatomy Lesson of Dr Dreijman*. Most guidebooks tell you that today the Waag houses the Jewish History Museum of Amsterdam, but this is no longer true. It is now in the former German synagogue, opposite the Portuguese synagogue near the flea market on Waterlooplein.

From the Nieuw Markt walk left along Bloedstraat, turn right along the canal bank and left across the first bridge. You are now in the square housing Amsterdam's most venerable church, the Oude Kerk. Surprisingly enough, this also happens to be an area unique to Amsterdam where scantily-clad prostitutes sit in the windows beckoning customers day and night. They virtually surround the gothic Oude Kerk, consecrated in 1306, with its celebrated carrillon of 47 bells, cast in 1658, and its superb bell-tower of 1564. If you want to see the interior (with three lovely renaissance windows and the tomb of Rembrandt's wife Saskia), you can do so in the afternoon between 12.00 and 16.00.

On the north side of the church, with the girls in the windows waving at you, turn down Enge Kerksteeg and then turn right into Warmoesstraat. No.67 is a splendid coffee shop, and the house opposite displays the oxhead sign of a former leatherworker. A left turn takes you into Oudebrugsteeg, where duty was once levied on beer, grain and fuels. You can spot the customs building by the coat of arms of Amsterdam set in the gable, guarded by a couple of lions. Oudebrugsteeg brings you back to the Stock Exchange on Damrak, and a right turn leads to the central railway station, where this tour began.

It is surely time for a coffee, and where better than in the Noord-Zuid Hollands Koffiehuis on Stationsplein? Amsterdammers are particularly proud of this coffee house. It was built in 1911. When the authorities constructed the Amsterdam underground railway in the 1970s, they destroyed it. The general public rose up in arms, and the Noord-Zuid Hollands Koffiehuis was rebuilt in 1981.

Further delights

Sunday morning entertainment

On Sunday mornings at 11.00 an informal radio broadcast takes place in the mirror room of the Concertgebouw, called *Für Elise* since Beethoven's celebrated piece is its signature tune. The general public is invited, for a small entrance fee. Children sit on the floor on cushions. If they need to, they can walk out for a soft drink, during two hours of light classical music and interviews with the musicians.

An alternative venue at the same time is the Coffee Concert held in the Lutheran Church on the Singel, which has not been used for services since 1939. It is known as the Koepelkerk ('domed church') because Adrian Dortsman, who built it between 1668 and 1671, gave the building a monumental copper dome topped by a lovely cupola. Here every Sunday at 11.00 there is something different: poetry readings, intimate concerts and the like. The restored church is also used for banquets, parties and art exhibitions.

Don't miss the 'houses of the gold and silver mirrors' next door to the church, two exquisitely designed and symmetrical gabled houses of 1614, their homely intimacy contrasting with the monumental church. No one quite knows whether their name derives from the fact that they mirror each other, from the fact that mirrors were let into their gables or from the fact that they were built by a Mr Mirror (a soapmaker called Spiegel).

Anne Frank House

To call this visit a 'delight' is a misnomer, but the agile should not miss the Anne Frank House at no.263 Prinsengracht, five minutes' walk from Dam square. You need to be agile, since the steps from floor to floor are short but extremely steep. This feature is typical of many houses in old Amsterdam, since they had to be built long and narrow. Moreover, to let in light, they were usually built in two parts, with a courtyard in between the building on the street and what is known as the annex behind.

The Anne Frank House, dating from 1635, is exactly like this, and it was in the annex, dating in its present form from 1740, that the doomed family hid from their Nazi persecutors. Anne had been born in Frankfurt in 1929, the second daughter of Jewish parents, Otto and Edith Frank. They came to Amsterdam in 1933, the year Adolf Hitler became Chancellor of Germany, driven there to escape the increasing persecution of Jews which Hitler immediately instigated.

Seven years later Holland capitulated to the German army. Otto Frank had just begun a business in herbs and spices at no.263 Prinsengracht. Fearing the worst from the Nazi anti-Semites, he immediately began converting his annex into a hiding-place. Two upper floors and the attic were cut off from the rest by a hinged bookcase. The windows were covered with thick curtains. In 1942, when the Nazi policy of deporting Jews to their eventual deaths in concentration camps became patently clear, he and his family went into hiding, along with their friends the Van Daan family. Their problem was actually eased by the occupying Germans' decree that at night every window in Amsterdam was to be blacked out, as a precaution against Allied air raids.

On her thirteenth birthday Anne Frank had been given a diary. For twenty-five months she noted down the daily events of this extraordinary and precarious life, a diary which, when published in 1947, became world-famous. Four of Otto Frank's former employees, two typists (Miep and Elly), Mr Koophuis and Mr Kraler, smuggled food and clothing to the hideout, as well as books, magazines and the necessities of life.

It could not last. On 4 August 1944 the Nazi police broke into the annex and arrested the Franks and the Van Daans. They were transported to Auschwitz, ironically in the last such transport of Jews from Holland. There Edith Frank died of starvation and Mr Van Daan was gassed. His son Peter was forced to join a German army contingent and never seen again. In October 1940 Anne, her elder sister Margot and Mrs Van Daan were deported to Belsen concentration camp. All three died of typhus. Only Otto Frank survived, liberated from Auschwitz by the Russians.

All this is movingly set out in the Anne Frank House. Here are pictures of her adolescent heroes, pinned on the walls: Rudy Vallee, Deanna Durbin in the movie *First Love*, Ray Milland, Greta Garbo in *Ninotchka*, Ginger Rogers. Lines on the wall of the room where Otto, Edith and Margot Frank slept show the children's growth.

Peter Van Daan slept in the attic, his parents in what doubled as the kitchen and living room.

Exhibits here also chart the rise of Nazism and the history of World War II. The Anne Frank Foundation, which now runs the house, arranges fascinating exhibitions and seminars here on contemporary neo-Nazism, the history of anti-Semitism and related subjects. The house is open daily from 09.00 to 17.00 (on Sundays and holidays from 10.00 to 17.00).

Rembrandt's house and the Waterlooplein flea market

The house of Holland's greatest artist, Rembrandt van Rijn, is at nos.4/6 Jodenbreestraat. It can be reached by the underground railway, by trams nos.9 and 14, or by a gentle walk from Nieuw Markt down Sint-Antoniesbreestraat and across the canal.

Here the artist and his wife Saskia spent some twenty years of their lives, from around 1639 to 1660, when bankruptcy forced him to sell everything. Today 250 of his brilliant etchings are on display, together with some of his drawings and paintings by those who taught him and those he taught. The house is open daily from 10.00 to 17.00 (on Sundays and holidays from 13.00 to 17.00).

Jodenbreestraat means 'Jewish broad street', and in this Jewish quarter of the city the artist found models for his stupendous Biblical canvasses and etchings (including the famous *Jewish Bride*, which you can see in his former home).

Walk on past the former Jesuit church of Moses and Aaron, now a concert hall. Note the little statues of Moses and Aaron in the wall, Moses with the ten commandments etched on stones. In the seventeenth century Baruch Spinoza, the great Jewish philosopher, lived in a house (now disappeared) to the left of the church. He elaborated a philosophy based on the premise that 'man's chief purpose is to preserve himself alive', and was knifed to death by a Spaniard at the age of 43.

The huge flea market of Amsterdam, selling a treasure-trove of old and new junk, is in Waterlooplein across the square at the end of Jodenbreestraat. And another reminder of the haven given by Amsterdam to persecuted Jews in the seventeenth century can be found in Jonas Daniël Meijerplein (just south-east of Waterlooplein). The Portuguese synagogue here was inspired by the Temple of Solomon in Jerusalem and built by Elias Bouman in the 1670s.

Restored in the 1950s, its magical interior is open daily to the general public except on Saturdays and Jewish festivals.

The Jordaan

The entrancing Jordaan, deriving from the French *jardin* or garden, lies in the north-east quarter of Amsterdam and was offered by the city to the poorest of her citizens during the rebuilding of 1609. This was also the area settled by French Huguenots at the end of the century, refugees from the persecution of Louis XIV, and they are responsible for the French derivation of Jordaan. Bordered by Prinsengracht, Brouwersgracht, Lijnbaansgracht and Looiersgracht, it is a haven of narrow canals and streets, with some of the finest gabled houses in the whole city. Since 1960 students, musicians and artists have made it their home.

The great set pieces of the Jordaan (the Bloemgracht, Jordaan's 'gentlemen's canal', with its superb gables; Hendrik de Keyser's Western Church, the Westerkerk, with its carillon, crowned tower and splendid interior designed by Jacob van Campen, as well as a statue of Anne Frank set against the wall; and Herenmarkt, with the headquarters of the East India and West India companies) are not what draw me to the district, but simply the pleasure of wandering for an hour or two across picturesque islands and along unostentatiously lovely streets.

Diamonds

For 400 years Amsterdam has been the centre of the diamond industry. Wherever you walk in the city you are invited to buy them, and more delightfully to watch them being cut. The Diamond Centre BV, at 1 Rokin, opens daily from 10.00 to 18.00. You are welcome to tour the establishment and watch the cutting from 10.30 to 14.00. And this is but one of many similar places, all presenting a fascinating glimpse of a unique skill, all hoping you will take out your cheque book (which you need not do). Stones are first put in a clamp and split in one blow (or sometimes cloven by sawing). Next the corners are rounded off. Finally the diamond is polished to perfection. The diamond cutting establishments in Amsterdam include: Bonebakker at no.88 Rokin; Bab Hendricksen Diamonds at no.89 Weteringschans; Coster Diamonds at nos.2–6 Paulus Potterstraat; The Mill Diamond Centre at no.123 Rokin;

Reuter Diamonds at no.526 Singel; and A. van Moppes & Zoon at nos.2–6 Albert Cuypstraat.

The farmers' market in the Jordaan

Every Saturday in summer from 10.00 to 15.00 there is an old-fashioned farmers' market at Noordemarkt in the Jordaans, selling cheese, bread, fruit, vegetables and curds from twenty or so stalls.

Excursion to Monnickendam, Volendam, Edam & Zaanstad

The countryside, villages and towns around Amsterdam are so fascinating and charming that even on a visit lasting only a weekend you should hire a car and spend a day exploring them. Four places that should on no account be missed are the fishing village of Monnickendam, picturesque Volendam, the cheese town of Edam and the windmill village of Zaanstad.

Leave Amsterdam by following the signs for Amsterdam Nord and the N247. After driving through a tunnel you can pick up the signs for Volendam. Soon you are driving alongside a canal, with moored boats, running through green flat country grazed by black and white cows.

After 12 kilometres follow the sign that points right, to Monnickendam, on the Gouwzee. Immediately a huge brick church looms ahead. In its porch is the local tourist office. St Nicholas church, Monnickendam, dedicated to the patron saint of sailors, is one of those great gothic hall churches built in the fifteenth century that can be found in Holland in some of the tiniest villages. It is open 10.00 to 12.00 and 14.00 to 18.00, closing two hours earlier from October to April.

The church took 250 years to build. Its interior is even more magnificent than the exterior, with three barrel vaults decorated with stars, a superb organ case in red and gold and blue (with 500 pipes dating from 1530), intricately carved wooden screens, a magnificent pulpit, private pews set around the pillars and an ancient stone font. One part of the presbytery, set into the side of the church, carries the date 1626, and an older part leans perilously to the left.

Thirteenth-century Frisian monks founded this village, damming up the *see* to form a lake (hence the name Monnickendam). The street that leads beyond the church is delightful, and includes a house dated 1619. (Incidentally this is not a street paved for those wearing high-heels.) Stroll along, looking out for the lace work in the windows of the houses, intricately worked patterns of birds and other creatures set in carved wooden frames. At the sixteenth-century clock tower, which carries the second oldest carillon in Holland and houses the archaeological museum, turn left. Here are enticing fish shops and restaurants, and then the dam and lock, across which you reach the harbour, full of authentic old boats, yachts, fisheries and boat builders. The quayside is crammed with colourful fish shops, offering mussels, crab, mackerel, herrings and fishcakes, all succulently ready to eat.

Monnickendam boasts a town hall built in 1746, a seventeenth-century weigh-house and an orphanage of 1638. The restaurant 'Nieuw Stuttenburgh' displays a remarkable collection of old musical boxes. (The proprietor promises to 'make you feel like in granny's time while enjoying one of our 20 fish or meat specialities'.) But to my mind the charm of the place lies in its humble houses and its delicious smells — coming from the sheds where herrings and eels are being smoked. Over a doorway near the sheds is set the motto 'Love God above all', a reminder of the monks who created this beautiful spot 600 years ago. Every Saturday Monnickendam holds a street market, with extra street fairs put on during the tourist weeks of high summer.

Drive back to the N247 and turn right after 5 kilometres to Volendam. The route runs alongside canal bridges that seem to have come straight out of a Van Gogh painting. After another 2 kilometres turn right into Volendam, another fishing village, this one lying on the Ijsselmeer. Women here still wear long black dresses with striped aprons, quaint white hats and embroidered neck-bands. Men are seen in baggy trousers, shirts with huge buttons, and a kind of Russian fez.

The houses have sharply pointed roofs, in the traditional Dutch style. But Volendam has also geared itself to visitors, and now offers windsurfing, bowling alleys and swimming-pools, as well as tourist trips in motor boats. Here too are a good number of places for refreshment; you can drink Dutch gin (*jenever*) and eat a Dutch pancake (*poffertje*); and if you wish you can buy Dutch clogs, doilies, lace curtains and hand-made dolls. The so-called 'Golden Chamber' of Volendam ('De Gouden Kamer', at no.8 Oude Draaipad) is proud of its unique collection of cigar bands, 7 million of them, collected by a disabled fisherman and now pasted over the walls.

The town has a very curious coat of arms, including a foal with a fish on its leg. Apparently this foal fell in love with a young Volendam girl. Emerging from the sea, he made advances to her, only to be repulsed until he kicked a fish into her lap. Then she gave him an armful of grass. This unusual relationship developed so passionately that in the end the foal kidnapped the girl and carried her off into the sea. Incensed, the young men of Volendam set sail to rescue her, failed, and took up fishing instead — to the great prosperity of the small town.

Drive along Volendam harbour and continue to Edam by way of the dyke. At Edam look for the sign *Centrum* and turn right into the town. More than once I have driven in to the sound of a carillon and been happily able to park in Damplein near the town hall (which is dated 1737 on the façade). The Dam hotel serves excellent tomato soup, fried flounder fillets and ice-cream.

Again the name of the town derives from a dam, this time the damming of the River Ye. Once Edam boasted thirty-three wharfs, the result of digging a toll-free canal to the sea, but eventually the harbour silted up, in spite of strenuous efforts to prevent it. Edam declined in commercial importance and is, as a result, utterly unspoilt. Its cheese remains deservedly renowned. You can also buy samplers, brassware, clogs, delftware and cheese slicers.

The carillon, made in 1566, rings from the fifteenth-century bell-tower of the church of Our Lady, all that actually remains of the church. (Its extension is now Edam's tourist office.) There are five other churches in Edam, all fine, but only addicts should attempt to visit them all. However, it would be a shame not to glance inside the largest three-ridged church in Europe, Edam's St Nicholas, with two of its 22 pillars richly decorated with, among other motifs, crowned skulls, and 19 bells made in 1561 on display inside. Of its 31 seventeenth-century stained-glass windows, only one has been lost.

Edam has splendid cheese warehouses, many of them Louis XIV in style, and a cheese weigh-house dating from 1778. It also boasts a museum whose cellar floats on water. Built around 1550, some say by a mariner who never liked to sleep on firm ground, its entrance hall displays a couple of sea-chests, one of them once belonging to a whaling ship, and decorated with carvings of whale hunting. In the front room are three bizarre paintings, one of Jan Claeszoon Clees, the fat man, who weighed 35 stone when this portrait was painted in 1612. The second depicts Pieter Dirckszoon Langebaard, with a beard 3 metres long. The third is a portrait of the giantess Trijntje Cornelisdochter Kever, who stood 2.5 metres high and lived from 1616 to 1633. Her shoes are in a nearby glass case.

Leave Edam and follow the signs first for Hoorn and then for Pumerend. Keep a look out for more signposts as the scenic road zig-zags along, with many right-angled turns as it follows the irrigation channels on either side of the tree-lined route.

Though it is 800 years old, I find Pumerend neither beautiful nor ugly. Skirt the town, and follow the signs for Zaandam (be careful to follow the car route, not that intended for bicycles) which will lead you to the A7. Nine kilometres from Pumerend leave the motorway at the sign for Zaandijk.

Quite suddenly on the right appears the model village, Zaanstad, with its restored old Dutch houses, its pewter shops, its clock museum, a grocery shop a hundred years old, antique shops, cheese makers, and above all windmills. There are windmills of every kind and size here, brought from elsewhere and lovingly restored. 'De Kat' was first built in 1646, but burned down and was rebuilt in 1781. 'De Zoeker' dates from 1672. Some are thatched; all are in working order, and you can climb up and visit some of them in the summer months.

Zaanstad is not at all a dusty museum piece. People live in these houses with their clapperboard fronts and gables painted green and white. In a garden an old lady takes tea under a shade. Horses graze in the fields. Restaurants serve pancakes. You can go for a sail.

To return to Amsterdam, drive on towards Zaandam, take a left turn along motorway A8 and the city is only 7 kilometres away.

The whole day's outing has involved scarcely 50 kilometres of driving.

Food and drink

Next to the Amsterdam Ascot Hotel, just off Dam square, is a restaurant called the Red Lion (Roode Leeuw) which is utterly, typically Dutch — with four great carvings hanging from the ceiling, depicting a haywain dragged by four horses, bullocks pulling a carriage, a post-chaise and four other drays hauling a cart of beer barrels.

There I have eaten fine bouillon thickened with vegetables and rolled minced beef, schnitzel with cheese, fried round potatoes and a bland salad with mayonnaise sauce and chives, followed by a choice of ice-cream or cheese. This menu is one of several offered in Amsterdam hotels at tourist prices, a fact indicated outside by the sign of a fork carrying a tourist bag and wearing a hat with a flower.

These tourist menus offer a three-course meal at an extremely reasonable price. The food is not always Dutch. For well over a decade the Norwegian buffet-restaurant at no.65 Kalverstraat has been offering a self-service tourist menu which includes a bowl of soup, some sixty-five hot or cold fish and meat dishes and a selection of a dozen lip-smacking desserts.

Over 700 Amsterdam restaurants offer some sort of tourist menu. Another sign to look out for is a soup bowl garlanded with the words *Nederlands Dis*, sported by some 175 Amsterdam restaurants. These establishments offer a wide choice of traditional Dutch recipes and dishes.

The Dutch eat heartily. Breakfast in Holland is a revelation to those who normally take merely a croissant or toast and coffee. Dutch hotels serve three or four different sorts of bread (including the blackest, hardest imaginable), cheese, charcuterie and either tea or coffee. The Dutch also relish chicken soup (*kippesoep*), asparagus soup (*aspergesoep*), fish soup (*vissoep*) and vegetable soup (*groentsoep*).

In winter they often warm themselves on a pea soup (*erwtsoep*) thickened with smoked sausage, pork fat and sliced bread. They tuck into 'hotpots' (or *hutspots*, as they call them), made of potatoes, carrots, pieces of meat and bacon. As a fishing nation they love herrings, either fresh or smoked, and all the other produce of the sea.

The cheese board is by no means confined to Edam. Holland produces well over twenty different cheeses, including Gouda and the delicious Maaslandaerkaas. In an Amsterdam restaurant the cheeseboard with assorted Dutch cheeses (*kaasplankje met Hollandse kassoonten*) is packed with variety. Leidse, flat and round, is spiced with cumi; Roomkaas is creamy and delicious; Amsterdammer is a Gouda with a higher moisture count; Pompdour is enriched with garlic and herbs, as is Subenhara; delicate Kernhem has a rind that is light orange; Fresian is blended with cumin and cloves; and Maasdammer is a kind of Dutch Gruyère.

At lunch you may well also choose (from the *kleine kaart*) what is virtually a snack: fried eggs with ham, cheese or bread; a farmer's omelette (*boeren omelette*), or meat salad with toast (*husarensalade*).

Indonesian-based cuisine, a legacy of the Dutch Empire, is widely available. This always includes a dish of rice (the *rijstafel*), which serves as the base for peanut sauce, pork, bean sprouts, stewed meat (*daging*), fried coconut or fried bananas. And an Indian flavour has crept into many restaurants, so that you might well be offered chicken and curry sauce (*halve gebraden kys met kerrisaus*).

As for drink, the Dutch are renowned for having created gin, in the early seventeenth century. They drink the potent brew known as *jenever* neat, or with coca-cola or vermouth. Other delightful (though potent) Dutch liqueurs include curaçao, 'parfait d'amour' and 'triple sec'. And most restaurants offer French and sometimes German wines as well.

'Enjoy your meal' they say: '*Eet smakelijk*'.

Night life

No city in the world offers such a flamboyantly daring night life as Amsterdam. Its night-clubs, which flourish around the Rembrandtsplein and the Leidseplein, are far less innocuous than those of Paris or London. The largest night-club in Amsterdam is the Piccadilly, at nos.6–10 Thorbeckeplein. Rock bands play in Mazzo's (at no.114 Rozengracht) and in Paradiso's (at no.6 Weteringschans). The Jordaan is packed with bars and cafés that come alive at night.

These are by no means the only delights on offer in the city. The Concertgebouw Orchestra in its superb hall is the best-known of Amsterdam's cultural assets; but redundant churches, especially the Moses and Aaron church near Waterlooplein, also offer musical treats in the evening. The Dutch national dance company performs in the Stads Schouwburg in the Leidseplein, as does the Dutch national ballet. And the Carré Theatre (at no.115 Amstel) is only one of numerous fine theatre venues. As for opera, the Muziektheater presents performances of international calibre. Information and tickets are available at no.26 Leidseplein on weekdays between 10.00 and 18.00. Finally, try the Joseph Lam Jazzclub at no.8 van Diemenstraat, or the headquarters of the Amsterdam jazz community, BIM Huis, at no.73 Oude Schans.

No tickets are required for Amsterdam's plentiful discos. For concerts, theatre and the ballet tickets can be obtained from the tourist office (VVV-Verkehrsverein) at no.5 Rokin, open daily except Sundays from 10.00 to 16.00.

The most useful weekly magazine for the arts, culture, restaurants and shopping in Amsterdam is called *This Week*.

Important information

Banks in Amsterdam open on weekdays (not Saturdays) from 09.00 to 16.00, some of them staying open longer on Thursdays (which is a late shopping day). The airport bank at Schiphol is open every day from 07.00 to 23.00, and that at the central railway station from 07.00 to 10.45 (except on Sundays, when it opens an hour later).

As well as the usual public holidays, the Dutch also take 25 February (which commemorates the day in 1941 when the nation went on strike to protest against Nazi persecution of the Jews), 30 April (the Queen's birthday), 4/5 May, and 5 December when Sinter Claes leaves Amsterdam.

Public transport in Amsterdam includes 16 tram services, more than 30 bus lines and two underground railway lines (the most useful for weekend visitors running from Central Station by way of Nieuw Markt to Waterlooplein). Tickets are bought from bus and tram drivers, and in the underground stations. You must punch the ticket to validate it at the start of any journey. (Drivers do this for you on a bus; otherwise use the machines at the rear of trams and in the underground stations.) You cannot buy a single ticket, but must travel by means of a 'strip ticket' or *strippencard*, i.e. several tickets in one. A three-day ticket is even cheaper.

As well as travelling by canal cruiser, you can hire your own canal bike, a pedalboat seating two or four. These can be rented at Leidseplein, Prinsengracht at the Westerkerk, Keizergracht near Leidsestraat and by the Rijksmuseum/Heineken Brewery. You are given a set of routes as well as the bike.

Finally, rent-a-bike is one of the cheapest and best ways of seeing Amsterdam. You rent them at railway stations. Other rent-a-bike locations can be obtained from the city tourist offices, who will also give you a useful and picturesque route for touring outside the city.

Schiphol airport is said to have the cheapest duty-free shops of any airport in the world. Buses reach here from the centre of Amsterdam in 25 minutes.

Barcelona

*This city is a treasury of courtesy, welcoming of strangers, unrivalled
in its situation and its beauty. Barcelona was also a spot where my
adventures gave me no joy but instead much distressed me; yet I
suffered everything more happily since I had seen that place.*

Don Quixote de la Mancha, 1605

Barcelona, fiery capital of Catalonia, is a city of lamps. Some are spikily ornate, such as the turn-of-the-century ones that hang from the shady trees in the gracious Passeig de Gràcia, others double as fountains, with little taps so that the overheated passers-by can fling water over their faces and mop their warm brows.

For me Barcelona's charms are enhanced by the fact that it is a blend of four cities: a port and harbour, an ancient medieval quarter, the eighteenth-century Barceloneta, and the new town (the Eixample), laid out in the nineteenth century to the rigorous geometric designs of the engineer Idelfons Cerdà, whose parallel streets are enlived by the long, off-centre avenue called the Diagonal.

The pace of life in Barcelona is not the same as that of the other seven cities in this book. There is a different rhythm to the day, with a two-hour siesta from around two o'clock in the afternoon (though the larger shops and hotels tend to ignore this out of deference to tourists). From four in the afternoon many shops stay open till eight or even ten in the evening. Lunch is often the chief meal of the day. In the evening you start eating around nine o'clock, much later than in the other great European cities.

I remember eating one evening outside the Café Puda Manel in Barceloneta, on the Passeig Nacional across the road from the harbour. It was about eleven o'clock and the perilous chair lift over the water to the mountain of Montjuïc had long since closed down. As I tucked into my paella a couple of men beside me, one grey-haired and bald on top, the other handsomely moustachioed and with crinkly black hair, were relishing the largest mussels I had ever seen, squeezing lemon over them, breaking them open with their bare hands, and washing them down with a rosé wine. They followed the mussels with a huge platter of fried fish.

To my right a family of ten was eating, a baby kicking in its pram alongside the table. The noise of chatter was tremendous, the pleasure enormous, the food cheap and excellent. High above, in the distance, the illuminated ferris wheel on Montjuïc was still turning. After I had eaten, I wandered back to where I was staying past Barcelona's great gothic cathedral along narrow, rambling medieval streets.

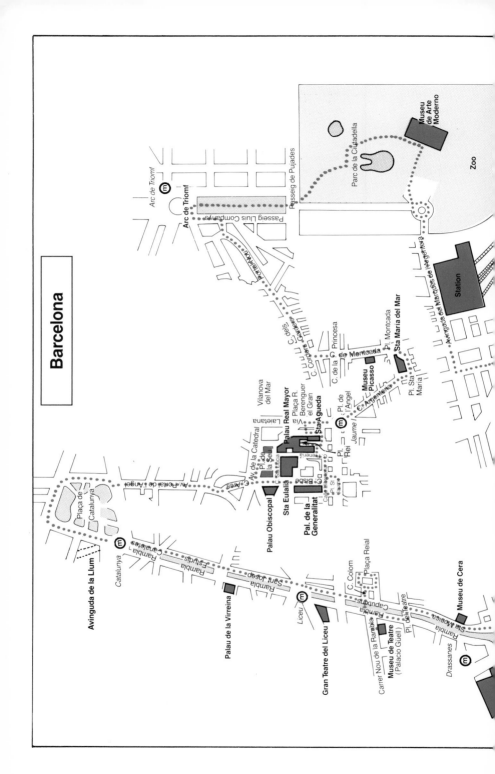

Barcelona

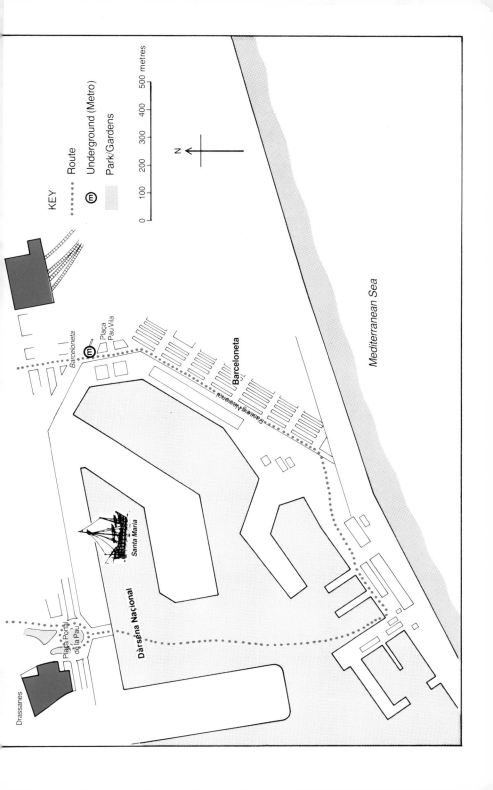

KEY

Route

(m) Underground (Metro)

Park/Gardens

0   100   200   300   400   500 metres

N

Drassanes

Plaça Portal
de la Pau

Darséna Nacional

Santa Maria

Barceloneta

(m)

Plaça
Pau Vila

Barceloneta

Passeig Nacional

Mediterranean Sea

A city tour

Barceloneta's extraordinary Passeig Nacional lies just south of the city's central railway station. You reach it from there by way of Avinguda del Marquès de L'Argentera, walking as far as the fountain and then left through the Plaça Pau Vila past the Metro station Barceloneta. On the right are the docks, with cranes and warehouses; on the left the Passeig Nacional. This area is crammed with shops, seafood restaurants, pavement cafés (their menus chalked on boards), banks and bars. There is also an aquarium (open daily from 10.00 to 14.00 and from 16.00 to 20.00), swimming-pools and a breakwater where lovers linger at night.

Can there be any other quarter of a great city so curious as Barceloneta, designed in the eighteenth century by a military engineer, Prospère de Verboom, with strict military precision? His grid street pattern survives to this day, with its narrow blocks of houses, every room possessing one window and access to the sun. Once the home of Barcelona's fishermen and sailors, Barceloneta still possesses a uniquely lively flavour, though today others have moved in to run the many fishing shops, bars and *bodegas* in its tiny streets, where both tourists and natives are served with ham on huge pieces of bread.

If you walk on to the end of the breakwater (keeping to the right of the aquarium and passing the chair lift) you can take a *gondolondrina* or water bus back to the romantically named Plaça Portal de la Pau, the square of the 'gate to peace'. Here, reminding us that this was once one of the greatest ports on earth, stands a huge monument to Christopher Columbus, who was received in triumph in Barcelona after sailing to the Americas in 1492. Gaietè Buiges Monravà designed the monument in 1886, topped by the explorer pointing out to sea. A lift inside the 50-metre column speeds you to the top for superb views of the harbour, the city and Montjuïc.

West of the Columbus monument stand the oldest surviving shipyards in the world, Barcelona's 'Drassanes'. Begun in the reign of King Jaime I (1213–76), they were well restored in our own century and are now a maritime museum housing great Spanish galleys, including the *Real*, flagship at the celebrated battle of Lepanto in 1571 when the Spanish and Venetians defeated the Turks. In the Dàrsena Nacional, an annex across the Plaça Portal de la Pau, sails a model of Columbus's ship the *Santa Maria*. You can visit the Drassanes from Monday to Saturday from 10.00 to 14.00 and 16.00 to 19.00.

Running north-east from the Columbus monument is Barcelona's most popular thoroughfare, the Ramblas. The busy traffic running up and down either side of this wide avenue flanks a central pedestrianized walk bordered with trees. Stroll up the right-hand side, with antique shops and a little passage running off to the wax museum (Museu de Cera), which is housed in a splendid former bank. Here, as in almost every wax museum I know, are utterly unrecognizable models of famous men and women (with the exception, in this case, of a fine model of the great Spanish cellist Pablo Casals). In the same little square is a bizarre museum of Satanism. Both open from 11.00 to 14.00 and from 14.30 to 20.00 on weekdays (carrying on until 20.30 on Sundays).

The Ramblas continues north, with open-air restaurants under awnings between the trees in the centre. Stalls sell newspapers and books, souvenirs and lovely leather goods. There is street theatre here too − clowns, sword swallowers and acrobats.

Just after Plaça del Teatre turn left along Carrer Nou de la Rambla. No.3 is one of several extraordinary buildings in Barcelona designed by the remarkable architect Antonio Gaudí i Cornet. If not his most noteworthy, it is still entrancingly bizarre. Known as the Palacio Güell (since it was designed for Gaudí's patron the English-educated industrialist Eusebio Güell), it dates from 1886 to 1891. From the outside Gaudí's unique genius is best seen in the splendidly sinuous wrought ironwork. Inside are bizarrely beautiful art nouveau capitals, ceilings, doors and stained-glass windows, as well as an entrancing parabolic dome above the central drawing-rooms. The chimneys are a riot of fancy, some covered in deliberately chipped pieces of multi-coloured ceramics. Happily you can get inside to see much of this sumptuous palace, since it is now Barcelona's museum of art and entertainment, open between 11.00 and 14.00 and 17.00 and 20.00 every day.

Around the Carrer Nou de la Rambla is the Barri Chino, possibly the seediest red-light area in Europe. The women and transvestites trading in the Celle de San Ramón are the kind that give a red-light area a bad name.

Return to the Ramblas along Carrer Nou de la Rambla, cross over the street and walk down Carrer Colom to the exquisite Plaça Reial. This regal square is surrounded by lovely neo-classical buildings, painted yellow and white, with identical columns on all four sides of the square. Palm trees provide a little shade. A fountain sprays refreshingly in the middle. Here are shaded seats, galleries, shops and bars, and on Sunday mornings the *plaça* springs to life as a coin and stamp market. Francesco Daniel Molina was the nineteenth-century architect responsible for this superb square. Gaudí designed its lamps.

Continuing once more up the Ramblas, the wide thoroughfare fascinatingly reveals that Gaudí had his talented predecessors. No.82 on the right is a house displaying Gaudí-like inspired madness. The narrow, entertainingly tiled no.77 across the street, though not by him, comes from Gaudí-land. This point is the start of the Ramblas flower market, with stalls on either side of the pedestrianized walk selling cut flowers, house plants, forced pot plants and bunches of dried flowers.

On the left is the opera house (the Gran Teatre del Liceu), opened in 1847 and sumptuously rebuilt inside after a fire gutted the place in 1861. A few yards farther along on the left is the entrance to the market known as *la Boqueria*, its archway graced with yellow bulls' eyes set in blue glass, with a flamboyant glass coat of arms hanging from cast-iron ropes of flowers. Inside the range of produce on offer is a feast for the eyes. Here are stalls selling every sort of dried fruit – succulent dates, apricots, sultanas, raisins and figs. Great chunks of fish, squid and octopus are laid out on ice, while vegetables and fruit include the biggest lemons I have ever seen.

Next, at the side of the baroque church of Mare de Déu de Betlem, comes the Palau de la Virreina. Built in 1778 for the widow of the Spanish viceroy of Peru and guarded by statues of two horsemen, it is now a superb art gallery housing (among much else) the collection made by Francesco Cambó, who died in 1947. The masterpieces he bequeathed to his native city include three superb Botticellis. (The gallery is open on Mondays from 16.30 to 20.30, and for the rest of the week from 09.30 to 13.30 as well, except for Sundays and holidays when you cannot get in in the afternoons.)

Ironically enough (since, as William Blake put it, 'a robin redbreast in a cage puts all heaven in a rage'), from the church of Mare de Déu de Betlem onwards the street-stalls start selling caged birds, as well as other live creatures. Finally, notice the former Royal Academy of Arts and Science at no.115, a wildly neo-romanesque building of 1883, now the Catalan Comedy Theatre.

Today this haunt of tourism – to be honest, slightly too much so – makes it hard to understand how, for a couple of years in the 1930s, Catalonia and its capital Barcelona were the centre of republican opposition to Franco's future dictatorship. In his *Homage to Catalonia* George Orwell described the impossible ideals of that era, a mixture (as he put it) of hope and camouflage, which he saw expressed in the Ramblas:

Down the Ramblas, the wide central artery of the town where crowds of people streamed constantly to and fro, the loudspeakers were bellowing revolutionary songs all day and far into the night. And it was the aspect of the crowds that was the queerest thing of all. In outward appearance it was a town in which the wealthy classes had practically ceased to exist.

To his regret, Orwell soon saw things returning to normal.

The Ramblas end at the huge Plaça de Catalunya, which boasts not only pigeons, a couple of splendid fountains – illuminated at night – and statues of (among others) a goddess, a shepherd and the naked spirit of Barcelona riding a horse and carrying a ship, but also an underground street, the Avinguda de la Llum. Built in 1928, it is lined with bars, cafés and a cinema. And since the Ramblas mark the western limit of the medieval quarter of Barcelona, this square is where you start exploring the Barri Gòtic.

Walk by the dolphin fountain at the south-east corner of the square, sculpted with more or less naked statues and fat little children, and make your way into the pedestrianized Avinguda del Portal de l'Angel. On the right there is a splendid department store where you can find excellent Spanish pottery (as well as caged monkeys and parakeets).

At the end of this narrowing street, walk left of the fountain, beautifully tiled in 1918, and then along the Carrer des Arcs. On your right rises Barcelona's art institute, its exquisite courtyard (housing Luis Montane i Mollfulleba's 1955 statue of Eve) a small foretaste of the delights to come. On the left is the modern college of art, a building that would scarcely merit a mention if Pablo Picasso had not sketched exceedingly playful drawings supposedly depicting the folklore of Catalonia on three of its sides.

Almost instantly you reach the marvellous cathedral square, the Plaça de la Seu, with the steps of Barcelona's majestic gothic cathedral of St Eulalia directly in front of you. Eulalia was a Spanish Christian put to death by the pagans in the early fourth century. Her body was hidden when Arabs invaded Spain in 711. It was miraculously discovered 165 years later and now lies entombed in the tiny crypt over which the present stupendous cathedral of Barcelona was built. Is it really St Eulalia's body? I like to believe so.

The church was begun in 1298 and finished, except for the façade, some 150 years later. A French architect, Charles Galtes, had come from Rouen to design it. By a miracle his plans survived in the cathedral archives, and in the nineteenth century one of Barcelona's wealthy industrialists (Manuel Girona y Agrafel) generously paid for the cathedral to be finished according to his original intentions. The great apparently thirteenth-century façade thus dates from 1892. The sons of this generous industrialist paid for the dome, which was completed only in 1913. Looking at the cathedral, you would never guess that some of it is so recent.

I love it. George Orwell hated it. He thought the anarchists showed bad taste in not blowing it up during the Spanish Civil War. At least, he conceded, they hung their red and black banner between its spires.

Do not expect to be allowed inside if you are a woman wearing shorts or displaying your bare shoulders. Since the clergy of this great cathedral are obliged to preach a faith which glorifies Mary, mother of Jesus, and pays homage to the One God who made human beings both male and female in an act of super-abundant creation, it is hard to accept this blatant anti-feminist ruling. But if you do not accept it, you will not get in and you will miss an interior that surpasses even the breathtaking charm of the exterior. The second chapel on the right-hand side contains a venerable sixteenth-century crucifix, the Holy Christ of Lepanto, which sailed on the flagship of Don John of Austria when he sank the Moslem fleet at Lepanto in 1571. The head of the crucifix leans slightly to the right. Pious Spaniards tell you that this is because the carved Christ did so in 1571 to avoid a potentially lethal cannon-ball.

More chapels house golden baroque altarpieces of the eighteenth century. Some of Spain's greatest saints lie in the other chapels of this cathedral, in particular the great compiler of canon law, St Raymond of Penafort, who died at the age of 100, and the brilliant missionary St Francis Xavier.

I find it hard to leave the glories of this cathedral, with its three great aisles and semi-circular apse. The splendidly carved pulpit and cathedral choir-stalls all date from the turn of the fourteenth and fifteenth centuries, the marble choir screen from 1562. The skill of their makers is matched by that of the unknown Pisan sculptor who made St Eulalia's alabaster sarcophagus in the crypt in 1327. Its carved lid even depicts the scene on 10 July 1339 when, in the presence of kings, nobles, bishops, princes and the papal legate, her sacred remains were placed inside it. Her original ninth-century tomb is set in the wall behind. Directly above her present sarcophagus is the high altar, with a fifteenth-century wooden altarpiece.

A white marble romanesque doorway leads to the cool cathedral cloisters. The cloisters themselves are flanked by yet more chapels with lovely wrought-iron screens, and blessed by a splendid mid fifteenth-century fountain. Curiously, for centuries these cloisters have been the home of the cathedral geese, sheltering and chattering under the ancient trees.

As you descend the steps from its great west doors, the cathedral square is flanked on the left by the delightfully irregular archdeacon's house – long, low arcading at the top, then two rows of shuttered windows, and finally a massive arched doorway below. Attached to it on the west side is a sort of tumbledown tower. This mishmash of a building dates basically from the eleventh century, though it was considerably enhanced 500 years later. Walk between the archdeacon's house and the cathedral along Carrer de Santa Llúcia, dedicated to the virgin martyr of Syracuse, St Lucy. The archdeacon's house is now a museum, and you should certainly take the opportunity of walking into and photographing its intimate courtyard, with a moss-covered fountain and a huge palm tree, the walls decorated with green, blue, yellow and white tiles. I find this courtyard infinitely more charming than the much grander romanesque courtyard of the archbishop's palace (Palau Obiscopal) straight ahead.

At the archbishop's palace turn left down the Carrer del Bisbe. Straight ahead on the other side of the Plaça de Garriga Bachs is the delicious and unreal Bishop's Gate — all fretted gothic tracery, like something out of a novel by Victor Hugo. This gateway actually stands on the old Roman wall of Barcelona, though its tracery dates from the twelfth century. The whole street beyond is cool and gothic, with overhanging balconies and gargoyles. In summer the sudden glaring sunlight of the wide and graceful Plaça de Sant Jaume at the end of the street comes as a shock.

Across the square rise the great white stones of the neo-classical façade of the Casa Gran, created in 1840 by Josep Mas to grace a gothic palace. Today this palace is known as the Ajuntament or city hall of Barcelona. Its noblest chamber, the 'Hall of One Hundred', where the civic leaders of Barcelona once met to rule this city, was begun in 1383 and sumptuously redecorated in the baroque age. The square is invariably roasting in summer; the dark, cool courtyards lit by chandeliers inside the Casa Gran are a welcome relief. On our side of the square, directly opposite the Casa Gran, stands another superb palace, the Palau de la Generalitat. Its sixteenth-century classical façade conceals another remarkable gothic interior, with exquisite courtyards, one of them boasting a gothic stairway and cloisters, another growing orange trees. Today the Generalitat is the seat of the president of the autonomous province of Catalonia. You can visit the building only on Sundays from 10.00 to 13.00, whereas the Casa Gran is open daily from 09.30 to 13.00 and also (except Sundays) from 16.30 to 19.00.

In the humid summer months the Plaça de Sant Jaume is to me enormously oppressive. A cool escape leads left, down another of Barcelona's narrow restful streets, the Carrer de la Llibreteria, filled with cakeshops, sweetshops, and bars. Now take the first turning left along Calle de la Frenería towards the cathedral. Down the second street right, Baixada de Santa Clara, you can see the slender thirteenth-century spire of the royal chapel of St Agatha rising from Barcelona's gothic Plaça del Rei. In my view this is the most entrancing square in the medieval city. And for the thirsty there is a water trough with a tap, much frequented by tourists.

A graceful, unprepossessing and beautiful staircase leads from the square into the superb Saló del Tinell of the Royal Palace. To its left rise the five classical storeys of the mid sixteenth-century royal watch-tower, the Torre del Rei Marti. To visit these great buildings (and I urge every weekend tourist to do so) enter by the gothic city museum (Museu d'Historia de la Ciutat) on the Carrer del Veguer (open except Mondays from 09.00 to 14.00 and from 16.00 to 20.30, closing on Sunday afternoons). Oddly enough, this whole building was transferred here from the Carrer de Mercaders to house the collection.

Inside the museum, before you reach the chapel and the Saló del Tinell, you unexpectedly stroll through a former Roman and Visigoth quarter of Barcelona. Superbly excavated, it includes a mosaic of three graces, a vulgar Roman statue (no longer intact), little benches where you can sit and contemplate the impermanence of human life, as well as a pre-Christian oil-store. Then wander through the display of little gems and bizarre baroque treasures of old Barcelona to the chapel of St Agatha. Its special treasure is a retable of the epiphany created by Jaume Huguet in 1456, depicting three glamorous Magi worshipping the Christ Child and surrounded by later Christian saints. My favourites are St Christopher, hand on hip, the heavy Christ Child on his right shoulder, crossing a river with his skirts tucked up, and another queenly saint (who can she be?) who carries flowers in her dress. Beyond the chapel you can see the immense arches of the mid fourteenth-century Saló del Tinell, the six powerful spans each stretching 17 metres.

When you leave these magical buildings, walk round the back of the chapel of St Agatha to see another marvel: the sunken garden known as the Plaça de Ramón Berenguer el Gran. Here you can see that the chapel of St Agatha stands on part of Barcelona's old Roman wall. Ramon Berenguer III, after whom the square is named, was Knight Templar, and his bronze statue (sculpted by Josep Llimona) still rides here.

He looks out from ancient Barcelona towards the modern city and dusty, busy Vía Laietana; but a few metres' walk and you can escape again, into the twisting medieval streets of the quarter known as the Vilanova del Mar. Turn right, cross the Plaça de l'Angel and take the narrow Carre de l'Argenteria to the left, leading down to the octagonal towers, magnificent porch and marvellous rose window of the church of Santa María del Mar. The soaring gothic interior lives up to what you can already see.

Walk round the church and down narrow Carrer de Montcada, named after the rich Guillem de Montcada who bought land here in 1153 to build his seigneurial palace. For the next 700 years this was the most aristocratic street in Barcelona, hence the palaces on either side, often severe on the outside but concealing beautiful courtyards. One of them is now the city's museum of costume.

Ahead you will almost invariably see a patient queue of devotees of Barcelona's adopted son Pablo Picasso, who was born at Málaga in 1881 but came here to study art when he was 14. The queue marks no.15 Carrer Montcada, where three adjoining palaces are now the Picasso Museum. They house a treasure-trove of his precocious youthful work, as well as proofs and prints stretching throughout his working life, not least forty-four remarkable prints given by the artist himself, his celebrated variations on the theme of Velázquez's *Las Meninas*. The museum is open from Tuesday to Saturday from 09.00 to 14.00 and from 16.00 to 20.30. On Monday afternoons, Sundays and festivals it is open only in the morning. People queue to get in even during the lunchtime breaks.

For a swift and easy way back to the central railway station you could take the Metro line 4 back to Barceloneta (in the direction La Pau) from the station Jaume I, at the corner of Carrer de l'Argenteria and Via Laíetana, and then stroll back to the Avinguda del Marquès de l'Argentera. But a much nicer route, taking maybe three-quarters of an hour longer if you do not hurry, would be by way of the Parc de la Ciutadella, Barcelona's city park.

To reach it continue along Carrer de Montcada, cross Carrer de la Princesa and keeping going until you reach the T-junction with Carrer Corders. Turn right and walk along into Portal Nou, which brings you to the upper end of the park, the Passeig Lluis Companys.

At the northern end of the grassy, flowery Passeig stands the bizarre brick Arc de Triomf, with guardian angels and noble figures on the plinth. The architect Josep Vilaseca designed it for the Universal Exhibition of 1888. Walk south through the park (which was also set out for the Universal Exhibition), with its palm trees, its cascade and its many delightful statues − including a huge elephant, an elegant lady with an umbrella and a monument to Walt Disney. Here are men playing boules and children on swings. Here hot fat dogs are carried by fat hot women underneath the shady plane trees. There is also a zoo (open except Mondays from 09.00 to 14.00, with free entry on Sundays and holidays). On either side are monumental buildings: the law courts, designed to intimidate wrongdoers and would-be wrongdoers; the quaint museum of natural history; the seat of the Catalan parliament.

In the middle of the park is the museum of modern art, essentially a collection of modern *Catalan* art, rather than of modern art in general. (It opens on Mondays from 14.00 to 19.30 and during the rest of the week from 09.00 to 14.00.) Its home is an interesting survival of Barcelona's strife-torn past. When the Catalans resisted King Philip V in 1715, he built a fortress (or citadel, hence the name Parc de la Ciutadella) to keep control of the city. In 1868 the Catalan patriot General Prim gave the citadel to the people of Barcelona, who tore it down twenty years later — except for the chapel, the governor's palace and the arsenal. Today the arsenal houses the museum of modern art. General Prim himself is commemorated with an equestrian statue in the park, where you turn right into Avinguda del Marquès de l'Argentera which takes you back to the central railway station.

Further delights

Montjuïc
Between Barcelona and the sea rises the hill of Montjuïc, 715 metres high. Does its name really derive from 'the mount of the Jews', a reference to the fact that these people took refuge here after the persecutions of 1391 and built a cemetery? Or from 'the mount of Jove', the Roman God Jupiter, a relic of the Roman occupation? For many years a bastion stood on Montjuïc, with an important defensive watch-tower. Then in 1929 Barcelona hosted an International Exhibition, and the citizens set themselves to transforming Montjuïc into its present fun-filled self.

Reach it by bus from the monumental Plaça d'Espanya (Metro

station Espanya), whose swashbuckling fountain by Josep Maria Pujol represents Spain offered to God, as well as the Mediterranean, the Atlantic Ocean and the Cantabrian sea. Here too stand the older of Barcelona's two bull-rings and the monumental congress hall. And passing between two brick towers modelled on the bell-tower which stands in St Mark's Square, Venice, but built for the Exhibition of 1929, Avinguda de Reina Maria Cristina leads to the mighty Palacio Nacional, with its multitude of cupolas. Another legacy of 1929, it is fronted by magnificent jets of water which are illuminated at night.

Today it is the home of the Museum of Catalan Art, with sixty-eight halls of marvellous romanesque and medieval creativity (open from 09.00 to 14.00, except for Mondays and holidays). This grandiose building also contains a ballroom 5000 metres square, capable of holding over 20,000 dancers.

Walk between the pseudo-Venetian bell-towers and take bus no.61 on the right. It takes you on a tour of Montjuïc, soon passing the Pueblo Español on the left. This creation of the painters Miguel Utrillo and Xavier Noguès was built by the architect Folguera and supposedly represents Spain in its unique splendour. If you get off the bus here you enter by a replica of the gate of San Vincente, Avila, and find yourself in a square flanked by famous buildings copied from the originals in Valencia, Tarragona, Madrid, Burgos and virtually everywhere else of note in the country. The village is packed with potters and trinket sellers, full-size copies of Spanish farms and reproduction churches (also life-size).

The bus continues past the site of the Montjuïc stadium, built for the Exhibition of 1929 and demolished in the 1980s to make way for an astonishing Olympic complex (for the games in 1992). More or less everything else on Montjuïc — the open-air Greek amphitheatre; the archaeological museum; the fun-fair — dates from 1929, but the Miró Foundation is another exception. This series of white concrete buildings appears on your left as the bus rattles on from the Olympic stadia. Its architect was Josep Lluis Sert, its inspirer the Catalan artist Joan Miró, and today it houses not only his own drawings, sculptures, water-colours and tapestries but also the many works of art he bequeathed to Barcelona on his death in 1983. It opens from Tuesday to Saturday from 11.00 to 20.00, closing on Sundays and holidays at 14.30.

The views of Barcelona from Montjuïc are astounding. There is also an extremely welcome open-air swimming-pool near the funicular railway and opposite the fun-fair, open in summer from 10.00 to 15.30 (closing half-an-hour earlier on Sundays and holidays). Here too stands the former castle, now a military museum. The fun-fair in the amusement park boasts a terrifying ferris wheel, and is open weekdays from 18.15 to 00.15, Saturdays for an hour longer, and Sundays from 12.00 to 00.15.

To settle your nerves, have a drink at one of the cafés and then take the precarious cable car from Miramar to Barceloneta back to the city, or (from the entrance to the amusement park) the funicular railway which tunnels under the cliff as far as the Metro station Parallel on line 3 (paying with a Metro ticket).

The works of Gaudí
Barcelona suddenly began to expand in the nineteenth century. The new cotton, iron and steel industries brought immigrants, and between 1850 and 1900 the population rose from 150,000 to 600,000. To house everyone, the area of the city grew from fewer than 20 hectares to over 200.

Fortunately, there was an architect of supreme genius on hand. Antonio Gaudí i Cornet was the son of a boilermaker, born in 1852 just as this colossal expansion was beginning. Great buildings and parks were needed for this new Barcelona, and Gaudí provided the most stupendously original of them. In 1873 he had joined the Provincial Architecture School of Barcelona. He did not really fit in with the prevailing modes of architectural thought there, but stuck out his apprenticeship and in 1878 was commissioned to design the lamps for the city's lovely Plaça Real. No one pattern of architecture dominated his mind. Eclecticism, complexity, the development of nineteenth-century gothic, and above all what the Catalans called *modernisme*, the equivalent of the French art nouveau and the German *Jugendstil*, fascinated him. He carried *modernisme* beyond anyone else's wildest dreams.

In consequence, until he was killed by a Barcelona tramcar in 1926, Gaudí created some breathtakingly original works of architecture and a fantastic city park that no visitor should miss on any account.

One of his masterpieces is a second cathedral, the Templo

Expiatorio de la Sagrada Familia (the church of the Holy Family). It remains unfinished and crazily spectacular. Reach it from the Barceloneta by taking Metro line 4 (direction Roquetes) and changing at Verdaguer station to line 5 (direction Horta), alighting at Sagrada Familia station.

At night the bizarre, moving spires of the Sagrada Familia are illuminated, from inside too. By day you relish its predominantly pink and grey undulating stone, with the words 'Sanctus, Sanctus, Sanctus' continually repeated on the spires and Gaudí's unique crosses (if that is the right word) crowning them in pink ceramic.

I find it hard to believe that Gaudí was not the sole originator of this miraculous building, but this is true. He took over from a far more mundane architect called Francesco de Paula del Villar in 1883, when Gaudí was only 31. Del Villar's plans were totally redrawn. Gaudí planned three façades for the building, one to represent Christ's birth, another his death, the third his resurrection. One was completed in 1921. Twelve soaring towers were to rise above the church, four from each façade. Gaudí had finished four by the time of his death, all of them 107 metres high. When the rest are finally built the church of the Sagrada Familia will drive people mad with ecstasy. You can go inside between 08.00 and 20.00 (09.00 and 18.00 in winter), ascend the towers and visit the crypt to pay homage at Gaudí's tomb.

To the west of the Sagrada Familia the Plaça de la Sagrada Familia is a shady children's park. A short downhill walk along Carrer Sicilia brings you to the wide thoroughfare called Gran Via de les Corts Catalanes, where a bus will whisk you west to the Passeig de Gràcia in order to see two more Gaudí masterpieces. They lie to the north of the intersection of Gran Via de les Corts Catalanes and Passeig de Gràcia.

Walk right on the left-hand side of Passeig de Gràcia and cross Carrer del Consell de Cent. Here are three enchanting art nouveau buildings, one by Gaudí, two by his artistic predecessors. Further on, on the corner of Carrer d'Aragó, stands the delicious Casa Lleó Morera, which was designed by Domènech i Montaner. Then, at no.41, stands the beautifully tiled Casa Amettler, its architect Puig i Cadafalch. And next to it, at no.43, the greatest of the three: Gaudi's stunning Casa Batlló, undulating, tiled in green, blue, orange and brown, with writhing balconies adding to its mad beauty. Here again, as with the Sagrada Familia, Gaudí took over an older building, this time transforming it between 1904 and 1906. He added a new rippling skin, redesigning the entrance, openings and apertures, topping it all with a tower that looks like a riotous flower bulb. Small wonder that you need to sink overwhelmed on to the bench thoughtfully provided here by Barcelona city council as you contemplate it all.

Cross the road and walk on to the intersection with Carrer de Provença further up Passeig de Gràcia. At no.92 on the corner is Gaudí's Casa Milá. Casa Milá was commissioned by the Milá family in 1906, finished in 1910, and dubbed by the Catalans *La Pedrera* (the stone quarry). Here Gaudí has totally eschewed colour and tiling in favour of a stone façade that dances sinuously and wildly around the corner. The metal-work is tortured. Two hugely strange glass and bronze porticoes lead inside into deliciously cool interconnected courtyards, with the most magical art nouveau doors opening out into them.

One of Gaudí's patrons, the financier Eusebio Güell, profited considerably from Barcelona's astonishing commercial expansion in the second half of the nineteenth century. In a philanthropic gesture, he turned over part of his estate to Gaudí for the creation of a city garden, an assignment which the architect completed between 1910 and 1914, using all his powers of imagination.

You can reach it by a fairly stiff fifteen-minute walk after taking Metro line 3 (direction Montbau) to Lesseps station, turning right through the little park in Plaça Fernando Lesseps and by way of the underpass into the not very prepossessing dual carriageway called the Travessera de Dalt. After ten minutes take the steep Carrer de Larrard left. I recommend this route only if you pause at one of the restaurants on the way for a drink (and maybe also to eat an extremely cheap and excellent *menú de dia*). Otherwise take a taxi.

As you ride (or climb) up the Carrer de Larrard, a bizarre blue-and-white Gaudí pillar, topped by a double cross, suddenly arises ahead. The entrance to Parc Güell appears, flanked by a couple of gateways that must have come, it seems, from some children's fantasy chocolate factory. Everywhere in the park you find crazily wonderful ceramic details, sinuous parabolic passageways and patchwork quilts of tiles. Nearby is a fountain tiled in the form of a huge lizard. The Hall of a Hundred Columns is in fact supported by eighty-six, all Doric in design, deliberately contrasting with Gaudí's own inventions, and with the lovely tiles cf his collaborator Josep Maria Jujol i Gibert. Jujol also tiled the rows of benches set on top of the platform in the great *plaça*, with deliberately broken pieces of multi-coloured ceramic. Parabolic arches hold back the earth in long curving viaducts, bordered with flowers. Fantastically wrought iron grilles and gates add their charm to the whole dream park. And there is a view across Barcelona to the sea from the great terrace.

You need not take a taxi back to Lesseps station, for it is easy enough to walk back down Carrer de Larrard and catch a bus running west along the Travessera de Dalt. Bus no.24 will take you all the way back to Plaça de Catalunya.

Excursion to buy wine and see the sea

Hire a car, pack a swimming costume and a wide enveloping towel (since Spain's beaches do not all offer numerous changing places) and drive out of Barcelona by following the signs for Tarragona and Lleida and the motorway A7. You turn left along a wide boulevard flanked by modernistic junk juxtaposed with lovely old buildings set in exquisite gardens that boast palms and pergolas.

Take the motorway A2 towards Lleida and Tarragona. As you drive onwards hills with little villages set in their crevices appear ahead of you. Just after Martorell the landscape ceases to suffer the intrusion of modern Spanish buildings and is suddenly covered with vines and blessed with old churches and villages. The motorway has somehow become the A7. Wine caves (*cavas*) began to advertise themselves with huge placards set among their vineyards. Villas perched on top of hills now command fantastic views of the entire countryside.

After 35 kilometres you reach exit 27 and the road to Sant Sadurni d'Anoia. More and more caves are advertising their Spanish champagne. If you turn immediately left you reach Cavas Freixant, fronted by ancient wine presses and boasting beautiful factory buildings tiled with ceramics depicting foaming champagne glasses, vines and grapes. There are guided tours around this wine factory on weekdays from 09.30 to 11.30 and from 15.30 to 17.30. If you arrive at lunchtime, all you can do is sample one of the products in the bar where the workers drink, just outside the main gates.

Then drive on, following the signs to the *Centre Urba* of Sant Sadurni d'Anoia. This is an extraordinarily pretty village, crammed with balconies and ancient towers, as well as buildings by the art nouveau architect Josep Puig i Cadafalch. It thrives on champagne, and caves painted with grapes are everywhere. In Plaça del Doctor Salvans stands a seventeenth-century church with an ancient six-sided bell-tower. The beautiful portico (dated 1706) has classical roundels portraying the symbols of the four Evangelists: St John's angel, St Mark's lion, St Matthew's eagle and St Luke's bull. The adjoining presbytery is equally charming, a sundial adorning its decorated wall.

This is an excellent spot to buy some Spanish champagne, since the vintners have been producing it here since the sixteenth century. Cava Canals & Munné, for instance, stands in Plaça Pau Casals, its delightful façade topped by models of four massive champagne bottles. You can also eat an excellent Catalan meal here. The proprietor's semi-dry Cristal Dore is incredibly inexpensive and is said to be three years old. So is the Semi-Seco-Dulce. The extra dry Reserva de l'Avi is twice that age. A bottle lasted me about half an hour, as I lay in a field outside the village after lunch.

From Sant Sadurni d'Anoia take the C-243a towards Villafranca del Penedés. The road twists and turns through rocky, sandy soil supporting the vines whose produce you will probably have just sampled and bought. On either side too are orchards of peach trees, bordered with the willows from which the Catalans weave their baskets. More restaurants appear, and after 16 kilometres Villafranca. At first the adjective that springs to mind to describe the village is unprepossessing, but this is the capital of the ancient region of Penedés. Follow the sign pointing right to the *Centre Historic*, and then another notice in the Carrer de St Bernat on your right, directing you to the Museu de Villafranca and the Basilica Santa Maria.

This will lead you to the main square of Villafranca, Plaça de Jaume 1, where you can park. In the centre is a modernistic statue depicting that crazy Catalan habit of men and boys balancing ever higher on each others' shoulders until someone possibly falls off. The museum turns out to be six museums altogether: a wine museum, the town museum, the art gallery, the archaeological museum, the local ornithology collection and the geology museum — all contained in a building dating from the twelfth to the fourteenth century. (If you want to visit any of these museums, they open, except on Mondays, from 10.00 to 14.00 and from 16.30 to 19.30.) According to a plaque, King Pedro II el Gran of Aragon died on 11 November 1285 in this venerable building. Its charming upper balcony is matched at the end of the square, beyond the lamplit trees, with that of the town library. Next to the museum is a romanesque-gothic chapel dedicated to St John. Opposite the museum stands the so-called Forum Balta, whose massive round doorway has the arms of Catalonia sculpted on its keystone. It also boasts an oriel window with two of the slenderest pillars imaginable, over which is a rustic seven-arched balcony.

If you turn round from reading Pedro el Gran's memorial plaque, you see first the powerful buttresses and medieval gargoyles of the gothic basilica of Santa Maria, the final touch to this altogether delightful Catalan country square. And next to it hangs the metal sign of a vintner, depicting a man and woman hurrying home from the harvest, carrying between them on a branch a bunch of grapes as big as themselves.

The neo-gothic façade of Santa Maria is modern and very fine too. To get inside, walk past the metal vintner's sign and along Plaça Santa Maria up to the bell-tower and the south entrance. Unlike Barcelona's churches, this one does not seem to close for a very long lunch. The interior (and exterior) happen to be in excellent condition; the modernistic stained glass at the east end is not offensive; and to the right of the entrance steps lead down to the medieval crypt, with two superb and huge roof bosses, one depicting Jesus dead on his mother's knee, the other portraying him rising triumphant from the grave.

The C-244 to Vilanova la Geltrú with its thirteenth-century castle, scarcely 2 kilometres away, is signposted from the main square of Villafranca del Penedés. Then go on another 21 kilometres to the coastal resort of Sitges. This is a twisting route of unexpected bizarreness with superb panoramic views of the Catalan countryside.

Sitges has a long history. Originally a Roman trading post known as Subur, it was walled in the fourteenth century (and still retains some of these fortifications). It is blessed with the baroque church of SS Thecla and Bartholomew, as well as an art gallery boasting a couple of works by El Greco. But this is not why most of us come here, for Sitges also has splendid beaches, most of them available free to anyone who wishes simply to park, lay a towel on the sand, sunbathe and swim, and perhaps drink half a bottle of Spanish champagne.

After sleeping off the effects, the excellent coastal road will have you back in Barcelona after a mere 36 kilometres.

Food and drink

Catalonian cuisine is as fiercely nationalistic as the Catalan people. Recognizably Spanish to a foreigner, it is none the less individual with its own quiddities. The chefs are masters at mixing game with succulent fruit or nuts, so your partridge will arrive at the table cooked with grapes and your rabbit served with almonds. Alternatively game and fish are tantalizingly served together, and your chicken arrives with lobster. A *niu* is a dish made from stockfish and young pigeons. If you choose rabbit, it will often have been cooked in rum.

Spanish brandy and white wine are often ingredients in the fish stew known as *zarzuela*, a mixture of squid, prawns, octopus, mussels, lobster and so on, all served on rice. These ingredients also produce a magnificent *bouillabaisse*, known in Catalan as *el suquet de peix*. As for rice, it is essential for the magical *paella*. In Barcelona the waiter will bring it to your table in the huge flat pan in which it has been cooked over the open fire, ladling it beautifully on to the plate. It is likely to contain some octopus, squid, mussels and shrimps and be accompanied by a huge slice of lemon.

Hors d'oeuvres in Barcelona often turn out to be virtually a meal in themselves. Order a simple salad for one (*ensalada de la casa*) and you look round for somebody to share it with. To make way for another course or two I recommend *empanadillas*, delicious pasties, stuffed with minced meat or fish; or else *croquetas*, again made of minced meat or crumbled fish but this time fried in breadcrumbs.

Look out for Catalan sausages (*butifarra catalana*) or spicy black puddings (*butifarra negra*). Unpretentious working men's restaurants will often serve *monchetas con butifarra*, delicious broad beans with an exhilaratingly spiced sausage. In the same restaurant you are likely to be offered an inexpensive, juicily cooked *bistec a la plancha con garnicion*. And another spicy (very spicy) dish much on offer in Barcelona is the red Asturian sausage, *choricitos asturianos*. The humblest bar will often have several pungent cured hams hanging from its ceiling, and a chalked menu offering spaghetti as a huge *hors d'oeuvre* (chalked up as *macarrones entremeses*); that pungent cold soup *gazpacho andaluz*, a dish deriving originally from Castile; rich salads; boiled and fried vegetables spiced with garlic (a potent dish often simply advertised as *verdura*); and veal chops (*chuletas*). *Almondigas in salsa* are one of my favourite ways of eating pork and beef — chopped, rolled into balls and cooked in butter, flour and white wine.

If you like squid, look out for *calamares a la catalana*, which means that it is fried with ham and onions. I confess that I have never yet dared order *calamares en su tinta* (often called *chipirones* on Catalan menus), a dish of squids packed with egg and ham and served on rice after cooking in their own inky black sauce. Another seafood dish is *gambas a la plancha*, shrimps which have been first boiled and then oven-cooked. *Bacalao* (Catalan for the Spanish *bacalado*) means cod, often served *al pil-pil*, that is in a stew of white sauce, potatoes, onions and parsley. Hake is *merluza* — served in the same way as *bacalao al pil-pil*, or poached, or fried.

Cooking over charcoal is typically Catalan. In Barcelona pork (*lomo*) is often done on a barbeque (*a la brasa*), as are quails (*condornices*), rabbit (*conejo*) and chicken (*pollo*).

What of puddings? *Flan de la casa* will usually turn out to be a delicious custard flan. *Crema cremada* is caramel custard. Ice-cream (*helado*) is served in twenty different varieties. And if you are in Barcelona during one of the religious festivals, try the seasonal dessert: ring-shaped cakes (*tortells*) at Epiphany; a fritter (*bunuelo*) for Lent; Easter buns (*monas*); and almond *panellests* for All Saints' Day.

Finally I recommend four Catalan specialities: *pimientos rellenos*, which are large baked peppers, stuffed with meats, cheese or ham; enormous slices of bread with tomatoes and smoked ham (*pan con tomate y jamón*); marinated trout, flavoured with herbs, called *truchas a la navarra*; and *conejo con ali-oli*, rabbit served with a mayonnaise sauce flavoured with garlic.

What do you drink with all this? Cheapest and usually perfectly acceptable is the *vino de la casa*. The waiter will bring red unless you specify white (*blanco*). People often dilute their wine with lemonade, thus creating their own *sangría*, which usually features on wine lists as either *sangría de la casa* or *sangría de champagne* (in which case it will probably have been made from the sparkling wines of Sant Sadurni d'Anoia). Rioja, red, white or rosé is drunk here, though not a speciality of the region, as of course is sherry (*jerez*) and cold beer (*cerveza*) of very variable quality.

Night life

Whether an evening's entertainment should include watching bulls being slaughtered is for some of us a moral matter. Ernest Hemingway loved bullfights, and his descriptions of the death are more than enough to put me off the sport ('Finally he killed, going in perfectly and hitting bone twice; then burying the sword in the red pommel guard. They gave him one ear although the crowd asked for both. But he had hit bone twice.') You can, however, very easily watch bullfighting on a weekend visit. Two arenas are situated on the Gran Via de les Corts Catalanes, the older one where it meets Plaça Catalunya, and the Plaza de Toros Monumental (a rather pretty brick-built arena, decorated with blue-and-white tiles and egg-shaped towers) where it meets Passeig de Carlos I. Fights take place on Sundays from 18.00, and you can buy a ticket at the entrance up to one hour before the fights begin. Pay a little extra to sit on the shady side of the arena.

Barcelona is a city of football fans, and the Fútbal Club Barcelona (known as the 'Barça') has over 100,000 members as well as a stadium on Montjuïc with a capacity for 120,000 spectators. In summer the city also hosts international music and theatre festivals. The Teatre del Liceu in the Ramblas specializes in opera and ballet. Concerts take place in the lovely art nouveau Palau de la Música Catalana, which Domènech i Montaner built between 1905 and 1908.

The city boasts its quota of Parisian-style night-clubs: eat or drink at the Scala (at nos.45–49 Paseo San Juan) and watch the floor show; or choose El Molino (at no.93 Vilá Vilá). Shows start around 22.45. There are night-clubs and strip-joints on the Ramblas and in some side streets (operating from 23.00 to 3.00), although not all are to be recommended. As for Flamenco dancing, though by no means a native-born product, Barcelona bows to tourist demand with a number of clubs, such as Los Tarantos at no.17 Plaça Real and El Cordobés in the Ramblas, offering food as well as a show. Jazz concerts are given regularly in (of all unlikely places) the church of Santa Maria del Mar, as well as the Zeleste club (at no.65 Platería) and at L'Eixample (in Diputació-Bailen). The main casino is outside the city, at Sant Pere de Ribes, opening from 18.00 to 05.00.

To keep up to date about entertainment in Barcelona, you should buy the weekly guide *La guia del ocio*.

Important information

You will find both Spanish and Catalan spoken in Barcelona. The Franco regime banned the use of Catalan, but Catalan nationalism is no longer suppressed and Catalan names are used throughout the region and in this text.

Banks in Barcelona open only from 09.00 to 13.00 on working days. They close on Sundays and public holidays, of which there are many: 1 January, 6 January, 19 March, Good Friday, Easter Monday, 1 May, 24 June, 11 September, 24 September, 1 November, Christmas Day and Boxing Day.

Getting around the city is extremely simple. On foot you can reach everywhere in the centre. Taxis, painted yellow and black, are plentiful, can be hailed if they are cruising free, and cost surprisingly little. The five Metro lines are fast, and you should buy ten tickets at once to save money, at any Metro station. Trains run from 05.00 to 23.00. Buses are frequent (and you can get a guide to them from the Tourist Office, at no.658 Via de les Corts Catalanes). With these too a strip of ten tickets saves money, obtainable from the kiosk in Plaça de Catalunya (ask for an *abono*) opposite the department store El Corte Inglés.

Arriving at El Prat airport, look for the RENFE signs for trains running every twenty minutes from 06.30 to 23.00 which bring you to the central station within fifteen minutes. At other times RENFE provides a bus service to and from the airport.

Berlin

All free men, wherever they live, are citizens of Berlin, and therefore as a free man, I take pride in the words, 'Ich bin ein Berliner'.

President J. F. Kennedy, 1963

Berlin is an intensely exciting city, partly because its history has been at once both creative and destructive, partly because it has risen in our own century from ashes, and partly because, despite its prosperity and its affable population, it still appears vulnerable. Set in the DDR (as East Germany is officially called), West Berlin can seem like an outpost of the German Federal Republic in a foreign land. The scars of World War II have disappeared, but since the four-power victory over Germany in 1945 the city is still divided into an American sector, a British sector, a French sector and a Russian sector.

And of course the Berlin wall divides the Russian sector from the rest – a further symbol of the scars of history. Small wonder that in 1987 on the 750th anniversary of the founding of the city, the West Berliners chose 'reminiscence' and 'renewal' as two themes of their celebrations.

A splendid symbol of Berlin's powers of renewal is the city's Congress Hall. The Americans built it in fifteen months, as a gift to the international building exhibition of 1957. In 1980 its daringly curved roof fell in, proving to have been built too fast and too daringly. The West Berliners have rebuilt it, taking more time, and constructing it just a little more solidly.

Yet Berlin is not an anxious place, submerged in its difficult past. The city really does celebrate – musically, with its world famous Philharmonic orchestra; in night life, where almost anything goes; in theatre; in eating and drinking; in sunbathing in the parks. The parks dominate the city. More than anything else memories of West Berlin combine themselves into a vision of one exquisite park.

A city tour

All three Kaisers lived in Berlin, and the first of them, Wilhelm I, made Berlin the capital of the German empire. On his death in 1888 the most celebrated among all the memorials raised to him was a splendid neo-romanesque church, the Kaiser-Wilhelm-Gedächtnis-

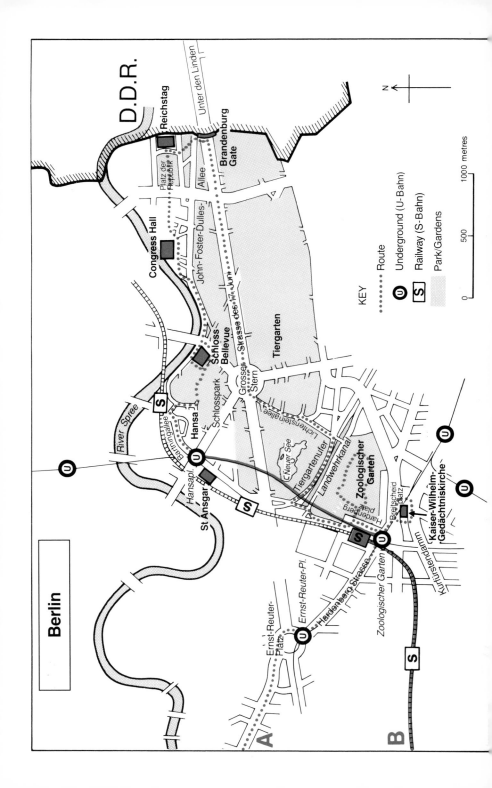

Berlin

D.D.R.

Reichstag
Platz der Republik
Congress Hall
Unter den Linden
Brandenburg Gate
John-Foster-Dulles-Allee
Schloss-Bellevue
Schlosspark
Strasse des 17. Juni
Grosser Stern
Tiergarten
Lichtensteinallee
C. Neuer See
River Spree
Bachstrasse
Hansa
Bartningallee
Hansapl.
St Ansgar
Tiergartenufer
Landwehrkanal
Zoologischer Garten
Hardenbergplatz
Breitscheid Platz
Kaiser-Wilhelm-Gedächtniskirche
Kurfürstendamm
Ernst-Reuter-Platz
Ernst-Reuter-Pl.
Hardenberg Strasse
Zoologischer Garten

A

B

N

KEY
Route
U Underground (U-Bahn)
S Railway (S-Bahn)
Park/Gardens

0   500   1000 metres

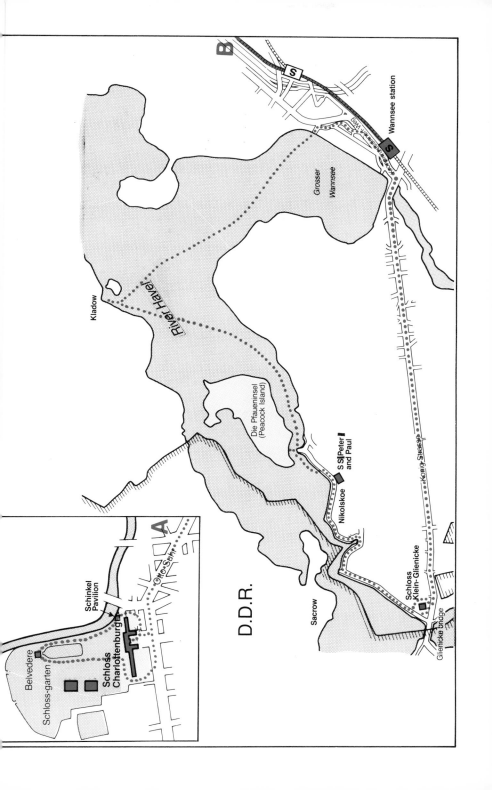

D.D.R.

River Havel

Kladow

Grosser
Wannsee

Die Pfaueninsel
(Peacock Island)

S S Peter
and Paul

Nikolskoe

Sacrow

Schloss
Klein-Glienicke

König-Strasse

Glienicke bridge

B

S

S

Wannsee station

Avus W99

A

Otto-Sohn

Belvedere

Schloss-garten

Schinkel
Pavilion

Schloss
Charlottenburg

kirche, built by Franz Schwechten between 1891 and 1895.

This church stands at the heart of West Berlin, a symbol both of its former grandeur and of the tragedy of its twentieth-century history. It was severely damaged by allied bombs in World War II, but they failed to destroy it totally. After the war the Germans decided to keep the church as a noble ruin. Another architect, Egon Eiermann, was commissioned to surround the ruined memorial with a new inconspicuous church (which nevertheless has coloured glass from Chartres and a glockenspiel designed by Prince Louis Ferdinand of Prussia). West Berlin grew again around this memorial to greatness and tragedy.

The church stands in Breitscheidplatz, just south-west of the railway station where all the trains from the Federal Republic of Germany arrive at Berlin. Part of the great rose window that adorned the west end still survives, a huge shattered hole. The tower points blankly to the sky. What remains has been used as the setting for a fascinating memorial exhibition (open except on Mondays from 10.00 to 18.00 and on Saturdays from 11.00 to 18.00). Miraculously, some of the original mosaics were spared, including gleaming representations of St Michael fighting the dragon and Christ Pantocrator.

Mosaics also record the former ruling family. The old Hohenzollerns begin with Elector Friedrich I, who founded the dynasty in Brandenburg in the fifteenth century, and end with Friedrich Wilhelm, 'the great Elector', who died in 1688. The more recent branch of the family begins with Queen Luise. She was the mother of Kaiser Wilhelm I, who proclaimed the German empire in 1871. Since his army had just defeated the French, this event took place in Versailles, not in Berlin. Over the Kaiser himself is a glorious baldacchino. On his right is poor Kaiser Friedrich III, who died after only 99 days on the throne, followed by the notorious Kaiser Wilhelm II, known as 'Kaiser Bill' during World War I. After the war Lloyd George wanted to hang him, but instead the Kaiser died in exile at Doorn in Holland in 1941. Finally the last of the line, Crown Prince Wilhelm (who died in 1951), is depicted at his marriage to his wife Cecilie.

There are, of course, biblical and Christian scenes here, as well as the heroes of the Reformation (Martin Luther, John Calvin, and so on, for this was a Protestant church); but the overall impression is that an imperial dynasty was being lauded here quite as much as the Christian faith. Other mosaics depict the Emperor Charlemagne and the Habsburgs, and four great wall reliefs illustrate the life of Kaiser Wilhelm I.

But what makes the memorial hall unforgettable is the extremely moving post World War II exhibition. Sixteen large exhibits depict the history of this doomed church, from the time it was built until it was seen in flames on 22 November 1943. The Berliners see the memorial hall as both an admonition against war and a call to reconciliation. Here they have erected a statue of Jesus which was once part of the destroyed altar of the church, with his own words inscribed on a plaque in front: 'Forgive us our sins, as we forgive those who sin against us.' And next to the statue is a cross made of nails. The nails came from England in 1987, collected from beams of Coventry cathedral after they had been reduced to ashes by a German air raid on 14 November 1940. Similar crosses made from Coventry cathedral nails are now in churches in Dresden, East Berlin and Wolograd (formerly Stalingrad) in the USSR.

Berlin shows itself at its sprightliest in the Kurfürstendamm which leads south-west from the Kaiser-Wilhelm-Gedächtnis-kirche. This splendid shopping street, abbreviated to the Kudamm, stretches for nearly 4 kilometres. In the sixteenth century Elector Joachim II laid it out as a fitting approach to his hunting lodge. Then in the 1880s it was widened and lined with exquisite art nouveau (*Jugendstil*) buildings. Alas, of some 250 houses 200 were destroyed in World War II. But today's thoroughfare bustles with life (two theatres, hotels, shopping centres, the Café Kranzler, cinemas, night-clubs, antique shops, restaurants) and exudes glamour, albeit of a different kind from that a hundred years ago. Not far down, Wertheim's department store has recently been refurbished with a startling façade and regularly changes the exhibitions in its huge window. For Berlin's 750th birthday celebrations the display consisted of thirty-eight different birthday cakes, one of them depicting Marlene Dietrich in her *Blue Angel* outfit succulently crossing her legs amidst the cream.

On the other side of the Kaiser-Wilhelm-Gedächtniskirche is a jolly modern fountain, designed by someone called Schmettau in the mid 1980s and named 'Wasserklops'. It is decorated with little figures (including humans), water pouring out of them. Sit in the sun outside the café to the east of Wasserklops, sipping a coffee. In really hot weather you can watch the children on the other side of the fountain taking off their shoes and socks and sometimes all their clothes to run up and down a water staircase.

Go down the steps beyond Wasserklops into the Europa Centre: a huge complex of cinemas, restaurants, bars, a cabaret and a casino where you can play baccarat, roulette and black jack. In the middle of the Europa Centre is a hugely entertaining water clock, which speedily empties itself with many a gurgle at 13.00 and then starts its 24-hour cycle again.

No trip to Berlin is complete without a visit to the zoo (Zoologischer Garten), one of the most famous zoos in the world. Walk from the Europa Centre north of the station to the zoo entrance in Hardenbergplatz. The Berlin zoo was founded in 1841 under the direction of the great African explorer Martin Lichtenstein and with gifts of animals from King Friedrich Wilhelm IV of Prussia. Prussian diplomats throughout the world enthusiastically shipped beasts back to Berlin. By 1939 this was the most important zoo in the world, possessing an animal collection approaching 4000 beasts as well as some 1500 species of birds and an aquarium stocking 8300 reptiles, amphibians and fish. In addition there were another 750 species of invertebrates.

Only 91 animals survived World War II, but the zoo and aquarium have risen again. Today there are in the region of 11,000 beasts, birds and fishes on display, nearly 1550 species in all. A weekend in Berlin could be totally consumed trying to see half of them. But a visit is essential. (The zoo opens daily from 09.00 till dusk, and on Sundays from April to September it opens an hour earlier. The aquarium opens daily from 09.00 till 18.00.) Everything is labelled in German, French and English. The elephant house is a must. Berlin zoo keeps African and Indian elephants, with some fine subspecies, in roomy outdoor enclosures, separated from visitors by narrow dry moats (and oddly accompanied by young rhinos). These intelligent beasts are highly trained and lumber through daily semi-acrobatic performances.

Here are lakes with coots and tufted ducks, mallards and herons. The pelicans have their own pond. More exotic species include the Caucasian porcupine, or the largest rodent in the world, the capybara. Baboons live on specially constructed rock formations which enable the less tough ones to escape or hide from the bossy or bullying ones. Here too is a house for the magnificent great apes, including a troupe of the rare orang-utans. Since fewer than 2500 wild orang-utans survive, Berlin zoo (like most others) refuses to buy them. The first ever orang-utan born in captivity was bred here, as long ago as 1928. Today the zoo possesses a dozen such apes, nearly all of whom were born in Berlin.

After the ape house comes the monkey house, and then the tropical house, with tree kangaroos, beautiful ruffed lemurs and the red-faced Japanese macaque. Two-toed sloths amble along hanging upside down from the branches, since they cannot walk upright. The sea-lion fountain is a rare survival from the pre-war zoo and is graced by a colony of Cuban flamingoes.

From here a staircase leads directly to the magnificent aquarium (fronted by a statue of the extinct giant lizard known as the iguanadon). Another feature not to be missed is the crocodile hall. Berlin zoo breeds some of its own crocodiles, feeding them on fish and rats, and it boasts one Chinese alligator — another extremely endangered species — which survived the war. As for the tigers, you are separated from them by nothing more than a glass window, except in the case of the Siberian tigers, which for some reason are encircled by a wide moat filled with water (this looks much safer). Striped hyenas, Bengal cats, jaguars and yellow mongooses all live in Berlin zoo, as do zebras, antelopes and delightful pandas. The European brown bear, Berlin's own symbol, is matched by snowy polar bears and Asian black ones. If you go to see the hippos, look out for Knautschke. Born in 1943, this beast is another rare survival from World War II.

Leave the zoo by the same entrance, turn right into Hardenbergplatz and right again into the Tiergarten, a nature park some 3 kilometres long and 1 kilometre wide, enhanced by one of the most brilliant of European landscape gardeners, Peter J. Lenné (1789–1866). This was once the private hunting park of the prince-electors. More than a million trees have been planted since 1949 to remedy the destruction of the last war. Old gas lamps are a delightful feature of the park. Go across the lock on the Landwehr canal and you will see a charming series brought from Brussels, Great Britain, Dublin, Zurich, Copenhagen and Leiden.

Then turn right along the Tiergartenufer, and wander along

another romantic gas-lit avenue, the lamps on the left from Düsseldorf, Hanover, Munich, Nuremberg, the Krumme Lanke housing estate and Frohnau, those on the right from Budapest, Chemnitz (now Karl-Marx-Stadt), Dresden, Würzburg and Leipzig. If you continue along this peaceful bank you will reach a bridge after a while, with a reminder of past treachery on the other side of the canal. A plaque marks the spot where the bodies of the socialist leaders Rosa Luxemburg and Karl Liebknecht, brutally murdered by soldiers, were thrown into the canal in 1918.

If you want to avoid this grisly spot go left without crossing the bridge. Here there is a grassy picnic place (a *Liegewiese*, where no ball games are allowed), or else you can make your way to the lakeside Café am Neuen See where you can hire a rowing boat as well as eat.

Then continue into the old Tiergarten diplomats' quarter. Lichtensteinallee, which still houses the Spanish consul general. Straight on, the elegant tree-lined Fasanienallee leads through statues of spirited, savage huntsmen as far as Berlin's Victory Column. The statues, created by Carl Begas in 1904, happily portray some of the animals getting their own back on their hunters.

The Victory Column stands 67 metres high in the middle of the important road junction known as the Grosser Stern. It carries a gilded figure of Victory and was put up in 1873 to the designs of Heinrich Strack on the orders of Kaiser Wilhelm I to celebrate Germany's victory over Denmark in 1864, Austria in 1866 and France in 1870–1. You can climb all 285 steps of the spiral staircase inside the column (between 10.00 and 17.30) for a magnificent panorama.

To the right Strasse des 17. Juni leads directly past the impressive Russian war memorial to the dead of 1941–5 (flanked by World War II tanks, with a guard of honour always present) to the Brandenburg Gate. At the far side of the gate is the famous Unter den Linden, but that is in East Berlin and there is now no way through. Nevertheless the gate is still superb. Based on one set up when Unter den Linden was first planned in 1734, Carl Gotthard Langhans created the present gate between 1788 and 1791. Modelled on the entrance to the Acropolis, Athens, it stands 26 metres high, 11 metres broad and 65.5 metres wide. The chariot and horses on top, bearing the goddess of Victory, were sculpted by Gottfried Schadow and added three years later. Napoleon had

Victory, her steeds and her chariot removed to Paris in 1806. They came back after his defeat in 1814. Lower down on the gate are sculptures representing the goddess's triumphs and scenes from Greek mythology. On the north and south sides are statues of Athena and Ares. Another twenty reliefs illustrate the life of Hercules.

For over a century the square on which the Brandenburg Gate stands was the rallying point for political parties and the scene of great military parades. Today it is fenced off, though you can climb up to platforms and photograph East Berlin.

Fifty metres to the left of the Brandenburg Gate stands the Reichstag building. Walk to the front (the Platz der Republik). Across a great sports field you can see the sweep of the roof of the restored Congress Hall, elegant and daring, but not quite so much as before it fell down. Between 1884 and 1894 Paul Wallot designed the massive Reichstag, once the home of the German parliament, in the style of the Italian high renaissance. Over the porch during World War I was inscribed 'Dem Deutschen Volk'. On 27 February 1933 a mysterious fire here gave Adolf Hitler a pretext for banning the German communist party and thus consolidating his own hold over Germany.

The entrance is at the far side. Exhibitions are held here daily, except on Mondays, from 10.00 to 17.00. There is a permanent and fascinating display on German history, brilliantly set out, with a great many free hand-outs. There is also a little self-service restaurant where everyone has to stand up, so nobody stays there too long, but if you go further inside, you find both a sit-down *Stube* and a fully-blown restaurant.

The Reichstag stands on the edge of the River Spree, which here marks the border between East and West Berlin. Crosses in memory of those who have been shot dead by East German guards as they tried to cross over flank the western side. You are allowed to fall into the water here, but not to jump in without serious risk of suffering the same fate. If you fall in, your friends are not expected to jump in after you to save you. Instead, they call the emergency services from the boxes thoughtfully provided close by.

Walk to the Congress Hall by way of the sports field, take the little road to the left along the bank of the River Spree until you join John-Foster-Dulles-Allee, and then turn right to reach the exquisite

Schloss Bellevue set in its equally exquisite Schloss park. The architect Michael Philipp Boumann created the Schloss in 1785 for Prince Ferdinand, youngest brother of Frederick the Great of Prussia. Carl Gottfried Langhans designed its interior. Today it is the official residence of the President of the German Federal Republic, and a perfect example of what the Germans revere as an 'English garden'. Take time to have a cup of tea or a beer, a coffee or an ice cream, in the thatched park house. The park house does not serve substantial food, except for *Wurst* (which is virtually universally available in this city).

Directly west of the Schloss park is a remarkable complex of buildings: the Hansa quarter of Berlin. This residential district was the scene of the international building exhibition of 1957, when no fewer than forty-eight famous architects contributed work: men of the quality of Arne Jacobsen, Walter Gropius, Oscar Niemeyer, Sten Samuelsen and Fritz Jaeneck. Gerhard Siegmann and Klaus Müller-Rehm designed and built flats for the unmarried here — a socially revolutionary idea in the 1950s. I have stayed in one of the multi-storey flats in Bartningallee and can testify that, although in general the 1950s was not a great era in international architecture, these do work extremely well. A useful notice on Bartningallee tells you which architect was responsible for each building.

I cannot similarly praise the Hansa church of St Ansgar, designed by Willy Kreuer in 1957, with its bells in a sort of open bell-tower and its weedy stations of the cross by Ludwig P. Kowalski. Even its decent copper doors by Ludwig Gabriel Schreiber scarcely make it worthwhile passing the Hansa U-Bahn station (slightly hidden amongst a little block of shops, a fast food bar and a bank), from which you can ride speedily back to Zoo station (on line U9 in the direction Rathaus Steglitz).

Alight from the U-Bahn and take bus no.54 from Hardenberg-platz in the direction of the airport to see the magnificent Schloss Charlottenburg. It opens daily (except on Mondays) from 09.00 to 17.00, the last tour beginning at 16.00. Elector Friedrich III, who became King Friedrich I in 1701, commissioned gardeners to begin laying out the grounds in the late seventeenth century, and the *Schloss* is fittingly named after his second wife, Sophie Charlotte. When she died in 1705 he was still adding to the palace that had been started in 1695 under the direction of the architect Arnold

Nering. Next the Swedish architect Eosander van Göthe transformed Nering's building into a three-winged *Schloss*. When Friedrich died in 1713, building was by no means finished. In particular Frederick the Great employed the brilliant Georg Wenzeslaus Knobelsdorff in the 1740s to build a new wing.

Frederick the Great's own successors continued to enrich the building, above all with a theatre, designed by Karl Gotthard Langhans (creator of the Brandenburg Gate) and added in 1788, and with a delicate pavilion, east of the main building, designed by Karl Friedrich Schinkel and put up in 1825. Marvellously, all these diverse architects respected each others' intentions and styles, and the result is a splendidly harmonious *Schloss* in yellow and white with a green copper dome. Moreover, it was beautifully restored after World War II.

An equestrian statue of the Great Elector by Andreas Schlüter stands in its courtyard. The interior is furnished with tapestries, lovely paintings, marble (including a sunken marble bath whose bronze taps are shaped like dolphins), chinoiserie, fine furniture, porcelain, mirrors, chandeliers, faience, damask and gold braid.

The gardens are as beautiful as the *Schloss*. Walk round the Knobelsdorff wing to see Schinkel's pavilion, on the bank of the River Spree. Sophie Charlotte loved the French gardens created by Le Nôtre at Versailles, and she hired Le Nôtre's pupil Siméon Godeau to make her a garden here. Friedrich I enlarged the garden without changing its character. 'I wish your serene highness were here,' he wrote happily to the Elector of Hanover in 1706. 'The garden is twice as large as before, and truly it will tire you out.' Langhans was employed to create a baroque belvedere in 1788, sensitively designed to complement the other buildings.

The nineteenth century, with its love of romantic 'English gardens', could not resist some more transformations. In 1810 Heinrich Gentz added a royal mausoleum, where Queen Luise and later King Friedrich Wilhelm III were laid in sarcophagi designed by Christian Daniel Rauch. Later Kaiser Wilhelm I and his empress were laid to rest here. Yet nothing has spoiled Sophie Charlotte's original beautiful garden.

A line of classical busts guards the house. The first one portrays Julius Caesar, flanked by Livia. Next comes Tiberius Caesar and his wife Aggrippina. Nero and Messalina are here, neither looking particularly evil. Occasionally an imperial mother joins this row of emperors and their consorts. To the right stretches the formal garden and in the distance is Langhan's green and white belvedere. Leave the gardens at the far end near the mausoleum. The former theatre on the left now houses a museum of pre- and early history (open daily except on Fridays from 09.00 to 17.00). For those with children, there is a play park and picnic area nearby.

The route back to Zoo station on the 54 bus is filled with architectural treats, such as the *Jugendstil* Charlottenburg town hall, built around 1900 with a tower 88 metres high, and Ernst-Reuter-Platz with its fountains and the modern television building (80 metres high and infinitely uglier than the town hall). Bernhard Heiliger sculpted the modernistic statue *Die Flamme* in Ernst Reuter's honour in 1963. The bus continues along Hardenberg Strasse, passing the green and glass High School and the classically styled music school on the left on the way to Zoo station.

The rest of the tour – to Wannsee and the Peacock island – continues from here, but it requires another day. Take S-Bahn 1 from Zoo station to Wannsee. After the station for Charlottenburg, it continues south through the forest known as the Grunewald and reaches Wannsee after twenty minutes.

Turn right outside the station and stroll down to the harbour. Here you can buy a single ticket to sail across the lake to the Peacock Island (die Pfaueninsel), which you can visit from March till October from 09.00 to 17.00 (extended for up to three hours in high summer), and from 10.00 to 16.00 from November to February. While you are waiting for the boat, you can sample sausage and chips, ice-cream or schnitzel at the nearby bars or restaurants (though on holidays it is best to stay in the queue and delegate a companion to visit the nearby stalls). Or else you can refresh yourself on the boat, in the *Schiffsrestauration*, where they will almost certainly sell Schultheiss beer, alcohol-free drinks (including tea and coffee), wine and *Sekt*, *Wurst* with bread, bread with cheese, or even more complicated hot or cold foods.

Take the boat in the direction *Rundfahrt über Kladow-Pfaueninsel–Moorlake–Glienicke Brücke*. From the Grosser Wannsee lake it sails into the River Havel, while the tannoy plays traditional merry songs about this stretch of water. In choppy weather those sitting in the prow of the boat can enjoy the spray! If the weather is

Berlin

hot there will be people sunbathing on Wannsee Strand, Berlin's best beach, created in 1907. Over 8000 Berliners have their own yachts and boats here and there are 157 sailing clubs. Catamarans, rowing boats and yachts are everywhere, with the occasional long black barge bringing building materials from the DDR.

The boat stops at Kladow, with its hostels looking out over the lake, its fishermen and sunbathers. The next stop is for the Pfaueninsel. From here a little ferry boat (the *Fähre*) takes you across to the Peacock Island itself.

We owe this island to a Prussian king's passion for hunting. In the late eighteenth century Friedrich Wilhelm II avidly shot the snipe and ducks in the thick reeds, a mere 21 kilometres from the centre of his capital city. At this time the island itself belonged to an orphanage. In 1793 Friedrich Wilhelm bought it. He would come here as some Rousseauesque lover of nature, camping in an oriental tent under the trees. These were years when the rich constructed follies representing fake medieval ruins; Friedrich Wilhelm ordered his court carpenter, Johann Gottlieb Brendel, to build him one on the Peacock Island. A dairy, a barn, a poultry shed and a peacock pen (disguised as a haystack) were built here too.

Friedrich Wilhelm died of dropsy before he could fully enjoy his extraordinary creation, but his successors continued his work – a little more soberly. Stags, sheep, wild boars and buffalo were bred here. In 1802 a gothic, perfectly serviceable byre was built next to the dairy. Two years later a couple more stables, a farmhouse and another barn were put up in the middle of the island. Finally, in the 1820s, Peter Joseph Lenné was brought in to landscape everything.

As the nineteenth century progressed, the Prussian monarchy enriched the island with imported trees, and with houses for monkeys, eagles, kangaroos, llamas, beavers and goats. A lovely aviary was added, as well as a rose garden containing 3000 specimens. Around 1830 Albert Dietrich Schadow designed a luxurious palm house.

The exotic animals were eventually transferred to the new Berlin zoo. Many of the exotic buildings remain, though the llama house burned down in 1842. Schinkel built a Kavalierhaus (princely home). Walking round the island today is magical, past pergolas and Friedrich Wilhelm II's bizarre *Schloss*, past great swooping trees with peacocks perched in them. The Pfaueninsel is a protected nature reserve and you must not smoke or take your dog. And you can picnic only in the *Liegewiese* (where there are toilets).

Return to the mainland and take a boat onwards for one stop. (This is for the hardy and healthy; the more infirm could go by boat as far as the Glienicke bridge.) Then walk right, past the restaurant, and follow the path which leads romantically along the lakeside. Soon the Nikolskoe Church appears high up on the left, called after the property created here for Charlotte, the daughter of Friedrich Wilhelm III, and wife of the future Tsar Nicholas. Dedicated to SS Peter and Paul, it was built in the Russian style in the 1830s by August Stüler. Beware: the church can only be reached by 200 irregular steps up the hillside, and it is usually closed. Its onion-domed tower carries a glockenspiel which plays regularly from Easter to the feast of the Ascension. Even if the church is closed and the glockenspiel silent, in summer the nearby restaurant serves cheesecake, apple strudel and pancakes (with or without cream).

There are numerous places to stop for food and refreshment along this route, such as the Wirtshaus Moorlake with a sunny veranda looking out on to the Havel. It is also close to the border with East Berlin. On the other side of the water you will see the walled village of Sacrow, with its redundant church of the Saviour (by Schinkel) and its abandoned houses. The inhabitants were forced to leave by the East German authorities, who considered that the place offered too easy an access to the west and closed the whole village down. Boundary signs soon appear in the middle of the water, declaring that you are in danger of leaving the American sector.

The end of the tour is Schloss Klein-Glienicke, with its orangery and its park. Schinkel's classical *Schloss*, built in 1826, is flanked by two classical pergolas, a few gothic elements adding to its charm. From the front you can look over the River Havel into the DDR at the ruined Pfingstberg, a bizarre construction built for Frederick the Great to supply water to Schloss Sans-Souci. A water cistern was set on top of it to work the fountain in the park. To the right is Bornstedt church.

The park laid out by Lenné round Schloss Klein-Glienicke is the finest in Berlin, with the exception of the Tiergarten. Artistically placed ruined pillars lie fallen, half-buried in the garden, and there are little classical fountains. A circular gazebo with Corinthian columns occupies one corner. It overlooks the Glienicke bridge, where spies are exchanged and where notices once again proclaim that you are about to leave the American and enter the Russian sector. The Glienicke bridge is called the 'Bridge of Unity', as one Berliner observed to me, 'because it divides us'.

Finally you come to what Karl Friedrich Schinkel intended as the entrance to Schloss Klein-Glienicke. Schinkel embellished the entrance with a grand, yet simple fountain. Next to it a lady caryatid holds up the roof of a semi-circular gazebo. A carved horn of plenty pours out its goods. Two sphinxes guard an ornamental trellis archway.

You can picnic in the park, taking care to leave everything as spotless as the Germans do. Then cross the road and take bus 6 back to the S-Bahn station at Wannsee. Alight from the bus just before it turns left to the station, cross the road and turn right parallel to the railway track. Here a sign directs you to the grave of Heinrich von Kleist, who was born in 1777 and killed himself on 21 November 1811 'because,' as he said, 'there is no one left to help me on earth.' The grave overlooks the Kleine Wannsee. It is inscribed with Kleist's words, 'O Immortality, you are wholly mine.'

The S-Bahn takes you directly back to Zoo station (direction Friedrichstrasse).

Further delights

The Olympic stadium
Take the U-Bahn line 1 from Zoo station in the direction Ruhleben and get out at Olympiastadion. From here the gentle uphill walk to the 1936 stadium takes five minutes. The ugly concrete block of flats beyond the trees is a little-known work by the celebrated architect Le Corbusier.

At the far end of the impressive stadium where Hitler staged the 1936 Olympic Games are bronze portrait medallions of past luminaries of the Olympic world, including Otto March, who built the first stadium here in 1913, and his son Werner March, who built the present stadium. Here too you can read the names of those who won, among them the incredible American Jesse Owens, who won the long jump, the 110 metres and the 200 metres in 1936.

Berlin's Olympic Stadium cost 42 million Reichsmarks, and 2600 workers were employed in its construction every working day between 1934 when building started and its completion two years later. They used 30,500 cubic metres of natural stone and 17,200 metric tonnes of rolled iron. However much the stadium was intended to glorify National Socialism, Werner March's achievement remains a magnificent architectural statement. Today the whole Olympic complex includes not only the original stadium but also a swimming stadium, a hockey stadium (with artificial grass), a riding stadium and an open-air theatre that seats 20,000 spectators. The wooded slope of the Murellenberg provides a stunning backcloth to the stage.

Werner March's famous oval stadium at the heart of the complex is now a classified monument. On a platform at the western end stands the bowl for the Olympic Flame. Here too is the Marathon Gate, through which you can see the restored bell-tower that once housed the famous Olympic Bell. This was rung to call competitors to the Berlin games in 1936, but it was badly damaged in World War II and can no longer ring (the tower was completely destroyed). The bell is now displayed close by the southern gate of the Olympic Stadium, the German eagle on it still clutching the Olympic rings in its claws. The original inscription has also survived: *Ich rufe die Jugend der Welt* [I call the youth of the world].

The return journey to Zoo station is by the same line in the direction Schlesisches Tor.

The Brücke Museum

The small and magical Brücke Museum in Dahlem is open daily (except on Thursdays) from 11.00 to 17.00. Bus no.60 runs there from Hardenbergplatz. On the way, if you look left in Mecklenbergische Strasse, you will see where the Steglitz motorway actually passes *through* a block of flats that was constructed over it. Alight at Pücklerstrasse, which is along Clayallee.

The Brücke Museum is well signposted and less than a five-minute walk through the trees from the bus stop. This gallery was set up in 1966 to house the remarkable works of the Brücke school of artists, a revolutionary group who came together in Dresden in 1905. These men and women produced some of the greatest German Expressionist paintings, sculptures, water-colours and drawings. When you reach the museum you see precisely how great (and revolutionary) the school was.

A list of my favourite works would include Emil Nolde's 1915 portrait of Gustav Schieffler, in top hat and gold pince-nez with an all-purple face and a green moustache, and Karl Schmidt-Rottluff's 1913 portrait of a red-faced man in a wine bar. The exquisite sunflowers Schmidt-Rottluff painted in 1928 are milder, but still wild. Ernst Ludwig Kirchner's 1913 nude before a mirror is more extreme. Painted green and blue, smoking a pipe, with pink soles to her feet and blood red hair, she nevertheless really does look like a recognizable woman. After these delights it is no surprise to see that when Karl Schmidt-Rottluff painted a dyke bursting its banks in 1910, the waters are red; or that Erick Heckel's lovely naked young man and girl are both yellow.

The Brücke Museum is intimate, and a visit (including the bus journeys) could be made in two hours or so. On the way back you might care to travel a couple of stops beyond Hardenbergplatz and alight at the vast Wittenbergplatz. The largest department store in Berlin, the Kaufhaus des Westens, is in Tauentzienstrasse to the west, known to Berliners as the *KaDeWe*. Tauentzienstrasse, as fine a street for shopping, eating and drinking as the Kudamm, leads back in five minutes from Wittenbergplatz to the Kaiser-Wilhelm-Gedächtniskirche and Zoo station.

Berlin's flea market
The flea market lies between Nollendorfplatz and the former Bülowstrasse main railway station, some of the stalls entrancingly flourishing in restored turn-of-the-century railway carriages. It is open every day except Tuesdays from 11.00 to 19.00. Reach it from Zoo station by U-Bahn line 1 in the direction Schlesisches Tor, getting out at Nollendorfplatz. (The return journey is by the same line — take the lower platform in the direction Ruhleben.)

Excursion to East Berlin

East Berlin, the capital of the DDR, is accessible for members of EEC countries without obtaining a visa beforehand – though you need to take your passport. If you have a car you can drive through Checkpoint Charlie. But it is much easier to go across the border by S-Bahn 3 from Zoo station, getting out at Friedrichstrasse. On the way you see the Victory Column and the Hansa quarter to the right. The train crosses the River Spree. Through the trees you can spot the Congress Hall. After Lehrter Stadtbahnhof the train crosses an eerie no-man's-land, with watch-towers and a splendid view of the Reichstag building.

At the station foreigners should make towards the sign *Anderen Staaten* for passport control. Every time you cross in to the DDR at present you have to change 25 West German marks into East German currency. This gives you enough to buy, say, a couple of meals at seven or eight marks each, or a book or two, or the price of a visit to an art gallery.

Turn right outside the station and follow Friedrichstrasse to Unter den Linden, then turn right again to see the Brandenburg Gate from the East German side. Shops in Unter den Linden open from 13.00 to 19.00 on Mondays, from 10.00 to 19.00 on other weekdays, and from 09.00 to 13.00 on Saturdays. There is a fine university bookshop on the left as you walk towards the Brandenburg Gate and further on the Soviet Embassy which the Russian architect A. P. Strijewski designed in the early 1950s.

Retrace your steps and continue along Unter den Linden past Friedrichstrasse. I never cease to be astonished at the way East Berliners have restored their magnificent buildings. The state library on the left (once the Prussian state library) is housed in a massive neo-baroque building of 1913. Next to it is the Humboldt University, built as a neo-baroque royal palace and designed by Johann Boumann between 1748 and 1768.

A monarch, Friedrich II, actually rides up the street in this democratic republic, in an equestrian statue by C. D. Rauch. A plaque on the wall to the north of Friedrich II's statue marks the notorious spot where on 10 May 1933 the Nazis burnt books they had proscribed. Opposite the Humboldt University is the State Opera House, which G. W. von Knobelsdorff designed for Friedrich the Great in the 1740s in the style of a Corinthian temple. The statues in the niches represent Euripedes, Menander, Aristophanes and Sophocles.

A breathtakingly fine group of buildings surrounds the State Opera (in Bebelplatz). The former Royal Library, which the Berliners call the 'dressing table' because of its curved front, was built by Johann Boumann to designs by the great Viennese master Fischer von Erlach. Behind the Opera House stands St Hedwig's Catholic cathedral, modelled by the architect Jean Legeay on the Pantheon, Rome. On the farther side is a palace which Karl Ferdinand Langhans built in 1836 for Wilhelm I, and finally a palace of 1733–1811 which is now the Opera Café.

I find it almost impossible to believe that so many of these buildings were savagely bombed in World War II and that so much has been lovingly restored. The other side of Unter den Linden does, however, contain a reminder of the war years. The splendid Neue Wache which the architect K. F. Schinkel modelled on a Roman Temple in 1816 is now a memorial to the victims of militarism and fascism. They include the Protestant martyr Dietrich Bonhoeffer. Soldiers mount a guard of honour, which is changed daily at noon and 16.30. You can photograph anything you like in East Berlin apart from military personnel and installations, but an exception is made in the case of this guard of honour.

The museum of German history further down the street was once Berlin's baroque arsenal. Opposite it stands the former palace of the Crown Prince, behind which you can see K. F. Schinkel's stone Friedrich-Werdersch Kirche, built in the early 1820s.

And if this fantastic display were not enough, just across the stone bridge which spans the Spree is the huge Marx-Engels-Platz, with a series of imposing and excellent modern buildings to the south and the massive Protestant cathedral to the east, designed by Julius Raschdorff and built between 1894 and 1905 in the style of the Italian high renaissance. For once a modern architect has used plate glass with singular imagination, for the Palast der Republik opposite beautifully reflects the cathedral. Much damaged in World War I, the *Dom* is being slowly and meticulously restored. The cathedral incorporates a mausoleum set up in 1535 by Elector Joachim II and containing some 90 Hohenzollern sarcophagi.

On the north side of Marx-Engels-Platz is East Berlin's fantastic Museum Island. The museums themselves are works of art, all but one restored after World War II: the mid nineteenth-century National Gallery is like a huge Corinthian temple; the Pergamon Museum, named after the famous Pergamon altar displayed here, dates from 1909; the Bode Museum was designed by Ernst von Ihne at the end of the nineteenth century; the Altes Museum is a lovely classical building by Schinkel. All are usually closed on Mondays and open for the rest of the week from 09.00 to 18.00 (from 10.00 on Fridays).

The Museum Island really is an island, since the Spree divides here and its two streams also embrace the Protestant cathedral and Marx-Engels-Platz. If you cross the east stream from Marx-Engels-Platz, Karl-Liebknecht-Strasse takes you past a busy covered market on the left (where fish stalls, clothes sellers and toyshops spill out into the open air). On the right of the street is the lovely Marienkirche, a brick gothic building begun in 1380. Among its treasures are a bronze font dating from 1437; an early eighteenth-century organ by Joachim Wagner; a flamboyant pulpit created by Andreas Schlüter in 1793; a medieval dance of death painted in the porch under the west tower; and an altar of 1762 by the architect Andreas Krüger. Beautiful paintings hang on the walls.

In the same square rises the symbol of East Berlin, its television tower, with a restaurant 200 metres above the ground (although you do not have to eat to admire the panorama). If you prefer to eat at ground level, walk south-west across the square, past Reinhold Begas's superb Neptune fountain of 1891 (where 560 jets play on each hour). Turn left down the side of East Berlin's town hall – a splendid building in red brick, created by the architect Friedrich Waesemann between 1862 and 1869. A narrow street, Am Nussbaum, leads you to the right into a picturesque little complex containing Berlin's oldest surviving building: the thirteenth-century church of St Nicholas. When I was visiting Berlin in the 1970s it was still partly ruined as a result of the war. Today, naturally, it is virtually restored.

This is a region of good small restaurants, frequented by the East Berliners as well as by visitors, some of them well known ('Zum

Nussbaum' and 'Ahornblatt'), none of them serving gastronomic delights but all eminently serviceable.

Return to West Berlin by Friedrichstrasse station, this time looking for the signs *Ausreise* and once again passing through the controls marked *Andere Staaten*.

Food and drink

Food in East Berlin is, I think, more basic than in the west part of the city. For instance, a *Pökelkamm mit Mostrichstippe Berliner* is a pork chop from the pig's fatty neck, served with a kind of mustard dip. *Brühkartoffeln* are potatoes in a meat stock. Berliners are also fond of outrageously mixed drinks: *Berliner Weisse mit Schuss* is beer mixed with raspberry syrup or sometimes strawberry syrup. And they will add red wine to their oxtail soup.

Beer is a favourite drink in West Berlin, with many varieties available. Engelhardt's beer and Schultheiss are both brewed in the city. These help to wash down the often massive meals, which may start with vegetable soup (*Gemüsesuppe*) or onion soup (*Zwiebelsuppe*). Lighter, but still substantial are the green salads (*Kopfsalat*) and tomato salads (*Tomatensalat*), all the more filling if you follow them with a pork chop and chips (*Schweinkotelette panierte mit pommes frites*), or a veal cutlet (*Kalbschnitzel*) done in the same way. Liver in Berlin (*Leber Berliner Art*) is cooked with plenty of onions and served with apple purée and mashed potatoes. Naturally you can eat countless varieties of sausage: *Bockwurst, Bratwurst, Bierwurst, Jagdwurst,* and the inevitable pickled cabbage known as *Sauerkraut.* When a Berliner asks for *pommes frites,* he simply demands *pommes,* stressing both syllables.

Other dishes served in typical Berlin restaurants include *Eisbein,* a very fatty salted knucklebone of pork, and herrings of every variety (*Matjeshering, Rollmops* and *Brathering*). Other typical fish dishes include fresh eel with cucumber salad, usually also served with potatoes and known as *Aal grün mit Gurkensalat*; perch (*Barsh*) cooked in beer, and tench (*Schleie*) with a dill sauce. *Buletten* (known as *Frikadellen* elsewhere in Germany) are balls of minced beef and little pieces of soaked white bread, bound together with two eggs (or one if you pay less) and then fried in a pan.

In Berlin the *Kneipe* is a bar serving cheaper food. Every *Kneipe* will offer pickled gherkins (*Saure Gurken*), and *Schusterjungs*, i.e. a bun made of meal which has been boiled in water, vinegar and salt. Patrons pile lard lavishly on their *Schusterjungs*. Small wonder those who relish them often also drink *Molle mit Korn*, i.e. beer mixed with corn schnapps.

Berliners also relish Italian food, especially pizzas, for many of them holiday in Italy (though today they tend to regard Turkey, France and Greece as more fashionable). In addition, many Italians came here to work in the 1950s and 1960s and, not wishing to toil in factories, set up their own establishments.

Night life

Night life in Berlin is extraordinarily prolific. The city has built up a tradition of tolerance. There are no licensing hours, and many *Nachtlokale* seem willing to stay open so long as the patrons can survive. In the early morning the bars and cafés on the Kurfürstendamm will still be full. And on the Kudamm alone are enough night spots to last a lifetime, with names like 'Joe's Bier-Salon', 'One five One', 'Big Eden', 'Coupé 77', 'Subway', etc. Wander anywhere in the centre of Berlin and you will find countless more. If you want a transvestite cabaret try 'Chez nous' at no.14 Marburger Strasse or 'Chez Romy Haag' at no.24 Welser Strasse.

Berlin's celebrated satirical cabarets still flourish, including 'Die Stachelschweine' in the Europa Centre; 'Die Wühlmässe' in the Theater an der Lietzenburger; and 'Klimperkasten' on Otto-Suhr-Allee.

Since the nuances of their performances may well be lost on the foreign visitor, it might well be better either to visit one of the twenty or so theatres in West Berlin, or to spend an evening listening to the Berlin Philharmonic in its celebrated concert hall (Kemperplatz, Tiergarten), which the brilliant, uncompromising architect Hans Scharoun designed in 1963. Those with a taste for gambling may like to seek out the Europa Centre Casino, in operation from 15.00 to 03.00.

Important information

Banking hours in Berlin vary from bank to bank. Most open only Monday to Friday, perhaps from 10.30 to 18.30, but there is one in Wertheim's department store on the Kudamm which is also open on Saturdays from 10.30 to 14.00 (extended to 18.00 on the first Saturday in the month). The Berliner Bank (at no.24 Kudamm) opens from 09.00 to 18.30 on weekdays and from 09.30 to 13.30 on Saturday mornings. The airport bank opens from 08.00 to 20.00. There are also limited facilities for obtaining cash at post offices.

Travel on buses, the S-Bahn and the U-Bahn in Berlin is integrated. Buy tickets for 24 hours or for the whole weekend in a kiosk at the stations. Tickets can also be bought from the automatic dispensers at the stations.

One ticket will take you anywhere – one way, not return – hopping from U-Bahn to S-Bahn and on to buses, provided your journey lasts no more than two hours. Punch your ticket with the time stamp only at your first boarding. A child travels free with an adult. Children under five never pay.

Airlines fly in and out of Tegel Airport, Berlin, from the Federal Republic and from abroad. An airport bus takes you inexpensively into the centre of the city in about half an hour.

Florence

*What it is that infuses so rich an interest into the general charm is
difficult to say in a few words; yet as we wander hither and thither
in quest of sacred canvas and immortal bronze and stone we still feel
the genius of the place hang about; . . . as the weeks go by and you
spend a constant portion of your days among them the sense of one
of the happiest periods of human taste — to put it only at that —
settles upon your spirit. It was not long; it lasted, in its splendour,
for less than a century; but it has stored away in these palaces and
churches of Florence a heritage of beauty that these three enjoying
centuries since haven't yet exhausted.*

Henry James, 1873

Henry James forgot to mention the great river – not great in width or depth, but important in Florence's history, never far from one's thoughts (or occasionally nose). The romantic poet Percy Bysshe Shelley could scarcely contain his enthusiasm for the city merely after having walked along the river bank:

Florence itself I think is the most beautiful city I have yet seen. It is surrounded with cultivated hills and from the bridge which crosses the broad channel of the Arno the view is the most animated and elegant I ever saw. You see three or four bridges, one apparently supported by Corinthian pillars, and the white sails of the boats, relieved by the deep green of the forest, which comes to the water's edge.

The forest no longer reaches the water's edge, but the vale of the Arno with its sloping hills and villas still enfolds Florence as it did in Shelley's time, 'first the hills of olive and vine, then the chestnut woods, and then the blue and misty pine forest, which invest the aerial Apennines, that fade in the distance'.

Florence is the city in which I most share the excitements and ecstasy of those who visited it in the past. 'The day before yesterday, as I was descending upon Florence from the high ridges of the Apennines, my heart was leaping wildly within me,' recorded the French novelist Stendhal. 'What utterly childish excitement! At long last, at a sudden bend in the road, my gaze plunged downward into the heart of the plain, and there, in the far distance, like some sparkling dark mass, I could distinguish the sombre pile of the cathedral of Santa Maria del Fiore with its famous dome, the masterpiece of Brunelleschi.'

A similar excitement, childish or not, tends to come over every visitor to Florence. The city of Dante and Boccaccio, of Michelangelo and Botticelli, has left us more astonishingly beautiful and inspired works by its great men and women than any other. Here you are instantly involved in some of Europe's most savage history, most sublime architecture, greatest art and most piquant literature. The briefest visit should also include shopping in a few of the world's most elegant establishments (not all of them expensive), and wandering through the open-air markets – to buy leather, lace, straw hats and ceramics, or just a few succulent Tuscan peaches.

Beneath all its renaissance splendour and modern glamour Florence dates back to the Etruscans and the Romans. In that

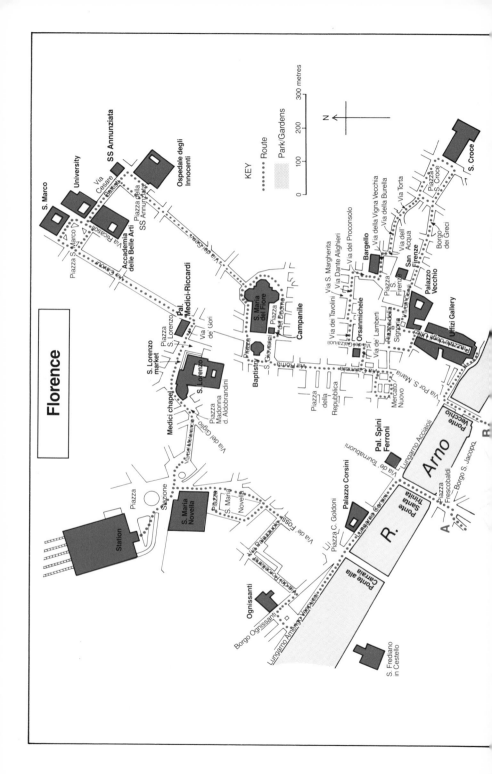

Florence

KEY
······· Route
Park/Gardens

0   100   200   300 metres

N ←

S. Marco
University
SS Annunziata
Ospedale degli Innocenti
Via Cesare Battisti
Via Ricasoli
Piazza della SS Annunziata
Accademia delle Belle Arti
Piazza S. Marco
Via Camillo Cavour

Pal. Medici-Riccardi
Via de' Gori
Piazza S. Lorenzo
S. Lorenzo market
S. Lorenzo
Medici chapel
Piazza Madonna d. Aldobrandini
Via Melarancio
Via del Giglio

S. Maria del Fiore
Piazza del Duomo
Campanile
Piazza S. Giovanni
Baptistry

Via dei Servi

Via S. Margherita
Via Dante Alighieri
Via del Proconsolo
Bargello
Via della Vigna Vecchia
Via della Burella
Via dell' Acqua
Via Torta

San Firenze
Piazza S. Firenze
Palazzo Vecchio
Piazza Signoria
Orsanmichele
Via dei Tavolini
Via dei Calzaioli
Via de' Lamberti
Via Calimala

Piazza S. Croce
S. Croce
Borgo dei Greci
Uffizi Gallery
Piazzale degli Uffizi

Via Roma
Piazza della Repubblica
Mercato Nuovo
Via Por S. Maria
Ponte Vecchio

Station
Piazza
Stazione

Piazza S. Maria Novella
S. Maria Novella
Via de' Fossi
Via de' Banchi
Via de' Panzani

Palazzo Corsini
Piazza C. Goldoni
Pal. Spini Ferroni
Via de' Tournabuoni
Lungarno Acciaioli
Ponte Santa Trinita
Piazza S. Trinita
Piazza Frescobaldi
Borgo S. Jacopo

Arno
R.

Ognissanti
Borgo Ognissanti
Lungarno Amerigo Vespucci
Ponte alla Carraia
S. Frediano in Cestello

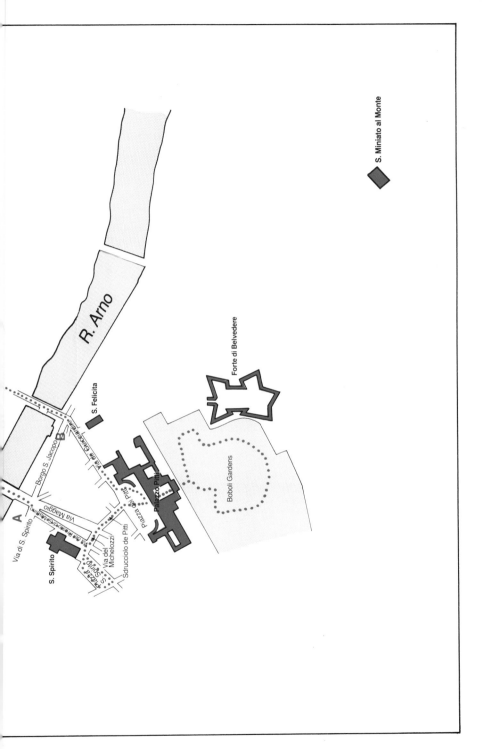

R. Arno

S. Miniato al Monte

Forte di Belvedere

Boboli Gardens

S. Felicita

Borgo S. Jacopo

Via de' Guicciardini

Palazzo Pitti

Piazza de' Pitti

Via Maggio

Via di S. Spirito

S. Spirito

Via del Michelozzi

Sdrucciolo de Pitti

Via S. Agostino

refreshingly cool hill-top town of Fiesole close by, from which Florence developed and which the Etruscans founded, there are superb remains of the Etruscan walls, an Etruscan temple dating from the sixth century BC, Roman baths, a Roman temple and an amphitheatre large enough for 3000 spectators.

Yet Florence remains no mere museum piece. I think it the most sophisticated city in all Italy, its leatherware (by such internationally renowned firms as Gucci and Raspini) leading the world, its citizens elegantly dressed and filled with fun, apparently oblivious to the fumes of their traffic-filled streets and rising refreshed after their long midday siesta for another afternoon's work and another evening's pleasure.

Florence is an old city and a modern one too. I once sat in the sun beside the roof-top swimming-pool of the Hotel Kraft and looked over an astonishing vista. I could see the seventeenth-century church of San Frediano; the long, powerful façade of the Pitti Palace; the renaissance bell-tower of Santo Spirito; the Belvedere fortress up on its hill with the elegant Kaffeehaus just below it; the medieval bell-tower of Ognissanti in front of me; the famous tower of the Palazzo Vecchio with its clock facing me; the minaret-like bell-tower of Santa Croce in the distance; the delicate six-sided tower of the Badia; then Giotto's famed campanile and the great dome of Florence cathedral; finally lovely Santa Maria Novella, with its own superb bell-tower and dome. Over to the left I could see as far as Fiesole; and all was surrounded with rounded hills and wooded slopes. In that sophisticated spot, I felt the truth of Augustus Hare's brilliant observation that in Florence you meet the past contending with the present; 'and in turn, each has the mastery'.

A city tour

This tour of Florence starts and ends close by its railway station, partly because most people arrive there from the airport, partly because in itself this is a noble building (dating from 1935) and above all because the greatest gothic church in Tuscany, Santa Maria Novella, stands across the piazza with its back to the station.

The façade of the church is covered in magical multi-coloured marble, the lower half the work of the Dominican friar Jacopo Talenti in the mid fourteenth century, the upper half designed by Leon Battista Alberti in the second half of the fifteenth century. The rich Florentine merchant Giovanni di Paolo Rucellai paid for Alberti's work and his family symbol (a ship's sail) appears in the façade, as well as that of those most famous wealthy Florentine patrons of the arts, the Medici (a ring with ostrich feathers).

Santa Maria Novella, as well as a masterpiece in itself, has been immortalized in world literature. In 1348, so the story goes, seven women met in this church one Tuesday morning. The place was virtually deserted, for Florence was suffering the deadly bubonic plague which was devastating all Europe. The women decided to make their escape from the poisonous air of the city to a country estate. With them they took three men, one devoted above all to love, another 'crushed by love' and a third a worshipper of the goddess of sensual love. Each day, out of the plague's reach, they sang, danced, wrote poetry, played draughts and chess. Every day they each told a story. In ten days they had produced a hundred tales between them. These form Boccaccio's *Decameron*, a sparkling and brilliant creation inspired by the deadly plague which he himself had witnessed.

The church in which the *Decameron* begins is crammed with wonders, not least the high altar crucifix by Giambologna. Behind the high altar there is a light switch to illuminate the sanctuary frescoes, masterpieces by Domenico Ghirlandaio, vividly depicting life in Florence at the end of the fifteenth century. Boccaccio himself is immortalized in the little Spanish chapel (the Cappellone degli Spagnuoli) in the cloisters. Here Andrea Bonaiuti painted a fresco in which he portrayed the most illustrious citizens of fourteenth-century Florence. Boccaccio appears in the centre of one segment, dressed in crimson with a white fur hat, holding a copy of his book, paying no attention to what is going on around him but looking straight out at us. His eyes seem to peer into the distance, as if envisaging some new literary diversion. Nobody knows much about the artist, Andrea Bonaiuti, but this one fragment of a fresco painted in the mid fourteenth century convinces me that he was a genius. The witty frescoes of Old Testament scenes in the cloister are by Paolo Uccello.

The pentagonal piazza in front of the church contains a couple of curious obelisks pointing to the sky. In 1563 Cosimo de' Medici made this square the start of an annual chariot race, setting out the course by wooden obelisks. Forty-five years later his successor Ferdinando I de' Medici replaced them with marble ones. Four unhappy-looking bronze tortoises still support them.

On the other side of the piazza is the Loggia di San Paolo, a lovely late fifteenth-century building, decorated under the portico with a charming terracotta medallion by Andrea della Robbia, depicting St Francis of Assisi meeting St Dominic. Andrea della Robbia put some unusual personal touches into his work on this loggia. The first medallion on the left is his own self-portrait. The one on the extreme right is a portrait of his uncle Luca.

Walk down the Via de' Fossi on the left-hand side of the Loggia di San Paolo, where elegant shops sell antiques and old pictures. Turn right into Via Palazzuolo and then left into Via del Porcellana which leads to Borgo Ognissanti. On the way you pass more antique shops, excellent inexpensive restaurants and some fashionable dress shops.

To the right along Borgo Ognissanti you reach the church of All Saints (Ognissanti). A weekend in Florence cannot possibly include an exploration of every religious masterpiece in the city; but Ognissanti possesses a treasure which should not be missed. In the chapel to the left of the high altar is the actual habit worn by St Francis of Assisi on that miraculous day when, praying on the mountain of La Verna in September 1224, he received the stigmata of his Lord. Thenceforth, it is said, Francis bore the same wounds in his hands and feet and side as those inflicted on the crucified Jesus.

There are a few other treasures worth seeing in Ognissanti.

Sandro Botticelli's painting of St Jerome translating the Bible hangs on the north side of the church. I very much like the saint's spectacles, hanging by his reading desk. (His eyes must surely have suffered from his hugely laborious task.) And I envy his red cardinal's hat. On the opposite wall hangs a Botticelli painting of another great doctor of the church, St Augustine.

On this same wall is a great curiosity: a portrait of the man who gave his name to America in 1507, the explorer Amerigo Vespucci. He appears as a youth in the second altar fresco on the right from the entrance to the church, dressed in red, between the Virgin Mary and an old man. The picture, by Domenico Ghirlandaio, depicts the Virgin Mary protecting the whole Vespucci family. As well as Amerigo, the Madonna is also shielding his beautiful cousin-in-law Simonetta, who was not only the mistress of Giuliano de' Medici and lusted after by Lorenzo de' Medici but also served as the model for Botticelli's celebrated *Primavera*.

As you go out, look back at Ognissanti's façade. Although the church was begun by an order of friars in 1251, it was given its Tuscan baroque front by the architect Matteo Nigetti in 1637. Nigetti was sensitive enough to include a lovely terracotta lunette of the Virgin Mary which Benedetto Buglioni had sculpted in 1482. As for the bell-tower, nobody thought to alter it, and it remains its old thirteenth-century self.

In 1966 Florence was overwhelmed by a disastrous flood. A mark on the wall to the left of the church, at a height one and a half times that of an average man, shows the point the waters reached on 4 November. Then walk across the Piazza di Ognissanti to the River Arno. In a city filled with astounding renaissance and baroque statues, it is refreshing to come across a modest, but fine art nouveau piece here: Romano Romanelli's 1907 sculpture of a naked man fighting a lion.

Walk left along the Arno for one of those thrills that vistas of Florence always bring. Across the river rise the dome and still unfinished façade of the church of San Frediano. Straight ahead you can see the marble façade and tower of San Miniato al Monte high up above the city. Spanning the river is the Ponte alla Carraia. Its history is a reminder that flooding in Florence is an age-old malady. The Ponte alla Carraia, like its neighbour the Ponte Santa Trinita further down the river, has been swept away an amazing number of times since it was first thrown over the Arno in the thirteenth century. In 1304 when a huge crowd of Florentines was standing on it to watch mummers on a floating stage simulate the torments of hell, it suddenly collapsed. Only when the brilliant Bartolomeo Ammannati redesigned both the Ponte alla Carraia and the Ponte Santa Trinita in the 1570s did any real stability come to either. Then the Germans bombed both to pieces in World War II, and both had to be rebuilt, happily to Ammannati's original plans.

Walk left along the Lungarno Corsini towards the Ponte Santa Trinita, past the 1873 statue of the dramatist Carlo Goldoni. Do not miss some fine, often forgotten Florentine palaces on the way. On the left stands the present home of the Leonardo da Vinci society, a lovely baroque palace with its terraces filled with statues created for the rich Corsini family by Pier Francesco Silvani and Antonio Ferri in the mid seventeenth century. Just before you turn right across Ponte Santa Trinita there is a complete contrast to the Palazzo Corsini in Via Tornabuoni to the left – the medieval Palazzo Spini-Ferroni, a massive three-storeyed, crenellated fortress built in 1269. The Palazzo Gianfigliazzi facing it dates from the same century. And no.9 Via Tornabuoni is the Palazzo Larderei, a magnificent high renaissance palace built in the late sixteenth century and designed by Giovanni Antonio Dossi. The column bearing the statue of justice was brought to the Piazza Santa Trinita in 1565 by Cosimo I de' Medici, from the baths of Caracalla in Rome.

Much could be written about some of the most glamorous if expensive shops in the city that are housed in the streets on this side of the Arno. In Borgo Ognissanti you can buy superb art deco and art nouveau antiques, as well as fine books, lovely Florentine papers or exquisitely embroidered dresses. The Profumeria Inglese selling delicious soaps and scents at no.97 Via Tornabuoni was founded a century and a half ago. Seeber's bookshop at no.68 is almost as old. There are also superb leather goods for sale along this street.

Cross the river by the Ponte Santa Trinita, from which you get a marvellous view of the precariously balanced shops on the next bridge along, the celebrated Ponte Vecchio. Across the river, walk along Via Maggio. In spite of its magnificence (no.40 is the fifteenth-century Palazzo Rosselli del Turco and no.26 was built in 1566 by the architect Bernardo Buontalenti (and was once the home of Francesco de' Medici's mistress Bianca Cappello), turn almost immediately right along Via di Santo Spirito.

Then turn left down Via del Presto di San Martino – and ahead of you is the massive basilica of Santo Spirito. This was the last majestic creation of Filippo Brunelleschi, the architect of the dome of Florence cathedral. Brunelleschi designed Santo Spirito at the age of sixty in 1440 and Baccio d'Agnolo added its bell-tower sixty years later. The piazza too is a delight. Irregular in shape, shaded by trees and bordered by palaces, it is enlivened each morning by a charming small market. Its Palazzo Guadagni of 1503 is probably by the architect Simone del Pollaiolo, whom everyone called *il Cronaca* (the gossip), though others say it is by Baccio d'Agnolo.

Walk out of the piazza along Via del Michelozzi, cross Via Maggio and continue along Sdrucciolo de Pitti which emerges in front of the magnificent Pitti Palace. Not surprisingly, Luca Pitti who ordered the building of this massive piece of architectural self-aggrandisement in 1475 was declared bankrupt long before it was finished. His rivals the Medici bought him out and, not content with finishing Pitti's own grandiose schemes, commissioned architects to enlarge on the original design. The Medici, the Austrians and the Grand Dukes of Lorraine all utilized it to display their dominance of Europe. When Italy finally got its own king, he too lived here for a time. Today the Pitti Palace is an art gallery (open weekdays except Monday from 09.00 to 14.00 and on Sundays from 09.00 to 13.00). It is well worth a visit (though this could take up a whole morning), not just to see its art collection but also the monumental staircase designed by Bartolomeo Ammannati. Ammannati is in fact responsible for the overall harmony of this great building, though the very first designs were those of Brunelleschi himself.

Behind the Pitti Palace you can wander in the superb Boboli Gardens. This delicious gift to Florence and to every visitor was the inspiration of Eleanor of Toledo, wife of Cosimo I de' Medici, the first Medici to own the Pitti Palace. An oasis of shade and tranquillity, with roses, cypresses and huge cedars of Lebanon, it includes a great amphitheatre (laid out in 1619); a late sixteenth-century grotto designed by Buontalenti (and housing Giambologna's statue of *Venus*); a splendid fountain (with another brilliant Giambologna statue, this time his *Oceanus*); and the Kaffeehaus, a pavilion built for Grand Duke Pietro Leopoldo I of Habsburg Lorraine in 1776. This Grand Duke was the first to let the general public into the Boboli Gardens, and today it is pleasant to take a drink here and remember him with gratitude. Then climb up to the Belvedere (if your legs will stand it), a fortress designed like a six-pointed star at the very top of the Boboli Gardens. There is a superb panorama of the whole city from here. (The Boboli Garden gate into the Belvedere is open every day, except Mondays, from 08.30 to 13.30.)

Stroll back down to the Pitti Palace and take Via de' Guicciardini right from Piazza Pitti to the Ponte Vecchio. A plaque on the wall of Palazzo Guicciardini, at no.15 Via de' Guicciardini, tells you that the Florentine chronicler and historian Francesco Guicciardini (1483–1540) lived here. Just before the Ponte Vecchio there is a little square, with the second-oldest church in Florence, Santa Felicita, to the right. Much rebuilt since it was founded in honour of a Roman martyr, it now houses some superb early sixteenth-century paintings by Jacopo Pontormo.

Even Adolf Hitler refrained from destroying the most venerable bridge in Florence. The Ponte Vecchio lies at the narrowest point of the Arno. There was a bridge here in Roman times, but the present structure is mid fourteenth century in origin. Its three arches support quaint shops that were built around a century later and are still trading – in pearls, silver, gold, jade, coral, bracelets, necklaces, rings, porcelain, tortoiseshell, enamel and cameos – with the cunning of their medieval predecessors. In the middle of the bridge the genial bust of Benvenuto Cellini, the brilliant Florentine goldsmith, renaissance sculptor, and an entertaining rogue to boot, presides over everything.

At the far end of the Ponte Vecchio, on the right-hand side of the bridge, are engraved some lines from Dante's *Paradiso*:

> . . . *conveniasi a quella pietra scema*
> *Che guarda il ponte, che Fiorenze fèsse*
> *Vittima nella sua pace postrema.*

> [. . . on that maimed stone
> Which guards the bridge
> The victim, when peace departed, fell.]

a reference to the murder here of Buondelmonte de' Buondelmonti, since when, Dante believed, Florence had known no peace.

Immediately at the end of the Ponte Vecchio turn right along the colonnaded bank of the River Arno. Then turn left to walk through the Piazzale degli Uffizi, braving the sellers of trinkets, leather goods, jewellery, silk scarves, masks and figurines of Michelangelo's statue of the naked *David*. Cosimo I de' Medici was responsible for these lovely buildings, partly concealed by the stalls. They must be the most elegant set of offices in the world. In 1560 he commissioned Giorgio Vasari to design them, and after Vasari's death the work was finished by Bernardo Buontalenti.

At the far end on the right is the entrance to the Uffizi Gallery, invariably boasting a daunting queue of would-be visitors during the tourist season. Ahead is the Piazza Signoria, with a copy of Michelangelo's *David* (the original of which is in the Accademia in Via Ricasoli) and a feast of other statuary.

Rightly the most prominent sculpture in the piazza is the equestrian statue to Cosimo I de' Medici, created by Giambologna in 1598, since he more than any other Medici dominated the architectural and sculptural brilliance of Florence at this time. A couple of decades earlier Ammannati had set up the luxurious fountain of Neptune behind Cosimo's statue. Neptune, it is said, represents Cosimo himself. The Florentine's exult in his massive sexual proportions, and call him *il Biancone* ('the white one'). Even Ammannati became ashamed at having created such a huge white object. I prefer the luscious syrens and sea deities surrounding him.

Donatello's remarkable statue of Judith slaughtering Holofernes used to stand in the Loggia dei Lanzi nearby. The sculptor was so pleased with his work that he signed it (with the words OPVS. DONATELLI. FLOR), an unparalleled occurrence for this genius. But the Florentines never liked having the statue here. First they were concerned that the notion of a woman killing a man would bring ill-fortune on Florence. Then they decided that the work was so brilliant that it needed protecting from the elements, and placed it in the Sala d'Udienza on the second floor of the Palazzo Vecchio. I wish the authorities would bring a copy back here.

While this example of women's potential powers of revenge against men has been removed, an even more virile representation of the savagery of men against women remains in the Loggia dei Lanzi: Benvenuto Cellini's *Perseus with the Head of Medusa*. Nobody supposed that even the brilliant Cellini could succeed in finishing this ambitious masterpiece. As the statue was being cast, Cellini accomplished the work only by casting all his pewter plates and vessels into the furnace.

Men continue to oppress women in the other masterpieces on display in the Loggia dei Lanzi, above all in Giambologna's *Rape of the Sabine Women*, a work which this brilliant immigrant from Douai finished in 1583. I love simply walking slowly round this entrancingly vigorous group, consisting of a superbly sensual woman, a lithe powerful youth and a conquered old man. From whatever angle you view them all, Giambologna offers a *tour de force* of proportion, twisting figures, artistic movement and powerful drama.

The Palazzo della Signoria, whose massive castellated bulk and slender tower dominate the square, is known to everyone as the Palazzo Vecchio. Florence became a republic in 1293 and this was the seat of government, built for the civic leaders or *Signori* by Arnolfo di Cambio between 1299 and 1310, when the tower was finished. Outside, it remains virtually as it was built, but Vasari completely restructured the interior when Cosimo I de' Medici decided to make it his ducal palace. You can visit the museum housed here free on Sundays between 08.00 and 13.00, and see Donatello's *Judith slaying Holofernes*. The Palazzo is open Monday to Friday from 09.00–19.00 (entrance fee).

If you walk round the Palazzo Vecchio and along Via de' Gondi you reach Piazza di San Firenze, a magical square. Immediately to the left is the Palazzo Gondi, designed by Giulio da Sangallo and finished in 1501. At the top of the square you see the massive tower and ancient walls of the thirteenth-century Bargello, once the seat of the Florentine people's representative (the *Podestà*). This was the place where unfortunates were tried and sentenced, but it is now the fabulously rich national sculpture museum. To its left rises the delicate six-sided spire of the Badia Fiorentina, once the Benedictine abbey church of the city. And across the square is the eighteenth-century baroque façade of San Firenze itself.

Cross the bottom of the piazza and walk along Borgo dei Greci and a yet more remarkable spectacle gradually comes into view: the pink, white and green marble façade of the church of Santa Croce, with its great blue star in the pediment bearing the symbol of the Holy Name of Jesus ('IHS'). This façade was entirely constructed in the nineteenth century and paid for by an Englishman named Sloane. Six centuries earlier all that stood here was a modest little Franciscan church. In 1295 the friars deputed Arnolfo di Cambio (in all probability) to start building the present huge basilica. Rival preachers condemned the grandiose scheme as ungodly arrogance. When the Arno flooded in 1333, some saw it as a heaven-sent reprisal. The Franciscans carried on building undeterred.

Their church became the pantheon of Florence's great ones. Some of them, such as Dante, are honoured by great monuments without actually being buried here. Others lie in sometimes splendid, sometimes overwrought tombs. The French novelist Stendhal, who visited Santa Croce in the early nineteenth century, was overwhelmed, as everyone else must be, not only by the monumental statuary but also by the giants who lie here:

Inside, to the right of the doorway, rises the tomb of Michelangelo, and beyond it there is Canova's portrait of Alfieri. I did not need a guide to recognise the features of the supreme Italian writer. Further on I found the tomb of Machiavelli; while opposite Michelangelo lies Galileo. What a race of men! And as well as those I have already named Tuscany can add Dante, Boccaccio and Petrarch. What an amazing group! The tide of emotion overwhelming me flowed so deeply that it could hardly be distinguished from the reverence of religion. My very soul, already moved by the mere idea of being in Florence, now was in a state of trance.

Santa Croce is open from 10.00 to 12.30 and 15.00 to 18.30 (closing at 17.00 in winter). Don't miss Giotto's superb frescoes of St Francis, St John the Baptist and St John the Divine in the chapels to the right of the high altar, or Brunelleschi's splendid Pazzi chapel, with its circular blue-and-white terracotta reliefs by Luca della Robbia. It is also well worth visiting the exquisite cloisters (entered from the piazza to the right of the church), where the Santa Croce museum displays a crucifix by Cimabue which, though restored, is still scarred by the flood-waters of 1966.

In the piazza in front of the basilica a statue of Dante, put up in 1865, glares angrily down at Florentines and tourists alike. There are also some interesting buildings here. No.1 is the Palazzo Cocchi Serristori, which Baccio d'Agnolo built at the end of the fifteenth century. No.21, the early seventeenth-century Palazzo Antellesi, is an interesting survival. This is one of the few Florentine palaces which still has frescoes on the façade, painted by Giovanni da San Giovanni and his assistants in twenty days. Perhaps they worked too fast, for the frescoes are certainly in very bad order today.

Walk back across the square and then through a warren of picturesquely twisting streets to the Bargello: Via Torta leads into Via della Burella, then turn right into Via dell' Acqua and left into Via della Vigna Vecchia. On the right is the Bargello. Its entrance is in Via del Proconsolo, which leads to the right from Via della Vigna Vecchia. The Bargello is open on weekdays, except Mondays, from 09.00 to 14.00, closing one hour earlier on Sundays. Although the Uffizi is one of the world's greatest art galleries, on a weekend visit I would prefer to spend time here, in this beautiful palace.

A short way up Via del Proconsolo turn first left into Via Dante Alighieri, the medieval street which contains the so-called house of Dante. Certainly Dante was born somewhere around here in 1265, and certainly this house (more or less rebuilt in 1910) once belonged to his family. Beatrice Portinari, with whom he fell in love having seen her once (when she was eight years old) and who inspired his greatest poetry, lies buried in the church in the Via Santa Margherita nearby. As he himself wrote, when she first turned her eyes on him and courteously saluted him, 'at that moment I seemed to see the heights of blessedness'. Beatrice died young. Canto XXI of Dante's *Paradiso* describes how she leads him to the seventh heaven:

> Again my eyes were fixed on Beatrice,
> And with my eyes also my soul, which in her looks
> Found all contentment.

Dante's house, which contains a museum, opens from 09.00 to 12.30 and from 15.30 to 18.30, closing in the afternoons on Sundays and public holidays.

Dante actually married a lady called Gemma Donati, and you can see the little church of San Martino al Vescovo where they married just round the corner left of Via Dante Alighieri. This small quarter is the oldest surviving part of Florence. The fortified tower known as the Torre della Castagna, in Piazza San Martino opposite the entrance to the little church, was built by the heads of the Florentine guilds so that they could live secure, without fearing the depredations of their powerful enemies. Continue past the church of

San Martino along Via dei Tavolini and you reach Via dei Calzaiuoli and, across it, the extraordinary guild church of Orsanmichele — extraordinary because the guilds combined a church and a granary in one building, and then commissioned the greatest Florentine sculptors to embellish it outside with religious statues. Inside is a marble tabernacle made by Andrea Orcagna in the mid fourteenth century and one of the masterpieces of Florentine gothic.

But Florence does not live only in the past. One of the city's most famous markets is the Mercato Nuovo, which opens every day in summer from 09.00 till 17.00 (closing on Mondays in winter). Follow Via de' Lamberti past the side of Orsanmichele and turn left at Via Calimala and you will be in the midst of its crowded stalls selling leatherware, ceramics, lace, linens and all sorts of trinkets. The market is traditionally known as 'il Porcellino', from the fierce, ugly bronze boar copied from an antique original by Pietro Tacca and set up here by Cosimo I. Two bits of the boar have been highly polished by countless stroking hands; his nose is stroked for good luck; another part for virility. The boar has also given his name to an excellent bookshop in this piazza, the Libreria del Porcellino.

Walk back along Via Calimala and into the spacious Piazza della Repubblica. Via Roma on the other side brings you to three pieces of world-famous Florentine architecture, the Baptistry, the cathedral (Santa Maria del Fiore) and Giotto's bell-tower. The Baptistry is the oldest of the three, a lovely romanesque building, delicately covered in green and white marble, with a pyramid-shaped roof added in the twelfth century. Andrea Pisano created the bronze doors on the south side around 1330. The other three are by Lorenzo Ghiberti, who beat all-comers in a celebrated competition to design them in 1401. Inside, the Baptistry is supported by Corinthian columns even older than itself, since they come from an earlier Roman building. Its dome is covered with a thirteenth-century mosaic of the Last Judgment, in which the torments of the damned are depicted with particularly savage glee.

The cathedral was begun in 1296 when the Florentines instructed Arnolfo di Cambio to replace the old church of Santa Reparata with 'the highest and most sumptuous building human invention could devise'. His plan was so ambitious that in 1419, when most of it was finally completed, the builders found themselves utterly unable to work out how to add a dome that would not collapse. The genius who solved the problem was one of those that had been beaten by Ghiberti in the competition to design the Baptistry doors, Filippo Brunelleschi.

Emilio de Fabris added the marvellous marble façade between 1871 and 1887. Florence cathedral is also embellished with exquisitely carved doorways. Other unsung late nineteenth-century masters (C. Cassioli and A. Passagli) added the great bronze doors. Inside the proportions of the cathedral are so excellent that you can scarcely believe that this is the fourth largest in the world. The art historian Jacob Burckhardt wrote of its 'almost terrifying power'. Giorgio Vasari took the opportunity of painting an equally terrifying fresco of the Last Judgment inside the dome. You can see it more closely as you climb the 463 steps that lead inside the two skins which Brunelleschi designed for his dome, before you emerge high on the roof for a superb panorama of the city.

Before you leave Florence cathedral, do not miss two remarkable wall paintings, both of fifteenth-century knights on horseback. One is in memory of Niccolò da Tolentino and was painted by Andrea del Castagno in 1456. The other, of the English mercenary leader John Hawkwood, was painted by Paolo Uccello twenty years earlier. Uccello's bizarre genius led him to paint everything in different shades of green: the horse, the plinth it stands on, and Hawkwood himself.

By the side of the cathedral is its exquisite bell-tower, 85 metres high and known universally as Giotto's campanile. Giotto took over as supervisor of works in 1334 when the cathedral was not yet half built. He immediately began building the campanile. Three years later he was dead, and Andrea Pisano followed by Francesco Talenti completed the work over the next fifty years. It had cost 11 million florins. John Ruskin, who was one of the first to teach the modern age to admire Giotto, confessed that 'when a boy, I used to despise that Campanile, and think it meanly smooth and finished.' He added, 'I have since lived beside it many a day, and looked out upon it from my windows by sunlight and moonlight,' slowly coming to love that 'surface of glowing jasper, those spiral shafts and fairy traceries, so white, so faint, so crystalline'. You can go up the campanile, for a view as good as the one from the cathedral.

From the east end of the cathedral, Via dei Servi runs to Piazza Santissima Annunziata, a processional street flanked by fine palaces

(the last one in brick, with great cornerstones) and specially built to
link the cathedral with the church of Santissima Annunziata. The
church itself has a kind of loggia entrance, matching the wings of its
delightful square. On the wall a plaque notes the height reached by
the floodwaters of 4 November 1966, thankfully not so high as
those that swamped Ognissanti.

On one side of the square is Brunelleschi's utterly charming
Foundling's Hospital (Ospedale degli Innocenti), built in 1519.
Opposite, dating from a hundred years later but gently
complementing Brunelleschi's loggia, is the loggia of the Servite
monks (notice their S's in the roundels). In the middle of the square
is a fine equestrian statue by Giambologna, of Ferdinand I, Grand
Duke of Etruria. The church itself boasts a magnificent golden
ceiling and a strange, superb altar to the Madonna, surrounded by
hanging lamps.

Walk left from the piazza along Via Cesare Battisti to the convent
and cloisters of San Marco, which Michelozzo di Bartolommeo
restored in 1452 at the expense of Cosimo de' Medici il Vecchio.
Giambologna added a couple of marvellous side chapels in 1580,
and the church was given its baroque façade 300 years later.

No weekend visitor should miss San Marco, not solely because
of these architectural splendours but also because of the astounding
frescoes painted by Fra Angelico and his pupils in the cloisters and
in the monks' forty-four cells. The entrance is at no.3 in Piazza San
Marco, to the right of the church. The cloisters open from Tuesday
to Saturday from 09.00 to 14.00, closing an hour earlier on Sundays
and public holidays. Inside, scarcely anything has changed since Fra
Angelico's time (he died in 1450), except that the monks have gone.
Cell 1 contains what must be his most famous work, the *Risen Jesus
meeting Mary Magdalen*; and at the top of the staircase that leads to
the cells you suddenly come across his breathtaking *Annunciation*.
Outside, the pompous statue in the square is of General Manfredo
Campi (1806–65).

Leave Piazza San Marco by Via Cavour. Just after a plaque on the
right telling us where the musician Rossini once lived stands
the Palazzo Medici-Riccardi, built for Cosimo il Vecchio by
Michelozzo. Inside its courtyard there is a staircase leading up to
the superb chapel, frescoed by Benozzo Gozzoli for the Medicis
with an extraordinary procession of the Magi on their way to

Bethlehem. With amazing but typical arrogance, Gozzoli was asked to paint several members of the Medici family into the procession. Gozzoli put himself in as well. The chapel is open (except on Wednesdays) from 09.00 to 12.00 and from 15.00 to 17.00, closing in the afternoons on Sundays and public holidays.

This area is Medici Florence. Turn immediately right along Via de' Gori and you reach the church of San Lorenzo and the celebrated Medici chapel. In the piazza is a statue of Giovanni de' Medici. Here too there is another open-air market, selling toys, sweets, jewellery, trinkets, clothes, gloves and fruit.

The great church is still unfaced with marble, pigeons nesting in the nooks of its façade. St Ambrose is reputed to have founded it in the year 393, but we owe today's lovely cool building with its great columns to Brunelleschi. Donatello designed the two bronze pulpits at the very end of his life, decorated with dramatic scenes of the crucifixion, deposition, resurrection and ascension of Jesus. The Medici symbols adorning the ceiling of the church look from a distance like great ladybirds. Brunelleschi designed the exquisite old sacristy off the south transept as a funeral chapel for Giovanni di Bicci de' Medici. Donatello decorated it. The so-called chapel of the princes, far more lavishly decorated and housing the tombs of the Medici grand dukes, is to my mind far less pleasing than Brunelleschi's.

Walk round the apse of San Lorenzo to reach Michelangelo's superb new sacristy, the Medici chapel (open except on Mondays from 09.00 to 14.00, closing at 13.00 on Sundays and public holidays). Michelangelo began building it in 1521. The two Medici buried here (Lorenzo, Duke of Urbino, and Giuliano, Duke of Nemours) are virtual nonentities, both of them represented as Roman generals. Their tombs are decorated with four of Michelangelo's finest sculptures: the figures of *Twilight* and *Dawn* on Lorenzo's, *Night* and *Day* on Giuliano's. Is *Night* the greatest of these four masterpieces? Close by is the sculptor's lovely *Madonna and Child*. This too was intended for a Medici tomb, that of Lorenzo the Magnificent.

Walk straight on from the Medici chapel along Via del Giglio, turn right along Via del Melarancio and you are back at Santa Maria Novella.

Further delights

San Miniato al Monte and the Piazzale Michelangelo

The church of San Miniato al Monte smiles down on Florence from its hill above the city, its green and white marble façade as well known as Giotto's campanile. You can reach it by bus no.13 from Via de' Pecori (just by the Baptistry). St Miniato himself walked there in the mid third century, in unusual circumstances if you believe the legend, since he had just been beheaded on the orders of the persecuting Emperor Decius and was carrying his severed head in his hands.

The present church replaced a small chapel dedicated to Florence's first Christian martyr in the eleventh century. Its exquisite romanesque façade was completed around 1090, with the exception of the thirteenth-century golden mosaic depicting Jesus between the Virgin Mary and St Miniato. The eagle above the pediment is the emblem of the Guild of Calima, wool-merchants who were once the guardians of the church. Baccio d'Agnolo built the bell-tower in 1518.

Inside, all is sober, geometrically and beautifully decorated in green and white marble. The pavement is a stupendous mosaic of 1207, displaying the signs of the zodiac. The raised choir covers a lovely romanesque crypt, which still houses the bones of St Miniato. Michelozzo created the splendid tabernacle, the 'Chapel of the Crucifix' at the end of the nave. On the north side Brunelleschi's pupil Antonio Minetti created the chapel of the Cardinal of Portugal in 1460, and Luca della Robbia decorated its ceiling. But the unity of the original building remains unimpaired. Its pulpit, dating from 1209, is a riot of romanesque carvings.

The monks of San Miniato al Monte still sell their own liqueurs from a shop in the piazza. And in the nearby cloister recently discovered fragments of frescoes by Paolo Uccello are displayed. As the sixteenth-century artist Giorgio Vasari noted disapprovingly, Uccello 'depicted scenes from the lives of the church fathers which totally ignored all the rules of consistency in colours, for he painted the fields blue, the cities red, and the buildings in whatever colour he felt inclined to.' Uccello, Vasari judged, was wrong to do so. We, schooled in the deliberate aberrations of the Impressionists, might well disagree and consider Uccello's oddities part of his genius.

Walk down from San Miniato al Monte to the Piazzale Michelangelo for one of the finest views of the whole city. Amongst the master's statues reproduced here is, inevitably, his *David*.

The Uffizi

Florentines call the Uffizi the world's greatest art gallery, and they could well be right. The gallery itself is a work of art. Vasari (and the architects who succeeded him) created a masterpiece of elegant corridors and loggias here. In six months in 1565 he also built the celebrated Vasari corridor, crossing the River Arno over the Ponte Vecchio to join the Uffizi with the Palazzo Vecchio. As Vasari wrote, 'I have never before this had to design something so difficult or dangerous, since its foundations are in the river and it virtually stands on air.' On the top floor of the Uffizi are more elegant corridors, designed by Vasari as the offices of the Grand Duke and now flanked with tapestries and busts.

Naturally Tuscan and Florentine art predominates in today's collection. Sandro Botticelli's *Birth of Venus* and his *Primavera* must be the most famous of the works housed here. (Rooms 10 to 14, entirely devoted to Botticelli, are invariably crowded.) One third of Paolo Uccello's *Battle of San Romano* is here, its horses frantically rearing, dying or kicking up their heels (the other parts are in London and Paris). Here you can see Giotto's Ognissanti *Madonna*, which he painted for the church by the Arno in 1310 or so. Then there are the two famous renaissance portraits painted by Piero della Francesca in 1465: of Federico di Montefeltro, with his bizarrely broken nose, and his sweet wife Battista Sforza, with her becomingly braided hair. Here too you can see Leonardo da Vinci's tormented *Adoration of the Magi* and his peaceful *Annunciation*. Room 25 contains Michelangelo's *Holy Family*.

As for the non-Tuscan geniuses whose works are here, I particularly like Tintoretto's *Leda and the Swan* and Titian's *Venus of Urbino*, and a lovely self-portrait by Rembrandt. Bellini and Giorgione are displayed in room 21. Finally, do not miss the

'Tribuna', a superb room designed by Bernardo Buontalenti in the 1580s to house the finest works of art belonging to the Medici. Today its centrepiece is the *Medici Venus*, a Roman copy of a Greek original, rediscovered in the fifteenth century. The Uffizi is open, except on Mondays, from 09.00 to 19.30, closing at 13.00 on Sundays and public holidays.

Fiesole

Lying 8 kilometres north-east of Florence, Fiesole is best reached by bus no.7 from the central station. (It also stops by the cathedral and in Piazza San Marco.) The Florentines and the citizens of Fiesole greatly disliked each other in the Middle Ages, and in 1125 most of the town was destroyed by Florence. Fortunately the episcopal palace and the cathedral, founded a century earlier, were still standing after this vicious act. The cathedral has an early romanesque crypt and some of its pillars were cannibalized from Roman buildings. The building you see today was the result of a monumental enlargement in the sixteenth century.

It stands on the north side of Piazza Mino da Fiesole, where the bus stops, and where the old Roman forum used to be. Fiesole's present city hall, the former Palazzo Pretorio, stands to the east, built in the fourteenth and fifteenth centuries. The coats of arms decorating it are those of the former city captains. Next to it is the charming renaissance church of Santa Maria Primerana.

Everywhere in the city are reminders of its ancient past. Walk up steep Via San Francesco between the episcopal seminary and the episcopal palace (on the west side of Piazza Mino da Fiesole) to find the basilica of San Alessandro, which stands where there was once a Roman temple to Bacchus. There is a stunning view of Florence from Via San Francesco. A few metres further on, the thirteenth-century church of San Francesco, with its lovely rose window and fifteenth-century façade, marks the site of the Etruscan acropolis.

Fiesole boasts Etruscan walls and an Etruscan temple. The Roman amphitheatre at Fiesole was excavated in the last century and dates from the first century BC. It could seat 3000 spectators. On its right are Roman baths which were built 200 years later and added to by the Emperor Hadrian. Treasures from the excavations are on display in the Roman museum (fittingly designed in 1910 to resemble a Roman temple).

Excursion to San Gimignano

A day's excursion by car to San Gimignano offers a chance not only to enjoy what is unquestionably the most beautiful of all Tuscan villages but also to drive through the delightful countryside outside Florence, perhaps stopping for a glass of Chianti *en route*.

Leave Florence by the Porta Romana and drive south-east on the route for Siena along the N2. After about 6 kilometres you reach Galluzzo, a town famous for its Carthusian monastery founded by one of Petrarch's dearest friends, Niccolò Acciaiuoli, in 1342. (There are guided tours every half hour from 09.00 to 12.00 and 16.00 to 19.00 in summer and from 14.30 to 17.00 in winter.)

After another 14 kilometres you pass through Sant'Andrea in Percussina, to which Macchiavelli was exiled for fifteen years and where he wrote his greatest works. Three kilometres further on leave the N2 at San Casciano in Val di Pesa, with its fine church of the Misericordia, and take the winding road south-west by way of San Pancrazio and Certaldo. Certaldo, 22 kilometres away, is a small wine-producing town, half modern and (in the upper part) still preserving its ancient character. Here Boccaccio spent most of his life, dying at Certaldo in 1375.

Thirteen kilometres due south of Certaldo lies San Gimignano, approached through lovely cypresses and vineyards, standing 324 metres above sea level and ringed with three walls. Thirteen dour medieval towers glower from inside the walls. The citizens say that there were once seventy-six, though so far archaeologists have been able to find the foundations of no more than fifty or so. These towers, built by rival families at odds with each other, are memorials to a savage past. Here each family group would retire for safety, emerging from time to time to fight with their enemies. This virtually perpetual civil war in San Gimignano eventually so weakened the city that the Florentines subdued it in 1353.

Today San Gimignano is everybody's dream of medieval Tuscany. The citizens devote themselves to making furniture and a delicious white wine called Vernaccia, and to welcoming tourists. Since there are so many visitors, it is best to park outside the city walls and walk through the 700-year-old Porta San Giovanni. Via San Giovanni is bordered by thirteenth-century buildings, as well as the romanesque church of San Francesco. The Fattoria Tollena sells wine made in the Franciscan convent. At no.40 is the elegant fourteenth-century Palazzo Pratellesi, which you can readily visit since it now houses the municipal library.

Towards the middle of the town is the triangular Piazza della Cisterna, surrounded by medieval palaces of all shapes and sizes and centred on a thirteenth-century well. Here too are restaurants and wine shops. And just round the corner is the centre of the city, the Piazza del Duomo, with lowering towers, the Palazzo del Podestà (dating from 1239) and the splendid cathedral church which the citizens call the Collegiata.

Inside the Collegiata, frescoes by Bartolo di Fredi, Barna da Siena and his pupil Giovanni d'Asciano cover the walls. (Barna was killed painting them, when he fell from the scaffolding.) Those in the south aisle depict New Testament scenes (with such homely touches as two angels carrying towels at Jesus's baptism). In the north aisle are lively scenes from the Old Testament: Noah getting drunk and then displaying himself naked; animals entering the ark two by two, the monkeys riding on other animals' backs.

And to the south side of the Collegiata is the open-air baptistry, with what ranks as my favourite Tuscan painting on its wall: a fresco of the Annunciation, painted by Domenico Ghirlandaio in 1482 and depicting both the Virgin Mary and the angel as tender youths.

The Palazzo del Popolo, designed by Arnolfo di Cambio, is reached from this baptistry, its massive Torre Grossa dating from 1300 and offering a splendid view of the surrounding countryside. The palazzo is now an art gallery, open from 09.30 to 12.30 and from 15.30 to 18.30 in summer, from 09.30 to 12.30 and from 14.30 to 17.30 in winter. Its chief treat is a set of 'profane' frescoes on the walls of the second floor, executed by Memmo di Filipuccio in the fourteenth century and depicting (amongst other subjects) lovers happily bathing or lying together in bed.

Walk back to the Piazza del Duomo and turn left into Via San Matteo, a feast of medieval palaces reaching the city gate known as Porta San Matteo which was built in 1262. If you turn right here and follow Via Sant'Agostino you reach a piazza boasting two churches: San Pietro, built in the eleventh century (and frescoed inside by the Siennese four hundred years later), and Sant' Agostino, a romanesque-gothic church dating from 1298 and containing some of the most remarkable and realistic frescoes in Tuscany, Benozzo Gozzoli's 1465 illustrations of the life of St Augustine.

Drive back to Florence by taking the road due east from San Gimignano. This forks left after 5 kilometres and reaches Poggibonsi (with its fifteenth-century castle) after another six. From Poggibonsi the N2 runs north for 27 kilometres to Florence.

Food and drink

Florentine food is superb because all its ingredients are rich: beef from Italy's finest cattle, raised in the Val di Chiana; seafood from the Tyrrhenian; trout, tench and eels from the abundant rivers; wild boar from the Maremma; lamb from the sheep grazing everywhere; succulent olive oil from Lucca; swelling beans, courgettes, peas and black cabbages from the fields.

In Florence beefsteak, at its best when the slaughtered beast has just ceased to be a calf, is cooked on a charcoal fire partly made of vine shoots. Seasoned with herbs and served with black pepper and salt, it appears on the table as *bistecca alla fiorentina*. Tripe is also served Florentine style (as *trippa alla fiorentina*), simmered with herbs, cut into strips when it is cooked, mixed with hot tomato sauce and flavoured with Parmesan cheese.

The fish stew known as *cacciucco* is invariably flavoured with garlic and emerges as a rich blend of several kinds of cuttlefish, tomatoes, hot chilli pepper, sole, hake, swordfish and squid. At least three cloves of garlic will go into preparing four medium-sized trout, which are often cooked in white wine. Another three cloves of garlic will have flavoured a dish of Florentine liver by the time it appears on the table, lightly fried, as *fegato di vitello alla toscana*. A lighter snack would be *crespelle alla fiorentina*, crêpes filled with spinach and cheese. Another splendid Florentine crêpe is the *fritella*, packed with raisins and served in wine.

Where to eat depends on your pocket. The cheapest places are students' canteens (known as *mense*), rising in price through *tavole calde* (bars which serve hot food at their counters) and the ubiquitous trattoria, the *rosticcierie* and the *fiaschetterie* to the celebrated and expensive Enoteca Pinchiorri in a fifteenth-century palazzo at no.47 Via Ghibellina. Bars flourish everywhere, as do the *gelaterie*, serving delicious ice-cream. The *pizzeria* is no Florentine invention, but it serves a palatable dish here as everywhere in Italy.

In a *vinaio* you can usually eat cheaply and drink a glass or two of wine without ordering a whole bottle. Vermiglio, Florence's own dry red wine, was renowned in the Middle Ages. Chianti Classico, a blend of wine from four grapes, is produced from over 70,000 hectares of vineyards between Florence and Siena. It bears the highest denomination possible for an Italian wine, *denominazione d'origine controllata e garantita*. If the wine has aged for two years, the label will also carry the word *vecchio*. If it has aged for three years the label says *riserva*.

Brunello di Montalcino is said by many to be even finer than Chianti Classico. It is certainly as expensive. But there is no need to look for such great wines in Florence in order to find an acceptable drink. Sassicaia, a delightful red wine, is not yet allowed to compete for the *denominazione d'origine contollata* label. And if you see the word *locale* on a bottle it by no means indicates rubbish but usually a handy, modest thirst-quencher that will not break your pocket.

Lunch in Florence is usually served between 12.30 and 14.30; dinner starts about 19.30 and is rarely available in restaurants much after 22.30.

Night life

Florence by night is not necessarily wicked but always lively and, in its discos and piano bars, much given to the young. There are floor shows at such venues as the 'Moulin Rouge', at no.12 Via Fosso Macinante, and 'Pozzo di Beatrice', at no. 5 Piazza Santa Trinita.

Florence's leading theatre is the dinky, elegant Teatro della Pergola, at no.32 Via della Pergola. The Teatro Communale at no.16 Corso Italia is the venue for concerts between October and November, opera from the middle of December to the middle of January, and the hub of a feast of opera, concerts and recitals (known as the *Maggio Musicale*) held throughout May, June and July. The best way of finding out what is happening in Florence at night is to buy the magazine *Firenze Spettacolo*.

Important information

Banks in Florence open only on weekdays, from 08.30 to 12.30, and they close on public holidays. Very occasionally you will find a bank that also opens from 15.00 to 16.00. The Banca Nazionale delle Communicazioni at the central railway station is open daily except Sundays from 08.20 to 19.00. A useful facility for weekend visitors is that in the summer months some shops in the centre are open all day on Sundays.

Nearly everything closes either entirely or earlier than usual on public holidays, which are 1 January, Easter Monday, 25 April, 1 May, 24 June, 15 August, 1 November, 8 December, Christmas Day and Boxing Day.

Getting around Florence is easy if you go on foot. Driving around Florence is tantamount to suicide or leads to madness. If you need to ride, take a bus. You buy tickets in a bar or at a tobacconist, either singly (a *biglietto semplice*) or in a book of eleven (a *biglietto multiplo*). If you see a bus bearing the sign of a hand holding a coin, you can pay when you get on it, but only if you have the exact fare.

Florence's airport is in fact at Pisa. Arriving by day is a breathtaking experience, since you usually descend from Genoa over the hills and then, reaching the coast, swing out over the sea and back before landing at the homely little airport. A comfortable and speedy train takes you from the airport directly to Florence in one hour, through vineyards, villages, hills and quarries, past yellow flaking houses, churches and the occasional palm tree. In the summer the fields are full of poppies and tiny gardens grow roses. Before the train reaches Empoli the country begins to roll a little. In the distance little towns cluster at hill tops, with an occasional monastery, and you may glimpse a tributary of the Arno from time to time.

London

If you wish to have a just notion of the magnitude of this city, you must not be satisfied with seeing its great streets and squares, but must survey the innumerable little lanes and courts. It is not in the showy evolution of buildings, but in the multiplicity of human habitations which are crowded together, that the wonderful immensity of London consists.

Samuel Johnson, 1759

I have often been amazed at the noise of people talking animatedly to each other on the S-Bahn or U-Bahn in Berlin. The same applies to the Paris Métro. By contrast, the staid British stolidly read newspapers, paperback novels and magazines on the tube (London's Underground railway), never glancing up or uttering a word to each other.

Yet Londoners are a welcoming race. If you ask the way, they will often walk along with you until they can be sure you are properly directed. They are proud of their city. When someone suggests an alteration in the great gothic pile that is St Pancras railway station, they petition Parliament and have the proposal thrown out. They queue in orderly fashion for their buses (unlike the Florentines, who will happily brush aside cripples and old ladies to board first); but if anyone in authority suggests changing a bus route or demolishing a redundant horse-trough, their passions are roused. They write to *The Times* or *The Independent*, they pester their Members of Parliament (whom they rightly regard as their servants), and nothing stands in their way until a tiny bit of London remains as it has been for a century.

In consequence, London's mighty monuments (Westminster Abbey, St Paul's Cathedral, the Houses of Parliament, Harrods, the Royal Academy) are only one face of this intriguing city. It is also crammed with charming nooks and crannies, with alleyways and little passages, and with quaintly old-fashioned quarters that in, say, Paris, would have been demolished long ago by a planner such as Baron Haussmann, bent on creating a rationally designed capital city. London, thanks to the temperament of its citizens, will never be rational and will always present the unexpected.

A city tour

Just before two o'clock in the morning, on 2 September 1666, a man in Farriner's bakery, London, smelt smoke and woke his companions. He, the baker and his family, climbed out over the

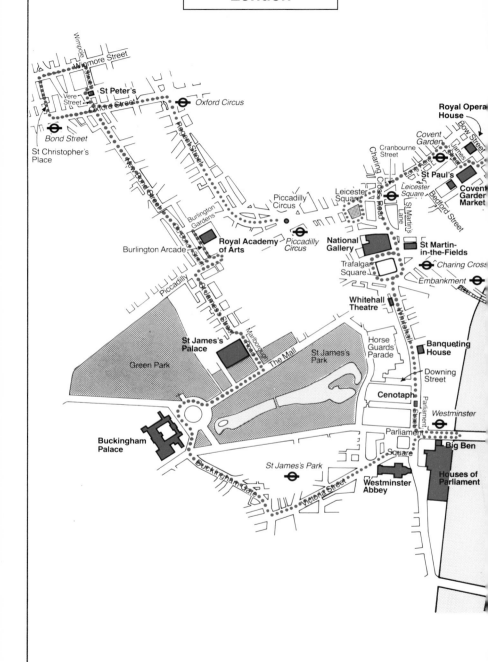

London

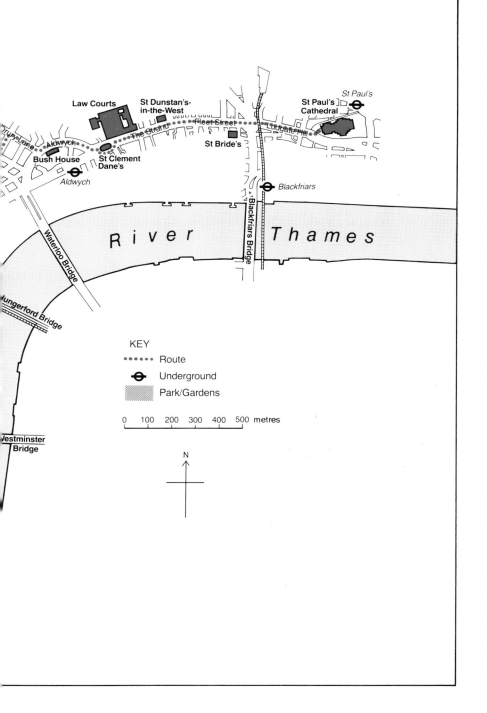

Law Courts

St Dunstan's-in-the-West

St Paul's

St Paul's Cathedral

Drury Lane

Aldwych

Fleet Street

The Strand

Ludgate Hill

Bush House

St Clement Dane's

St Bride's

Aldwych

Blackfriars

Blackfriars Bridge

R i v e r   T h a m e s

Waterloo Bridge

Hungerford Bridge

Westminster Bridge

KEY

• • • • • • Route

Underground

Park/Gardens

| 0 | 100 | 200 | 300 | 400 | 500 | metres |

N

rooftop and were saved. Their frightened maid refused to follow. She was burnt to death.

So began the great fire of London. Only eight other people lost their lives. But by the time the fire had burned itself out, over 13,000 houses had been destroyed in the flames, as well as 87 churches and 44 livery companies. A Frenchman named Robert Hubert confessed that he had set fire to the bakery. He was hanged at Tyburn.

The disastrous fire offered a unique opportunity to one of the greatest of all British architects, Sir Christopher Wren. The great fire had reduced the medieval cathedral of St Paul's to ashes. Dr Wren, as he then was, became surveyor-general to St Paul's. He designed the present magical building, the greatest baroque church in London. Wren himself laid the first stone of the new cathedral in 1675. Acts of worship began again in 1697. The final stone was set at the top of the lantern in 1710, when Sir Christopher, at the age of seventy-eight, was too infirm to climb so high himself. His son laid the stone on his behalf.

This is where a tour of London should start (go to St Paul's station on the Central line of the Underground). The dome of St Paul's is topped by a cross 111 metres above ground level. Great Tom, the largest bell in the cathedral, not only rings out the hours but also tolls the death of every member of the British royal family. The interior demonstrates the work of some of the greatest artists of the seventeenth century. Sir James Thornhill was commissioned to produce the frescoes of the life of St Paul which decorate the inside of the dome. You see them best from the whispering gallery, over 30 metres above the floor of the cathedral, where everything you murmur against the wall is heard perfectly on the other side, over 30 metres away. While Thornhill was painting these frescoes, he stepped backwards, to the very edge of his platform. His assistant, afraid to shout out in case he startled Sir James and the artist tumbled to his death, was inspired to smear over one of the paintings. Sir James leapt forward in anger, and thus his life was saved. Grinling Gibbons carved some of the choir screens and stalls, as well as the organ-case above them, while the French iron master Tijou forged the gates of the north and south chancel aisles.

Wren was one of the first persons to be buried in the crypt of his own cathedral. On a slab of black marble are carved the words,

'Lector, si monumentum requiris, circumspice' [Reader, if you need a monument, look around you]. Here too is buried Admiral Horatio Nelson, hero of the battle of Trafalgar. He lies immediately under the dome in another man's tomb, designed for Cardinal Wolsey in the sixteenth century by a Florentine artist, Benedetto de Rovezzane. When the Cardinal fell from favour at the Reformation, King Henry VIII took away his tomb. It was kept at Windsor Castle until someone had the brilliant idea of using it to honour Nelson in 1806.

St Paul's has become the last resting-place of numerous fighting men. The corpse of the Duke of Wellington, another foe of Napoleon, also lies in the crypt at the west end in a great sarcophagus of Cornish porphyry resting on a base of granite, designed by the German architect Gottfried Semper. It weighs 18 tons, and twelve black horses were required to pull it at the Duke's funeral in 1852. Just over a hundred years later, a new, lovely high altar and the baldacchino (or canopy) that shelters it were designed by Stephen Dykes Bower, one of Wren's successors as surveyor, as a memorial to the dead of the British Commonwealth in the two world wars. The style of this memorial so cunningly matches Wren's baroque that few realize it was built here nearly 250 years after the original architect's death.

Leave St Paul's Cathedral down the monumental flight of steps at the west end and walk down Ludgate Hill to the traffic lights at Ludgate Circus, crossing into Fleet Street. Jump on a bus (checking with the conductor that it goes on down the Strand) to ride along what used to be the heart of Britain's newspaper world. (The street is called after an ancient river, the Fleet, which now runs underground nearby.) Two lovely churches grace its length. The first, St Bride's, very shortly on the left, is another masterpiece by Sir Christopher Wren, bearing his tallest steeple. Like St Paul's Cathedral, it was built after the great fire. The second, on the right, is St Dunstan's-in-the-West, built 250 years later. This has a delightful clock outside with two giants striking the hours and quarters with their clubs.

A third fine church, St Clement Dane's, divides Fleet Street from the Strand. This is another masterpiece by Sir Christopher Wren — not because the earlier church was destroyed in the fire of 1666 but because it was found to be unsafe in 1679. Alas Hitler's bombs wrecked the interior in 1941. Since the allied air forces raised the cash for its restoration after the war, much of the interior is now embellished with air force insignia and badges. The names of 1900 American airmen killed in action are inscribed here (in a book under the west gallery). This church also has pride of place in a rhyme Londoners have sung for generations, which begins:

> Oranges and lemons,
> Say the bells of St Clement's,

St Clement Dane's stands just beyond the London Law Courts, a huge gothic construction on the right put up to the designs of the architect G. E. Street between 1868 and 1882. By the time Queen Victoria opened the courts, Street was dead, the result of a stroke brought about by the enormous problems involved in this vast project. When the courts are sitting you can visit this magical Gothic pile on weekdays from 10.30 to 13.00 and from 14.00 to 16.00, and gaze upon the architect's statue in the main hall. The statues over the entrance represent Jesus, flanked by King Solomon and King Alfred of England.

Leave the bus here and walk right round the Aldwych, skirting Bush House, home of the World Service of the BBC. Turn right up Drury Lane, past the Aldwych Theatre and then left into Russell Street. This will lead you straight into Covent Garden, but you could make a detour right up Bow Street to see the Covent Garden Opera House. In the evening the sumptuous mid nineteenth-century façade is magically illuminated. Covent Garden represents an Italian piazza in the heart of London. The market hall was built in 1830 and for over 150 years a fruit and vegetable market flourished here. In George Bernard Shaw's play *Pygmalion* (which became the celebrated Hollywood musical *My Fair Lady*), the waif Eliza Doolittle sells flowers here until she is transformed into a gracious lady by her tutor Professor Higgins. Today Covent Garden market still sells fruit and vegetables, but much more too: books, clothing, ironmongery, antiques and straightforward junk. Here you can sit and drink coffee or wine, or have a steak, or a slice of cake with a cup of tea. And in fine weather there is usually street theatre or music outside the portico of St Paul's church, sometimes of an astonishingly high standard.

The Italian architect Inigo Jones designed this church in 1830.

Today it is known as the actors' church and plaques on the wall inside commemorate such entertainers as Noël Coward and Ellen Terry (not all of whom are buried here: Ellen Terry is; Coward isn't). You enter from Bedford Street, on the opposite side from the market.

North of Covent Garden, just beyond its underground railway station, turn left into Long Acre (housing Edward Stanford's, the world's biggest map-seller and a specialist travel bookshop). Cross St Martin's Lane into Cranbourne Street which leads to Leicester Square. A bronze statue of Charlie Chaplin stands in the square, complete with baggy trousers, walking stick and bowler hat. It was made in 1981 by the artist John Doubleday.

Retrace your steps to the noisy artery known as Charing Cross Road, lined with booksellers and graced with three theatres, and walk right down to Trafalgar Square. In the centre is Nelson's column, with the admiral perched on top of it, complete with eyepatch and cocked hat. Fountains play round about and bronze lions rest benignly at his feet. Nelson is in good company. Here too are King Charles I, General Sir Charles Napier and General Sir Henry Havelock, sitting statuesquely on their horses. And everywhere there are pigeons, with children feeding them. At Christmas-time you can hear carols sung underneath an enormous fir tree.

On the north side stands the National Gallery, packed with masterpieces and open Mondays to Saturdays from 10.00 to 18.00 (Sundays 14.00 to 18.00). The works of the great British landscape artist John Constable are a must here, as well as the exquisite (though invariably flattering) eighteenth-century portraits of English gentlemen and their ladies by Gainsborough. But the National Gallery is also stocked with masterpieces by non-British artists; you can, for example, see a third of Paolo Uccello's *Battle of San Romano* (the other thirds are on show in Paris and Florence). Each summer the Gallery commissions a distinguished artist to make his or her own selection from the whole collection and then to devise an original way of displaying the works.

Entrance to the National Gallery is free. The building is guarded by two further statues: James I and George Washington. George Washington's statue is a copy of one by Jean-Antoine Houdon in Richmond, Virginia. The Commonwealth of Virginia gave the copy to the National Gallery in 1921. Next to it on the east side of the square is the church of St Martin-in-the-Fields, built by the architect James Gibbs in the 1720s. (The interior is not by him and is far less pleasing than his portico and the lovely steeple.) If you are lucky enough to arrive at lunchtime, you may well be able to sit for half an hour and listen to one of the many delightful concerts put on here.

Then walk down Whitehall, south of Trafalgar Square, a street crammed with ministerial offices, some slightly pompous, others examples of fine civic architecture. Here, for instance, you can see the British Foreign Office, the Treasury and the Ministry of Defence. The Whitehall Theatre stands at no.14. William Kent, a mid eighteenth-century architect of genius, designed the Horse Guards building half-way down on the right. The sovereign's horse guards sit on guard here every day of the year, sweltering in summer, both steeds and riders virtually motionless. The horses do not even twitch a muscle at the flash of camera bulbs.

On the other side of the road is the Banqueting House, a masterpiece designed by Inigo Jones and built 1619–22. King Charles I paid Rubens to decorate its ceiling with a painting depicting his own just rule. Ironically in 1649 the king was escorted through one of the Banqueting House windows on to a scaffold and beheaded. You can visit it every day, except Mondays and Sunday mornings, from 10.00 to 17.00.

In the centre of Whitehall stands Britain's most important war memorial, the Cenotaph, designed by Edwin Lutyens after World War I. Since those who fought for the British Empire included Sikhs, Hindus, Christians, Moslems and Jews, Lutyens wisely decided to construct a memorial without the slightest hint of a religious symbol in order to avoid offending any of them. Just before the cenotaph Downing Street leads right. No.10 is the official home of the British Prime Minister, but security considerations mean that you cannot (as was once possible) have yourself photographed outside. From the Cenotaph southwards Whitehall becomes Parliament Street and soon opens out into Parliament Square. Here you can see two great national monuments separated by 500 years – the Houses of Parliament and Westminster Abbey. But just before you cross the road to the Houses of Parliament it is worth walking left to Westminster Bridge, simply to have a look at London's great river, the Thames.

Like St Paul's Cathedral, the present Houses of Parliament were rebuilt after a disastrous fire (this time in 1834). The architects were two men of genius, the classicist Sir Charles Barry and the inspired gothicist Augustus Welby Pugin. Work began in 1840. Four years later Barry decided that a great tower, clock and bells were needed. Benjamin Vuillamy, Queen Victoria's clock-maker, designed the clock. Both it and the tower are known as 'Big Ben' after the famous 14-ton bell. Shortly after entering service, the great bell cracked. It has remained cracked ever since, and tolls the hours slightly out of tune.

Westminster Abbey is far more venerable, its foundation stone laid in 1245, its architect almost certainly a Frenchman. Here is the gothic of northern France — of the cathedrals at Amiens and Reims, as well as of the Sainte-Chapelle in Paris — brought to London. The abbey was finished only in 1380. Then it was enhanced, added to and enriched over the centuries, above all by a huge chantry chapel for King Henry VII. The countless monuments to the dead include some masterpieces of sculpture, such as the gothic tomb of Henry VII's mother, made by the brilliant Italian Pietro Torrigiani. The monks who once lived here have long gone, but the chapter house, built in 1250 or so, remains pure and beautiful. A splendid large cloister leads to the oasis of the little cloister. You will almost certainly have to queue to get in (between 09.00 and 16.45 on weekdays, closing two hours earlier on Saturdays) and on Sundays you can walk around freely only by avoiding the numerous services with their splendid music.

Walk south-west from the abbey along Victoria Street and turn right into Buckingham Gate which leads to Buckingham Palace. King George IV decided to have the palace built in the early nineteenth century, but died before it was finished. So did his successor. Queen Victoria had been ten years on the throne before it was ready, the original architect, John Nash, having been dismissed and replaced by Edward Blore. This mighty pile has more than 600 rooms, is graced by gardens where the English monarch invites the favoured to parties, and boasts an art gallery in the south wing where some of the royal paintings are on view to the general public for a small fee (open Thursday to Saturday, 10.30–17.00). A treat that costs nothing (apart from the need to arrive early for a decent view) is the ceremonial changing of the royal guard outside the palace every day in summer at 11.30 (and every other day at the same time in winter).

Walk back along the Mall, a wide street set out in the 1660s and now ideal for the royal or ceremonial processions that are a feature of London life. London boasts the loveliest open spaces, and on the right is St James's Park. Here you can gaze on Buckingham Palace, feed the ducks on the lake with pieces of bread, or listen to the band (in summer).

Turn left out of the Mall along Marlborough Road and you reach St James's Palace. This red-brick Tudor building (commissioned by King Henry VIII) is far more ancient than the monarch's favoured home, Buckingham Palace.

St James's Street leads north-west from here to Piccadilly. A few paces to the right across Piccadilly stands the Royal Academy of Arts (invariably shortened to the Royal Academy). It is Britain's oldest society dedicated to the fine arts, founded under the patronage of King George III in 1768. A statue of its first president, the artist Sir Joshua Reynolds, stands in the courtyard, frequently garlanded with flowers. Its greatest treasure is Michelangelo's *Madonna and Child with the Infant St John*.

This is the moment to pursue some of those innumerable little lanes and courts that Dr Samuel Johnson believed contributed essentially to the charm of London. West of the Royal Academy you can wander up the delightfully old-fashioned passage known as Burlington Arcade. Wander down again to turn right from Piccadilly into Old Bond Street. London is famed as the art centre of the world, and Old Bond Street is known for some of the great dealers who operate from here. The galleries are open to anyone and the works on display can be bought by all those with several thousand pounds to spare (sometimes less, sometimes more). Famous names include Thomas Agnew on the left at no.43, and Colnaghi on the right at no.14, a firm established in 1760. Old Bond Street also boasts other internationally-known names from the world of fashion, perfumes and cosmetics: Yardley House, Pierre Cardin, Gucci, Chanel, Lowwe, Tiffany and Co. Here you can buy beautiful, if expensive, shoes and suits, and a Persian carpet or two.

Just before you pass into New Bond Street, notice the entrancing art deco Atkinsons building of 1926 on the right, on the corner of Burlington Gardens. The jewellery firm of Cartier is situated in New

Bond Street, as well as numerous rivals, silver and gold dealers, antique and furniture shops, clothing emporia and porcelain vendors. No.10 on the right, Clifford Chambers, is a delightful building in the Dutch style, built in 1877. On the right too is Sotheby's, the famous auction house, founded in 1744. Saint Laurent is also here, continuing the tradition of haute couture in this elegantly expensive part of London. Then suddenly you emerge into Oxford Street, with its great department stores, generally far more suited to people's pockets than any shop in Bond Street.

Turn left along Oxford Street, cross to the other side of the road when you reach Bond Street tube station, walk a few paces further on past Lilley and Skinner's store and you will be moments away from one of London's hidden gems. Perched on a pole on the pavement is a clock with the words Saint Christopher's Place inscribed on its face. A sign points right along an exquisite arcaded alleyway that leads to shops, pubs and restaurants. The brilliant Victorian designer, poet and socialist William Morris had a workshop here. Today there are a couple of bookshops (one antiquarian), pavement cafés, patisseries, hairdressers and dress shops.

St Christopher's Place leads into Wigmore Street, and here you turn right. On the left is the accoustically magnificent Wigmore Hall, built by the celebrated piano-maker Friedrich Bechstein in 1901 and an ideal venue for intimate concerts. The premises of a rival piano firm, Bösendorfer, now adjoin the hall. Turn next right into Wimpole Street to return to Oxford Street. About half-way down on the right is the church of St Peter's, Vere Street, a most elegant building with a Doric portico by James Gibbs.

Take the first bus going left to ride for a moment or two as far as Oxford Circus. Regent Street leads south-east from here, designed on a beautiful curve by John Nash as far as Piccadilly Circus, and now one of London's splendid shopping streets (as well as the home of airline companies, tailors and banks). Piccadilly Circus is the direct result of Nash's work, for the site where Regent Street and Piccadilly intersected had to be totally reconstructed in 1819. In 1893 the sculptor Alfred Gilbert further enhanced the circus with his statue of Eros, cast in aluminium. Oddly enough this Greek god of love was cast in honour of a stern Christian philanthropist, the Earl of Shaftesbury. Eros *buries* his *shaft* or arrow in the ground, a pun on the earl's name. Here in summer the young recline, drinking from cans or simply drinking in the ambience of the heart of London.

Further delights

Two great museums

Two London museums must not be missed: the Victoria and Albert Museum in the Cromwell Road (tube to South Kensington) and the British Museum in Great Russell Street (tube to Tottenham Court Road). The Victoria and Albert opens Monday to Thursday from 10.00 to 18.00 (it is closed on Fridays), Saturday from 10.00 to 17.00 and Sunday from 14.30 to 17.00. The British Museum opens Monday to Saturday from 10.00 to 17.00, Sunday from 14.30 to 18.00.

London owes the Victoria and Albert not to Queen Victoria but to her enterprising husband Prince Albert, who founded it as part of a restless campaign to champion and inspire British designers by bringing together examples of excellence in each creative field. The architect, Sir Aston Webb, designed a museum of 150 rooms housed in a building that is such a mixture of architectural styles that no one could have foreseen how splendid it would look. Inside are Raphael cartoons, a medieval treasury, prints and ceramics, whole shop-fronts, tapestries, jewellery, musical instruments, sculpture, stained glass, the famous Great Bed of Ware (12 feet, 3.5 metres square) and a whole room designed by William Morris. The top floor of the Henry Cole wing houses a stunning collection of paintings by that most English of artists, John Constable.

Just up the road from the Victoria and Albert is Hyde Park, where you can listen to band concerts in summer. In the corner near Marble Arch the quirkiness of English life is perfectly demonstrated at weekends, for here cranks and geniuses, religious maniacs and prophets mount soap-boxes and preach their peculiar gospels, taking on hecklers, questioners and all-comers.

The British Museum is another architectural gem, but by contrast with the Victoria and Albert its design is restrained and disciplined, fronted by a huge neo-classical portico designed by Sir Robert Smirke in the 1820s. The treasures you can see here include the so-called Lewis Chessmen, a chess set of 67 ivory pieces made in Scandinavia in the twelfth century; the Mildenhall Treasure, a priceless collection of fourth-century Roman silver; the Parthenon marble frieze, which Lord Elgin brought back from Athens (and which Greece would like returned); a splendid collection of Egyptian mummies; two of the oldest Bible codexes in the world (Codex Sinaiticus and Codex Alexandrinus); beautifully illuminated medieval manuscripts; whole mosaics rescued from excavated Roman villas and painstakingly set out as new. So vast is the collection that the British Museum digs into its treasures several times a year and mounts special exhibitions: on Egyptian sculpture, on the art of printing, on Chinese ceramics, on almost anything imaginable.

Harrods

If you leave the Victoria and Albert Museum by the Cromwell Road entrance and walk left into Brompton Road you soon reach Harrods, one of the largest department stores in the world, housed in a remarkable terracotta building designed at the beginning of this century, its details picked out in lights when evening falls. The interior lives up to the exterior, especially the magical meat hall, which is decorated with hunting scenes. This part of London is crammed with fashionable boutiques, most of them pricey.

The Portobello Road

A more raucous and certainly cheaper shopping outing would be a visit to the Portobello Road market, held on Saturdays in Notting Hill. Take the Underground railway to Notting Hill Gate station, leave by the Pembridge Road exit and the Portobello Road is second on the left. The route takes you past the Gate Theatre (which is over the top of a pub dedicated to Victoria's consort Albert).

The exotic name Portobello derives from an obscure naval skirmish of 1739, when Admiral Edward Vernon sailed to Porto Bello in the Spanish West Indies with only six ships. Fortunately the

Spaniards were completely unprepared, and Vernon successfully captured the harbour, blowing up the Spanish forts. The British were delirious with joy, the admiral was granted the freedom of the city of London, and countless pubs throughout the country – and this long winding street – were named after him.

The tradition of cheap goods – dating from the early 1860s when Romanies started selling horses here – has not totally disappeared from the Portobello Road, though a richer clientele now comes along. Today, since most British banks close on Saturdays, money-changers do a brisk trade with the many foreign visitors. Stalls selling German sausages vie with the food sold in pubs. Folk singers wander about.

As well as open-air stalls selling trinkets, glassware, clothing and books, shops on either side of the road carry on their trade in reproduction 'antiques', protecting their reputation with the discreet words 'attributed to'. An effete nude is 'attributed to' the Victorian painter William Etty and a fine lady is 'attributed to' Romney. Genuine antiques can be found – though only for a price – and in addition some of the streets around the Portobello Road house galleries selling paintings and prints by contemporary artists, some of them locals. Here is where West Indians meet Turks, Americans meet the British and expensive ceramics mingle with junk. Even if you buy nothing, Saturday morning in the Portobello Road is hugely enjoyable. Dealers arrive at about seven o'clock in the morning (the best time for bargains), while the general public begins to fill the street about an hour later.

Excursion to Windsor

The swiftest way to Windsor is by train from Paddington station, reached on the London Underground by the Bakerloo, Circle or District lines. Paddington is itself something of an architectural masterpiece and a historical curiosity. The brilliant engineer Isambard Kingdom Brunel designed it for the Great Western

Railway in 1851, replacing an earlier station made of wood. The great central shed has a span of 31 metres. The architect M. D. Wyatt created lovely ironwork decoration. And another architect, Philip Hardwick, designed the Great Western Hotel at the front, opened in 1854 and restored inside in the 1930s.

Queen Victoria made her very first railway journey from Slough to here in 1842. For this excursion you travel in the opposite direction, from Paddington to Slough. Make sure to catch one of the fast trains, and not one that stops at every station *en route*. The latter can take more than three-quarters of an hour; the former scarcely more than fifteen minutes. From Slough a little train, running frequently, trundles to Windsor across meadows and over the Thames, with a view of the ancient buildings of Eton College on the left. It takes just six minutes.

At Windsor and Eton central station you could pause for a moment to see the entertaining exhibition, with life-size models, depicting the celebrations of 1897 in honour of sixty years of Queen Victoria's reign. Victoria came to the station to greet members of her own royal family who had come from all over the world for the occasion. The model of the dumpy old Queen looks exceedingly angry, in spite of the supposed joy of the event. As you walk out of the station the oldest and largest still inhabited castle in the world looms on your left. Windsor Castle's round tower rises 66 metres above the River Thames, and is topped by a 22-metre flagpole that bears the British royal standard when the monarch is there. The so-called 'Norman Gateway', built in fact by King Edward III, is flanked by a couple of drum towers. Beyond the castle is a magnificent park, an ideal place for a picnic on a hot day. A remarkable long walk, 80 metres wide, runs through the park from the castle for 3 miles (5 kilometres); it was laid out in 1665.

You can visit the state apartments of Windsor Castle (whenever the monarch is not in residence) on almost every day of the year from 10.30 to 15.00 (but not on Sundays). The rest of the castle is open to visitors on Sunday afternoons from mid June to the last week in October. You can visit the exquisite St George's chapel, with its Perpendicular gothic windows, on weekdays from 10.45 to 16.00 and on Sundays from 14.00 to 16.00 (closing fifteen minutes earlier in winter in both cases). Here many of England's monarchs rest in peace, including Charles I. In 1813 his coffin at Windsor was opened up. The royal head lay separated from the rest of the body by a clear cut through the fourth cervical vertebra. Charles's hair had retained its noted beautiful dark-brown hue, his beard redder than the rest. But to expose his body to the air was a mistake. The king's one remaining eye lasted just a few minutes, only to dissolve before the eyes of the witnesses.

A batallion of one of the five regiments of Foot Guards is always stationed at the castle, and the splendidly martial ceremony of changing the guard takes place daily.

If you have time when you leave the castle, stroll to the right down to the River Thames, either for a sail on a Thames cruiser or to cross Windsor bridge and walk along the charming high street of the village of Eton. This is not only the home of one of Britain's most famous private schools (which you can also visit), but also boasts excellent little art galleries and restaurants — not all of them expensive. (The Peacock restaurant, for example, part of the Christopher Inn in Eton High Street, has been highly praised in food buffs' guidebooks for over a decade, but has not made this an excuse for putting up its prices.) Then catch the train back to Slough and make sure to take a high-speed train back to Paddington.

Food and drink

Gastronomically speaking, England does not rate highly among the nations of the world. But London makes up for the lack of a national cuisine with an extraordinary variety of ethnic food which is frequently very cheap.

The Chinese came to London in the late eighteenth century, brought by the ships of the East India Company. Italians began to come here in such numbers in the nineteenth century that special Italian quarters were set up in Holborn and Clerkenwell; and many more came again in the 1950s. At this period too some 30,000 Asians settled in the city. Greek Cypriots had long felt welcome here, and around 10,000 sought refuge in London when Turkish troops invaded Cyprus in 1974.

The result is that today you can eat Chinese, Italian, Asian and Cypriot food almost everywhere in London. You can recognize Cypriot restaurants by the 'eyestones' they put in their windows, good luck charms that somewhat resemble glass eyes. Most so-called Greek restaurants actually serve Cypriot food. Part of Soho is officially designated Chinatown, with even the telephone boxes designed to look like pagodas. Soho and west Bloomsbury are also filled with Italian restaurants – some of them inexpensive trattorias, others dearer ristorantes.

Indian restaurants are usually cheap and usually also excellent. One of the most economical dishes is the various forms of biriani, pilao rice mixed with eggs, vegetables and pieces of lamb or chicken. In an Indian restaurant Bombay duck is not a cooked bird but a pungent form of dried fish. Chappati is bread made from unleavened wheat. Tandoori food has been marinated in sauce and then cooked in an oven made of clay.

Perhaps Britain's own contribution to London food is the ubiquitous 'pub grub', almost always very basic and generally stodgy: cottage pie; sausage and chips; steak and kidney pie, boiled potatoes and sprouts; baked potatoes filled with cheese; and such like. But such food is not expensive. The beer is served in pints or half pints, and some pubs even serve drinkable wine as well as decent beer. But above all London pubs are generally warm, friendly places. Another popular institution is the wine bar, where the food on offer is usually of the quiche and salad variety and where prices are generally higher than in a pub.

Night life

London is famed for its theatres, from the Theatre Royal in the Haymarket and the Old Vic just opposite Waterloo railway station to the Royal Court in Sloane Square. There is even an open-air theatre in Regent's Park in the summer where, for example, the mummers in Shakespeare's *A Midsummer Night's Dream* can spring out on the audience from the bushes. You will always be able to find musicals and variety shows as well as straight drama. And a kiosk in Leicester Square sells half-price tickets on the day of performance.

Opera flourishes too, not only at Covent Garden but also at the London Coliseum in St Martin's Lane. Classical music is on offer everywhere, on the South Bank (the Queen Elizabeth Hall, the Purcell Room, and the Royal Festival Hall), in the Barbican Centre and the Wigmore Hall, and in beautiful churches throughout the city. And from mid July to early September there are the Promenade Concerts in the Royal Albert Hall.

London boasts an energetic night life and cabaret scene, though Soho, once notorious for sleazy strip-tease, has long been cleaned up. Raymonds' Revuebar in Brewer Street still offers the sight of tastefully unclad girls. 'La Vie en Rose' in Great Windmill Street advertises sophisticated entertainment. Other clubs inviting you to dance and enjoy cabaret are 'Boulogne' in Gerard Street, 'Talk of London' in Parker Street near Drury Lane, and 'l'Hirondelle' in Swallow Street. Ronnie Scott's, at no.47 Frith Street, Soho, has for many years been the haunt of distinguished jazzmen, both British and foreign. You can also hear jazz in other pubs and clubs throughout the city. The young and energetic dance and drink at the Hippodrome in Leicester Square, while the Stork Club in Regent Street proffers cabaret of a more sophisticated kind.

Find out what is happening by buying one of the London daily newspapers or the excellent journal *Time Out*.

Important information

The London Underground (the tube) is stuffier and smellier than the Paris Métro, Berlin's U-Bahn or the Viennese subway, but it works. Red London buses, the natives say, always come in twos when you want only one, but perhaps this just reflects the Englishman's habit of poking gentle fun at his own beloved institutions.

Under fives travel free. Children aged 5 to 14 travel for half price. The best bargains for a weekend visitor are undoubtedly the one-day travelcard (if you are not planning to use the railway system) and the one-day capitalcard. Both allow you to use any bus or tube train. The capitalcard will also take you miles on British Rail (to Brighton and back if you wish; and certainly to Windsor and back) at any time after 09.30 on weekdays and all day long at weekends. Buy either card at tube stations (where you can also pick up a free map of the Underground system) and at main railway stations.

London taxis carry an illuminated sign when they are free, and the drivers are used to being 'flagged down', i.e. you just wave at them and they stop. Then the driver (or 'cabbie') winds down his window to find out where you want to go, before letting you into his cab. A meter clocks up your fare (with a standard addition if you have luggage) and drivers expect a tip – though not necessarily an excessive one.

London is served by two major airports: Heathrow and Gatwick. Although Heathrow is only 14 miles (23 kilometres) from London, the Green Line bus and the Underground railway (the Piccadilly line) can take an intolerable time reaching the city centre. Gatwick, 28 miles (45 kilometres) from the city centre, is served by the Gatwick express, a train which runs every fifteen minutes during the day and less frequently at night, and takes around half an hour to speed you in comfort to Victoria station.

In the matter of opening when their customers need them, British banks are probably the least satisfactory in the world. They open only on Monday to Friday from 09.30 to 15.30. They close on New Year's Day, from Good Friday for four days, for two variable holidays in May, on August 31, and on Christmas Day and Boxing Day. Happily, there are 24-hour banks permanently open at Gatwick and Heathrow airports.

Paris

I cannot tell you what an immense impression Paris made on me. It is the most extraordinary place in the world. I was not prepared for, and really could not have believed in, its perfectly direct and separate character. My eyes ached, and my head grew giddy, as novelty, novelty, novelty; nothing but strange and striking things; came swarming before me.

Charles Dickens, 1844

Flower stalls beside the church of the Madeleine, open-air bookstalls along the left bank of the River Seine; gargoyles on the cathedral of Notre-Dame; the Opéra; the Arc de Triomphe; artists in Montmartre; the Eiffel Tower; little cafés, bars and bistros; the art nouveau entrances to the stations of the Métro: these are the images of Paris that still come alive on any visit.

Scarcely less real are the images drawn from the past: Marie Antoinette on her way to execution; Napoleon lying in state under the Arc de Triomphe; Racine and Molière revitalizing Parisian theatre; Toulouse-Lautrec sipping absinthe and then hobbling to the bordellos to paint loving, realistic portraits of the girls, or finding his way to the Can-Can to portray his favourite dancers.

And Paris is small. You can easily walk across it in a day, peering into its secrets, its tiny alleys, its still unspoiled quarters — such as the Marais between the Centre Pompidou and the Seine. Beautifully developed from the sixteenth century, this region was untouched by Baron Haussmann's nineteenth-century replanning of the city and is now a prized conservation area, its old *hôtels* and narrow streets surrounding the magical Place des Vosges.

A city tour

Any tour of Paris must begin in the Place de la Concorde (Métro Concorde). 'Along the Paris streets, the death carts rumble, hollow and harsh,' wrote Charles Dickens in *A Tale of Two Cities*. 'Six tumbrils carry the day's wine to La Guillotine. All the devouring and insatiate Monsters imagined since imagination could record itself are fused into the one realisation, Guillotine.'

The six daily tumbrils rumbled into the Place de la Concorde. Before the Revolution was over they had brought no fewer than 1344 victims to be executed in this square. Here Marie Antoinette was beheaded in October 1793, ten months after the execution of her husband Louis XVI on 21 January. The square had been named

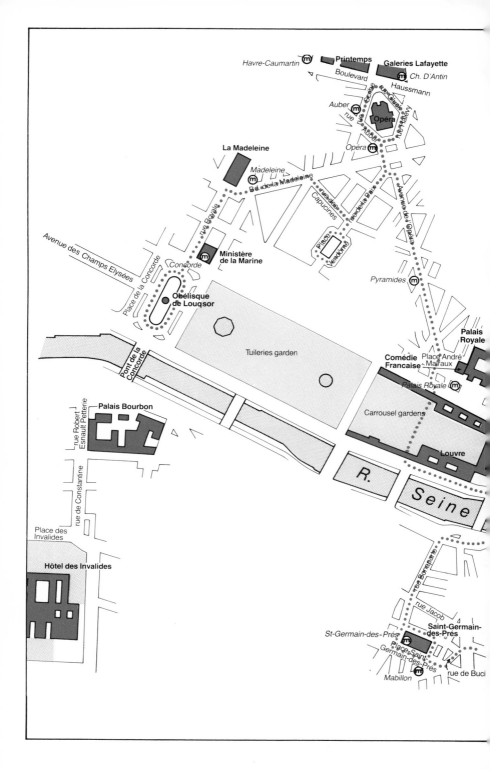

Paris

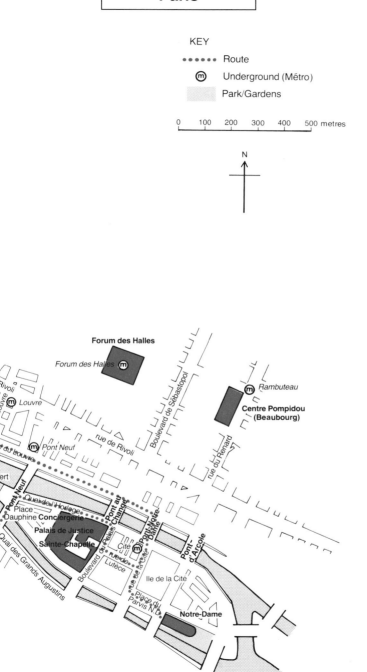

KEY

•••••• Route

ⓜ Underground (Métro)

Park/Gardens

0   100   200   300   400   500 metres

N

Forum des Halles

Forum des Halles ⓜ

rue de Rivoli

Boulevard de Sébastopol

Rambuteau ⓜ

Centre Pompidou
(Beaubourg)

Palais du
Louvre

Louvre ⓜ

rue du Louvre

rue de Rivoli

rue du Renard

Quai du Louvre

Pont Neuf ⓜ

Point du Vert
Galant

Quai de l'Horloge

Pont Neuf

Quai de Conti

Place
Dauphine Conciergerie

Palais de Justice

Sainte-Chapelle

Quai des Grands Augustins

Pont au Change

Boulevard du Palais

Cité

Cité ⓜ

rue de la Cité

Lutèce

rue de Lutèce

Pont Notre-Dame

Pont
d'Arcole

Ile de la Cité

Place du
Parvis N.D.

Notre-Dame

after and built in honour of his father, Louis XV, but its name was changed after the Revolution.

Some say it is the most beautiful square in the world. Its creator, Jacques-Ange Gabriel, beginning work in 1757, decided to set out a huge open space (84,000 metres square) instead of the usual hemmed-in Parisian square. On the north side of the Place de la Concorde he set two exquisite buildings: today's French Admiralty Office (on the right) and the Hôtel Crillon. Directly opposite, the Pont de la Concorde crosses the Seine — the first bridge ever designed without a hump-back, and moreover made out of stones cannibalized from the demolished Bastille. The classical building on the other side of the Pont de la Concorde, although it has housed the Assemblèe Nationale (the lower house of the French Parliament) since the Revolution, is still often called the Palais-Bourbon, since it was built in the 1720s for Louise-Françoise de Bourbon, illegitimate daughter of King Louis XIV and Mme de Montespan.

To the west, flanked by two prancing horses, is the entrance to the Champs-Elysées, which stretches as far as the Arc de Triomphe. In the centre of the square, in place of the dreaded guillotine, there is an obelisk from Luxor, which was presented to King Louis-Philippe in 1831 by Mohamet Ali. In the following decade the obelisk was flanked with two superb fountains, modelled on those in the square of St Peter's, Rome.

Turn your back on the Assemblée Nationale and you see the church of the Madeleine (up rue Royale between the Admiralty Office and the Hôtel Crillon). To the east of the great square is the Tuileries garden, its entrance guarded by two winged horses, sculpted by Antoine Coysevox who died in 1720. Supplemented by the nineteenth-century Carrousel gardens, this delightful open space in the heart of the city stretches to the Louvre, its tree-shaded benches sought eagerly by many a weary tourist.

Four elegant streets lead out of the Place de la Concorde. Choose the rue Royale, where virtually every house treasures a rich part of France's literary, dramatic or fashionable past. On the wall of no.1, a notice declares the general mobilization of 2 August 1914, which marked the start of World War I. In the eighteenth century, the writer Mme de Staël, opponent of Napoleon, lived at no.6. Subsequent architectural fashions have fortunately only enhanced and not spoiled the grand design of rue Royale. Two expensive restaurants here deserve especial mention, since they have retained their art nouveau interiors (that exotic sinuous style that made Hector Guimard, architect of the Paris Métro stations, famous). These two restaurants are Maxim's, which Louis Marnez transformed into art nouveau luxury in 1899, and the Lucas-Carton round the corner in the Place de la Madeleine, sumptuously refurbished by Louis Marjorelle in 1905.

Walk as far as the church of La Madeleine, standing 108 metres long and 43 metres wide and deriving its inspiration quite as much from Greek pagan temples as from Christian models. Napoleon had it built as a monument to the French army, i.e. his own glorification. Fifty-two Corinthian columns, each 19.5 metres high, form a colonnade around the building and support a richly sculpted frieze. Is this really a place of worship? As the British architectural historian Ian Nairn once observed, the church of La Madeleine has 'a distinctly raffish air'.

East of the church is a colourful flower market, open from nine in the morning till the early evening except on Sundays. From here the Boulevard de la Madeleine leads eastwards. Turn right into the rue des Capucines, with its Irish whiskey bar on the left, and then right again into Place Vendôme. Louis XIV's architect Jules Hardouin-Mansart created the present delightful octagonal square and the balconies still carry the Sun King's emblem. Chopin died in a house in this square, and here Napoleon III (1808–73) demanded the hand of his future empress, Eugénie. An equestrian statue of the Sun King (by François Girardon) was set up here in 1699 and torn down by revolutionaries in 1792. Napoleon then seized the opportunity of setting up a column in his own honour in its place.

From Place Vendôme the rue de la Paix leads north-east to the Opéra. Its architect, Charles Garnier, beat over 170 other entries in the competition to design it. Work began in 1862 and finished fourteen years and 34 million francs later. On top of the gable front Apollo stands with his lyre, supported by two female figures representing poetry and music. Inside, Garnier created unprecedented glamour that just falls short of vulgarity: a grand staircase of white marble with a balustrade of Algerian onyx; columns of pink marble; the Grand Foyer, decorated in gold; and a stage 52 metres wide, 60 metres high and 36 metres deep. To refresh patrons after a night at the Opéra, Garnier also built the Café de la Paix on the corner of the square.

Walk around the Opéra into Boulevard Haussmann, which contains two of Paris's loveliest department stores. The French have the knack of creating buildings that astonish by their daring and also work architecturally and functionally. The splendid Au Printemps at no.64 Boulevard Haussmann, and its neighbour the Galeries Lafayette are two remarkable early twentieth-century constructions, basically made out of reinforced concrete that has been transformed by *fin-de-siècle* mosaics, glass, and art nouveau metalwork. These stores are a cornucopia of fashion, lingerie, tableware, perfume, porcelain, crystal and jewellery. On Saturdays the pavements outside fill with stalls selling goods that range from junk to astonishing bargains in clothing or handbags. Bookstalls, crockery vendors, wig-makers and hamburger stalls crowd flower-sellers and (in season) Santa Claus into the busy Boulevard Haussmann itself.

The long Avenue de l'Opéra leads back to rue de Rivoli. At the end of the street on the left is the Comédie Française, and behind it the Palais-Royale, with its enchanting garden. The Palais-Royale was once known as the Palais-Cardinal, since it was built as a palace for Cardinal Richelieu in the seventeenth century. Subsequently enlarged but never spoilt, its arcaded garden is still exquisite.

As you come into the rue de Rivoli, the north-west wing of the Palais du Louvre stretches in front of you. Walk through the arches to one of the world's greatest art galleries, open daily (except on public holidays) from 09.45 to 18.30. Its Greek and Roman antiquities include the celebrated winged *Victory of Samothrace* and fragments from the Temple of Zeus at Olympia. Here too you can see one third of Paolo Uccello's *Battle of San Romano* (to see it all you must also visit the National Gallery, London, and the Uffizi, Florence). Addicts of Leonardo da Vinci will want to see his *Venus de Milo, Madonna of the Rocks, Virgin and the Infant Jesus with St Anne* and *Bacchus*.

Walk east from the Louvre along the River Seine (on the Quai du Louvre) until you reach the Pont-Notre-Dame, leading to the Ile de la Cité and the cathedral of Notre-Dame. The *quai* is lined with open-air stalls selling books and prints, the little show-cases fixed to the parapet above the river. Just before the Pont au Change the Conciergerie with its pepper-pot towers lines the opposite bank.

Across the Pont-Notre-Dame a little open-air market appears on Sundays, selling herbs, flowers and caged birds.

Curiously enough, though the cathedral of Notre-Dame is a masterpiece of the twelfth and thirteenth centuries, the Notre-Dame that is engraved on our consciousness is essentially (like Sacré-Coeur de Montmartre) a creation of nineteenth-century romanticism. In 1831 Victor Hugo described it as 'a vast symphony of stone'. He taught the world that here was 'the prodigious product of an era when, on every stone in a hundred ways, one can see emerging the fantasy of the worker disciplined by the genius of the artist.' Notre-Dame, he wrote, is 'a human creation as powerful and fecund as the divine creation – from which it seems to have derived its double character: variety and eternity.'

By the time these romantic words were penned Notre-Dame was in a sorry state, pillaged by mobs and dilapidated by time and neglect. Victor Hugo inspired its restoration. Two architects, Lassus and Viollet-le-Duc, were commissioned to restore the cathedral at a cost of 2,650,000 francs.

Lassus died in 1857. Single-handedly Viollet-le-Duc continued to supervise the gigantic work of restoration, which he completed in 1864. His zeal led him not merely to restore but to recreate what he perceived as an ideal Notre-Dame. The sum of $2\frac{1}{2}$ million francs was far from enough for Viollet-le-Duc's dreams, and a further 6 million were granted. Scrupulously, yet creatively, the statuary of Notre-Dame was renewed. Gargoyles, crockets, grotesques, pinnacles, new rose windows, the organ case, the altar, the treasury and the sacristy were built to the designs of the great nineteenth-century restorer. Viollet-le-Duc sought his models in the cathedrals of Amiens, Bordeaux and Reims. For inspiration he searched ancient documents and drawings. What he left was a cathedral in superb condition, but recreated according to the nineteenth-century dream of the Middle Ages. And this is what we see today.

Even so, much remains from earlier epochs. We can still discern the lineaments of the great cathedral which Maurice de Sully, Bishop of Paris, began in 1160. Sully's builders worked fast. They had virtually completed the choir by 1182. On 19 May that year the papal legate consecrated the high altar. By 1198 the roof of the transept was finished. By the mid thirteenth century the western façade and the towers were complete.

Then, under the master architect Jean de Chelles, the crossings to the north and south were extended. Finally the lovely chapels in the choir were completed during the first half of the fourteenth century. Notre-Dame stands 130 metres long and 33 metres high. The towers reach 69 metres, and Viollet-le-Duc's delicate *flèche* a graceful 90 metres. Initially the interior of the cathedral was dark. To remedy this, the windows of the nave were enlarged in 1240, and at the same time the original double flying buttresses outside were replaced by the present swooping single ones.

Fortunately, when much of the medieval stained glass was replaced with clear windows in 1756, the great rose windows were spared. The one in the north transept dates from 1257 and shows eighty Old Testament scenes. That at the west end of the cathedral – the biggest expanse of its era (1220–5) – is partly obscured by the mighty Cavaillé-Coll organ. The 110 stops and 8500 pipes of this instrument make it the largest in France. And to cap all this the portals of Notre-Dame and its interior are enriched with sublime medieval carvings.

As if Notre-Dame were not enough, the Ile de la Cité is also blessed with a second masterpiece of religious architecture: the Sainte-Chapelle. Whereas the glory of Notre-Dame is its sculpture, the glory of the Sainte-Chapelle is its stained glass. Although some of the fifteen windows have been renewed, much of the original thirteenth-century glass still remains, the oldest stained glass in Paris.

To reach the Sainte-Chapelle from Notre-Dame, retrace your steps along rue de la Cité at the end of the cathedral square and turn left into Place Louis-Lépine and along rue de Lutèce. The famous spire of the Sainte-Chapelle (topped with a crown of thorns) comes into view to the left. The rest of the building is concealed from the outside world by the Paris Palais de Justice. This was once the royal palace of Louis IX in the thirteenth century and it then became an increasingly toothless law court. It was virtually destroyed in a fire in 1776, but the architects who rebuilt it showed total respect for the medieval plan.

They were also persons of taste and sensibility. The superb wrought-iron gates were made by a smith named Thomas Bigonnet in 1783 at a cost of 200,000 francs. The magnificent Doric building opposite these gates, with its imposing flight of steps, dates from the same restoration. The Palais was richly decorated in the later nineteenth century by the architect Louis Duc.

The Palais de Justice also incorporates the notorious Conciergerie (open every day from 9.30 until 18.00 or 19.00, closed public holidays). Today this medieval bastion, with its twin towers (the 'tour d'argent' and the 'tour de César') is a museum and concert hall. Once it was used to house prisoners awaiting execution. The assassin of King Henri IV spent his last earthly hours here. So did nearly 3000 victims of the guillotine during the French Revolution. This Conciergerie museum displays a model guillotine, contemporary pictures of scenes of the Revolution, and Marie Antoinette's last will and testament. André George's observation seems particularly apposite on this spot: 'Paris arises from a bloodbath. . . . It has a double personality – one side revealing all that is gentle and intelligent, while the other is full of hatred.'

Yet the Palais de Justice and the Conciergerie should on no account be missed because of this brutal past. The 'Salle des Gens d'Armes', built between 1285 and 1314, is a magnificent gothic dining hall, the finest in Paris. The entrance to the Conciergerie, no.1, Quai de l'Horloge, is round the corner from the first public clock in Paris, given by Charles V in 1370. It is placed in a richly ornamented surround (including an appropriate statue of justice) made by Germain Pilon in 1585.

Beyond the Conciergerie is the oldest bridge in Paris, known paradoxically as the new bridge, the Pont Neuf. With a length of 330 metres, it spans the river on both sides of the Ile de la Cité. The first of Henri IV's public works to embellish his capital city, the Pont Neuf was begun in 1578 and completed in 1603. An equestrian statue of our benefactor, King Henri IV, by Pietro Tacca and Giambologna surveys his creation above the shady Place (or Point) du Vert-Galant – an excellent place for a picnic and exceptional in Paris for the fact that dogs are banned here. But here again André George's warning that the history of Paris reveals both intelligence and brutality is apposite. On this same spot Jacques de Molay, grand master of the Templars, was judiciously burned to death in 1314.

Opposite the statue of Henri IV is the entrance to an exquisite triangular court: the Place Dauphine. Created in 1607 in honour of the Dauphin Louis XIII, the Place Dauphine displays the genius with which Parisian architects created harmonious, uniform groups of buildings, in this case thirty-two dwellings of stone and brick. As John Evelyn noted in his diary, after visiting the city in 1643, 'Truely Paris, comprehending the Suburbs, is certainely for the material the houses are built with, and many noble and magnificent piles, one of the most gallant Cittys in the World, and best built.'

Walk across the southern half of the Pont Neuf from the Ile de la Cité to the left bank of the River Seine (the Rive Gauche), long the home of booksellers, students, intellectuals and salons. Here, the American hostess Natalie Clifford Barney set up house at no.20, rue Jacob in 1909, and for the next sixty years welcomed writers of the calibre of James Joyce, Ezra Pound, Guillaume Apollinaire, André Gide, Edna St Vincent Millay and countless others. Not far away, at no.21, rue du Vieux Colombier, Sidney Bechet began to play jazz clarinet in 1949 in the Club du Vieux-Colombier.

In truth the left bank has a far longer history than this. The Quai des Grands-Augustins, which runs south-east from where the Pont Neuf reaches the left bank, was the first quay to be built along the Seine in Paris. Its name derives from a thirteenth-century Augustinian convent, now completely disappeared, though it once stretched along the rue des Grands-Augustins as far south as the rue Christine. The restaurant on the corner of the rue des Grands-Augustins and the rue Christine was built in 1575 and still retains its original beams and woodwork. As for the Christine who gave her name to this street, she was the second daughter of Henri IV and his wife Marie de' Medici.

The left bank is now a bookish place. Before the French Revolution the rue des Grands-Augustins was pre-eminently a street of butchers. Today, no doubt helped by the proximity of the Sorbonne, the science faculties of the University of Paris and the École-Polytechnique, bookshops have taken over. Some of the booksellers of the twentieth century became legendary figures, in particular Sylvia Beach, without whom James Joyce's supposedly pornographic *Ulysses* would never have been published.

Walk right along the Seine from the Quai des Grands-Augustins, with a marvellous view of the length of the Louvre on the opposite bank, and turn left into rue Bonaparte. Laid out in the sixteenth century, this street is filled with lovely houses, fine art galleries and antique shops, with the Ecole des Beaux Arts on the right as you go down. It leads to the greatest monument of the left bank, the church of Saint-Germain-des-Prés. This splendid Benedictine abbey was founded by King Childebert I in 558, dedicated to St Vincent and the Holy Cross and re-dedicated to St Germain after that saint's canonization in 754. (Germain, born in Auxerre, was sent to Britain to combat the Pelagian heresy. He came upon a beleaguered British army about to be massacred by a force of Picts and Saxons. Germain led the British to a narrow ravine and made them shout 'Alleluia' three times. The shouts, re-echoing against the sides of the ravine, convinced the Picts and Saxons that they faced a huge force. They fled, and Germain happily baptised many of the rescued British.)

Around 990 the monks of Saint-Germain-des-Prés decided to build a new church. They finished the bell-tower some ten years later. It survives to this day, a powerful, dour romanesque keep, surmounted by a more graceful spire. The nave was completed in 1050 (though the present vaulting dates from the seventeenth century), but the choir was not consecrated until 113 years later by Pope Alexander III.

The Place Saint-Germain-des-Prés has become famous in the twentieth century not only for its abbey church but also for three literary restaurants: the Brasserie Lipp, the Café de Flore and the Café des Deux Magots, all excellent places to have a leisurely drink and watch the world go by. The Brasserie Lipp became the haunt of politicians as well as the literary world – Édouard Herriot and Léon Blum among the politicians, Antoine de Saint-Exupéry, Jean Giraudoux and Paul Valéry among the literary men. The Café de Flore was frequented by such writers as Guillaume Apollinaire and Charles Maurras. Les Deux Magots was patronized by Jean-Paul Sartre, Simone de Beauvoir, André Malraux and Albert Camus.

In her book *Exiles from Paradise* Sarah Mayfield records that she rarely passed Saint-Germain-des-Prés without seeing Ernest Hemingway either in the Café de Flore or les Deux Magots. 'Usually he was alone, bent over his notebook,' she recalled, 'writing slowly as if he weighed every word, cutting his sentences sharply, as he chiselled his gem-hard prose.'

In 1926 Hemingway had forsaken his wife and son to move into no.6, rue Férou on the left bank, with Pauline Pfeiffer, a journalist on the Paris edition of *Vogue* magazine. His current literary preoccupation was his novel *A Farewell to Arms*, and he returned to the United States after two years to finish it. Over twenty years later he was to observe, 'If you are lucky enough to have lived in Paris as a young man, then wherever you go for the rest of your life, it stays with you, for Paris is a moveable feast.'

Did Hemingway, I wonder, ever stroll a few metres along Boulevard Saint-Germain past the church and turn left into the delightful rue de Buci, with its cafés, restaurants, hotels and open-air Sunday market? Sitting at a pavement-table drinking a large *café au lait*, I find it hard to believe that the city gallows was once set up here, and that the massacres of 1792 began on this very spot.

Further delights

Montmartre

'On a gray day in Paris I often found myself walking towards the Place Clichy in Montmartre,' writes Henry Miller. 'From Clichy to Aubervilliers there is a long string of cafés, restaurants, theaters, cinemas, haberdashers, hotels and bordels. It is the Broadway of Paris corresponding to that little stretch between 42nd and 53rd streets. Broadway is fast, dizzying, dazzling, and no place to sit down. Montmartre is sluggish, lazy, indifferent, somewhat shabby and seedy-looking, not glamorous so much as seductive, not scintillating but glowing with a smouldering flame.' Less seedy today, Montmartre remains seductive.

From the Arc de Triomphe, from the orbital *périphérique* around Paris, from countless other vantage points in the city, you can see the dome, cupolas and gleaming white campanile of the basilica of Sacré-Coeur de Montmartre. To reach the top of the hill of Montmartre (97.5 metres above the River Seine) it is easiest to take the funicular railway, using a Métro ticket. Otherwise you can climb the 225 steps of the rue Foyatier. (A plaque tells that the Mayor of Montmartre rode down them on a bicycle in 1920.) And from

Sacré-Coeur you can look down over a stunning panorama of Paris. Arnold Bennett, visiting the basilica in 1903 even before the building was completed, felt that everything else seemed ordinary. 'I came out and surveyed Paris from the front,' he confided to his *Journal*:

I could distinguish most of the landmarks – Notre Dame, Panthéon, Invalides, Gare d'Orléans, St Sulpice, and Louvre. Never before had I such a just idea of the immense size of the Louvre. I could also see the Opéra. . . . And it looked so small and square and ordinary.

The Paris Opéra is certainly not small and square and ordinary. But after visiting Sacré-Coeur anyone can be forgiven for momentarily thinking it so.

Sacré-Coeur de Montmartre was built by the Catholics of Paris in expiation for what they considered to be the sins of the Paris Commune of 1871, in particular the execution by the Communards of numerous Dominican monks and the Archbishop of the city. It soon developed into a project destined to restore civic pride after the defeat of the French by the Prussians. In 1873 the National Assembly declared that 'By this work of expiation we must efface those crimes which are the final weight on our burden of sorrows.' By 1874 work had started. The architect in charge was Paul Abadie. Former episcopal architect to the diocese of Périgueux, he chose as the basis for his design the remarkable Byzantine-French cathedral of Saint-Front at Périgueux. Abadie died before the work was finished, but he was author of the plan of Sacré-Coeur: a Greek cross (as at Périgueux), topped by a huge dome, with smaller cupolas at the corners.

Abadie's successor as architect was Lucien Magne. He designed the campanile (known as 'the minaret' to the people of Montmartre), which stands 94 metres high. The four Catholic dioceses of Savoy paid for the famous bell which hangs there – the 'Savoyard'. Weighing 17,035 kilos, it was founded at Annecy-le-Vieux in 1895 and towed to Paris and up to the basilica by twenty-eight massive horses.

Ultimately it is the sheer scale of Sacré-Coeur de Montmartre that impresses. To support such a massive building on the weak sandstone of the hill 83 huge pits, each 30 metres deep, were filled with masonry to serve as foundations.

Devotion to the sacred heart of Jesus had been the special work of the Abbess Françoise of Lorraine, who inaugurated the cult in the church of Saint-Pierre de Montmartre, just west of Sacré Coeur, in 1675. For many years the religious authorities had frowned on this cult. Now it was granted superb architectural and artistic honour. Inside Sacré-Coeur Luc-Oliver Merson created a stupendous mosaic, 500 square metres in size, representing France's devotion to the sacred heart of Jesus. To the left of Christ (displaying his sacred heart) Merson placed St Joan of Arc and the Archangel Michael. To the right he depicted the guillotined Louis XVI, shown in his years of happiness, surrounded by his family, protected by the Blessed Virgin Mary.

Although Sacré-Coeur was not consecrated until 1919, the consecrated Body of Christ has been solemnly displayed over the high altar since 1885. St Louis VII, King of France, and St Joan of Arc were sculpted on horseback and set above the vestibule in 1927. (The sculptor was Hippolyte Lefebre.) Unfortunately the bombardments of World War II destroyed most of the original stained glass.

Visitors today can climb the dome or visit the impressive crypt (with its statues of Cardinal Guibert and Cardinal Richard, and a *pietà* on the altar by the sculptor Courtan). When you emerge from the Byzantine gloom of the interior, blinking in the sunlight, a few steps lead down to the rue du Cardinal-Dubois, where the Touring Club of France has usefully provided pay-telescopes and an orientation guide to the view over the rest of Paris. Immediately ahead is the Place Adolphe-Willette – in truth a delightful terraced garden, with clumps of trees and lawns and steps leading down to the Place Saint-Pierre.

Today musicians and street theatre enliven this part of Montmartre in summer. But the Place Adolphe-Willette has seen more stirring events. During the siege of Paris in the Franco-Prussian War, sixty-four balloons carrying a hundred would-be Parisian escapees were released from here. Gambetta escaped in one to organize the army of the Loire. Other balloons fell among the Prussian lines, and their passengers were taken prisoner.

Travel from Sacré-Coeur at ease by the funicular railway or walk down to the Place Saint-Pierre. Here what began as a small flea market developed (under the impetus of Parisian Jews and

Manchester merchants) into an important centre for the sale of cloth, a market rendered more colourful in recent years by Arabs and Algerians. There are rows of bookshops too.

The church of Saint-Pierre, oddly enough, is not here but lies to the west of Sacré-Coeur. Often forgotten in view of the stupendous basilica, it is in fact one of the most venerable buildings in Paris. Reach it from Sacré-Coeur by way of rue du Chevalier de la Barre, turning left into rue St Eleuthère. Close by this spot the legendary St Denis and his companions Rusticus and Eleutherius were martyred. Beheaded during the Decian persecution of Christians in the mid third century, the saint is not buried here since (according to the legend) he and his companions picked up their heads, washed off the blood in a nearby fountain, and walked to Saint-Denis (now a northern suburb of Paris), where a great Benedictine abbey was raised over their tomb. The fountain has long been identified as the one which is now in the Place Suzanne-Buisson (west of the church of Saint-Pierre, through the Place du Tertre and along rue Norvins). There is also a modern statue of St Denis in the *place*, dressed in Mass vestments and holding up his severed head, which is wearing a bishop's mitre.

Although the façade of Saint-Pierre dates from the eighteenth century, inside is a marvellous gothic church that incorporates an even older building. At the entry to the choir are four Roman columns which the Christians took from the ancient Gallo-Roman pagan temple they found here. The present church, consecrated in 1147, replaced the old oratory of Saint-Denis, which was destroyed in 944. Building did not cease in 1147. The five-sided apse dates from half a century later. As in Sacré-Coeur, the old stained-glass windows were destroyed by German bombs. Max Ingrand created the present post-Cubist glass of the nave in 1953.

As you leave the church of Saint-Pierre you see two more green marble columns from the old pagan temple on either side of the porch. Dedicated to the god Mars, this temple stood near another dedicated to Mercury. In spite of Sacré-Coeur and the church of Saint-Pierre, Montmartre has a long pre-Christian (indeed, pre-Roman) history. In 1798 the famous palaeontologist Cuvier discovered fossilized human bones on Montmartre, subsequently identified as people of the Stone Age. A plaque in rue Pierre de Ronsard marks where he found them:

Ici était l'entrée
des carrières de Montmartre
ou furent découverts
les ossements fossiles
qui servirent en 1798
aux études de Cuvier
créateur de la paléontologie.

[Here was the entrance
to the quarries of Montmartre
where fossilized bones
were discovered
that in 1798 were utilized
in the studies of Cuvier,
creator of palaeontology.]

And in spite of Sacré-Coeur and the church of Saint-Pierre, Montmartre has for long been noted for its lively secular life. This area has been the home of bohemians (Mürger, author of *La Vie Bohème*, lies in its cemetery) and above all of artists. Cézanne, Manet, Renoir, Van Gogh and Toulouse-Lautrec spent all or part of their working lives here. In 1907 Picasso and Braque looked at negro art collected by Derain and Vlaminck in Montmartre and were inspired to create Cubism – a manner of painting made notorious by Picasso's 'deformed' *Demoiselles d'Avignon*. Picasso became famous and installed himself in a great studio on the Boulevard de Clichy. Rue Fontaine, leading south-east from where the Boulevard de Clichy crosses the Place Blanche, was home to Toulouse-Lautrec, who occupied first no.19 and then no.30. The poet, critic and theorist of Surrealism, André Breton, took rooms at no.42 and there would entertain the likes of the left-wing propagandist Louis Aragon, that most humane of novelists, Georges Duhamel and the people's poet Jacques Prévert.

Rue Fontaine ends where rue Pigalle meets rue Chaptal. No.20 rue Chaptal (now known as the Cité Chaptal) was the site of the celebrated and radical Théâtre du Grand Guignol from 1896 until 1960. The Hot Club de France was founded next door in the 1930s, where Stephane Grappelli and Django Rheinhardt played host to countless other jazz musicians.

The artistic impulse has not yet quitted Montmartre. Its centre is the Place du Tertre, close by the church of Saint-Pierre – though today the paintings, sketches and portraits on sale here have as much to do with the tourist trade as with art. Galleries in the neighbouring streets ply a brisk trade during the tourist season. Cafés and cabarets add to the ambience, and street musicians entertain.

Equally fascinating, if more sombre, is Montmartre cemetery, west of the Place du Tertre, down rue Lepic (where the Moulin de la Galette still stands – one of the few survivors of the thirty or so windmills celebrated in countless paintings), from where a flight of steps descends into rue Caulaincourt. Here rest countless musicians, their spirits possibly harmonizing with the heavenly choir, Jaques Offenbach, Léo Delibes and Hector Berlioz among them. The novelist Stendhal lies here, as does the author of the most romantic of all lives of Jesus, Ernst Renan. Here too lies the German poet Heinrich Heine. Stendhal is commemorated by a portrait medallion by David d'Angers. Along the Avénue de la Croix a few metres west of his grave lies Chateaubriand's friend, the exquisite Mme Récamier. Not far away is buried Alphonsine Plessis, Alexandre Dumas's inspiration for *La Dame aux Camélias*. And Marceline Desbordes-Valmore, long-forgotten poet and comedienne, laments her fate in an epitaph which she wrote herself:

> *Mon Dieu! Que des pensées consolent de mourir!*
> *Mon Dieu! Que des pensées consolent de mourir!*
>   . . . .
> *Ainsi mourront les chants qu'abandonne ma lyre*
> *Au monde indifférent qui va les oublier.*

> [My God! What thoughts comfort us in death!
> My God! What thoughts comfort us in death!
>   . . . .
> Thus shall die the songs which my lyre abandons
> To a heedless world about to forget them.]

Le Marais
This elegant, former aristocratic area of Paris, encompassing most of the 3rd and 4th districts (*arrondissements*), was set out from the sixteenth to the eighteenth centuries on what was once marshland

(hence its name). The best way of assimilating its charm is to wander round the Place des Vosges, a magical arcaded square with a central garden, laid out in 1605–12. Once known as the Place Royale, it became the centre of court life and so the rich and powerful flocked to build their own mansions nearby. You can see some of these by walking along rich rue des Francs-Bourgeois running left from the north-west corner of the square. This is lined with splendid town houses or *hôtels* on either side. At no.14 in the adjoining rue Pavée is the Hôtel Lamoignon, built in the 1580s for Diane de France, the illegitimate daughter of Henri II and Filippa Duco. Opposite rue Pavée stands the Hôtel Carnavalet (you get in at no.23 in the adjoining rue de Sévigné), a mid sixteenth-century town house transformed by François Mansart in 1655. Here the great socialite and letter-writer Mme de Sévigné lived from 1677 until she died nineteen years later, and in its courtyard is a bronze statue of Louis XIV by Coysevox.

The treats of rue des Francs-Bourgeois also include the Hôtel de Coulanges at no.35, a magnificent early eighteenth-century town house, and the splendid Hôtel d'Albret at no.31, with its delicious Louis XV doorway. On the corner of rue des Archives stands the Hôtel de Rohan-Soubise, which is now a museum of French history. Its façade is sculpted with the four seasons; its interiors are magically rococo.

To reach Place des Vosges, take the Métro to Bastille. When you alight, take rue de la Bastille (at the north-west corner of the square) and then turn right along rue des Tournelles and left along rue du Pas de la Mule.

The Champs-Elysées and the Arc de Triomphe

The Avénue des Champs-Elysées (reached from the Métro station Champs-Elysées) is quite simply 2 kilometres of Parisian elegance. The promenade designed by the superb seventeenth-century landscape gardener Le Nôtre as far as the Rond-Point now stretches more than twice as far again to the Place Charles de Gaulle. In the older, eastern stretch of the avenue, the atmosphere is still that of a garden. North is the Elysée Palace, official home of the president of the French Republic. South are two delightful art galleries built for the Paris exhibition of 1900: the Grand Palais and the Petit Palais (separated by the Avenue Winston Churchill). Across the Champs-

Elysées from the Grand Palais is the Theatre Marigny (named after a brother of Mme de Pompadour); an open-air stamp market is held here on Sundays, Thursdays and most national holidays.

West of the dangerous traffic island known as the Rond-Point, enhanced since 1958 by luminous fountains created by Max Ingrand, the Champs-Elysées becomes a wide, busy, elegant thoroughfare, leading to the most famous monument in Paris, the Arc de Triomphe, conceived by Napoleon as an arch to celebrate the glories of his army and carved with the names of all 347 of his campaigns and of all his generals. (The names of those who died in battle are underlined.)

The body of an unknown soldier was buried underneath the Arc de Triomphe after World War I, and at half-past six in the evening, when the traffic has somewhat abated, a group of Old Comrades rekindles the eternal flame at his tomb. Climb to the top of the Arc de Triomphe for a superb view of the city. Twelve avenues radiate from here, completed by the city planner Baron Georges-Eugène Haussmann in 1854.

The Eiffel Tower

Almost as famous as the Arc de Triomphe, the Eiffel Tower was never meant to be permanent. Built as a gateway into the World Fair of 1889, it weighs 7000 tonnes, is made up of 15,000 separate metal pieces held together by 2,500,000 rivets, and – at 300 metres – is twice as high as the Great Pyramid of Giza. It was almost demolished when its lease ran out in 1909, but was saved partly because of its value for radio experiments. This remarkable landmark is now an essential feature of the Parisian skyline. 'I ought to be jealous,' said its designer, Gustav Eiffel. 'My tower is more famous than I am.' Until the construction of the Chrysler Building in New York in 1930, the Eiffel Tower remained the tallest structure in the world. I have only once been up it and then did not dare look over the side.

The speediest way to the Eiffel Tower is to take the Métro to Ecole Militaire. No one has any difficulty seeing the monument itself! Alight and simply walk north-west towards it.

The Beaubourg

A much newer Parisian phenomenon is the Centre National d'Art et de Culture Georges Pompidou built in 1977, situated almost directly north of Notre-Dame in the Place Beaubourg and known universally as 'the Beaubourg'. This often reviled building, described as all structure and nothing else, with scaffolding, tubes and escalators climbing the outside walls, has become a gallery of modern art attracting over 6 million visitors a year.

You can reach the Beaubourg swiftly by taking the Métro and alighting at Rambuteau. Rue Rambuteau runs along the north side of the Centre Pompidou itself. If you wish to walk from, say, Ile de la Cité, cross the north stream of the River Seine by the Pont-d'Arcole to the Place de l'Hôtel-de-Ville (with its vast town hall, rebuilt in 1882 after the Communards of 1871 had burned down an earlier one). Opposite the town hall, Avénue Victoria runs left from the middle of the square and reaches the pedestrianized rue Saint-Martin, where you turn right. The route crosses over rue de la Verrerie, running past the radiantly flamboyant gothic church of St Merri to the square in front of the Centre Pompidou.

Excursion to Versailles

A mere 25 kilometres south of Paris stands this glamorous example of the extravagance of the *ancien régime*, destroyed irrevocably by the French Revolution.

Louis XIII began its construction with a shooting lodge. Louis XIV, utilizing the incomparable skills of the gardener Le Nôtre and the architects Le Vau and Le Brun, brought it to completion. Here in 1715 Louis XIV died. Other brilliant architects enriched the palace: Hardouin-Mansart and Robert de Cotte especially are notable for creating the exquisite chapel.

Here are the state rooms of the doomed French monarchy (including the famous hall where seventeen mirrors reflect the light from seventeen windows opposite and where the treaty that ended World War I was signed in 1919). Here are situated le Grand Trianon, built for Louis XIV and Mme de Maintenon by Jacques-

Ange Gabriel (and redecorated by Napoleon after he married Marie-Louise of Austria), as well as le Petit Trianon, where Marie Antoinette would find refuge from the boredom of the French court. Here too Louis XVI commissioned the architect Richard Mique to build her a fairy-tale hamlet, with a dairy, a barn, a mill and thatched cottages. And from a balcony at Versailles, on 6 October 1789, both of them faced the mob that was to destroy them. Strangely, one room of the palace now carries portraits of the founders of independent America, including George Washington.

All is presided over by the equestrian statue of the Sun King, Louis XIV, in the courtyard, which greets you as you walk up the hill towards the palace. If you don't want to go in the palace, you can walk round the side into Le Nôtre's brilliantly composed gardens, which cover something like 100 hectares. Their fountains play only on the first and third Sundays in the summer months – small wonder, since they are said to use up to about $4\frac{1}{2}$ million litres of water in a single hour. The château is open (except on Mondays and public holidays) from 09.45 to 17.00.

A speedy suburban train runs along the left bank to Versailles (its stations include Gare d'Austerlitz and Gare des Invalides). Alight at Versailles Rive Gauche (RG).

Food and drink

Eating in Paris has its own peculiar fascination. When Edna St Vincent Millay was in Paris in the 1920s, she and her mother ate most days in the Café de la Rotonde on the Boulevard du Montparnasse. 'Mummie and I about live in this here cafe,' she wrote to her sister, 'We feed on *choucroute garnie*, which is fried sauerkraut trimmed with boiled potatoes, a large slice of ham & a fat hot dog, – yum, yum, werry excillint. That's about all they serve here in the cafe – that and onion soup and sandwiches. And mummie & I come here every day & eat the stinkin' stuff, & all our friends hold their noses & pass us by till we've finished.'

Clearly then, as now, it was possible to eat badly in Paris and to eat food that was both cheap and far from Parisian. Often, the well-served and unpretentious menus offer food that at first sight seems strange in the capital of France. Around the Gare du Nord, for instance, many restaurants are owned by Parisians whose roots are in Belgium and the Belgian accent spills over into the gastronomy as well as the beer. The food is often excellent.

France too is a country whose food has been enriched because it was once a colonial power. Vietnamese restaurants serve the delicate dishes of what was once known as French Indo-China. And the civilization of North Africa has brought an Algerian, a Tunisian and a Moroccan aspect to many a Paris thoroughfare. In consequence, restaurants serving, for instance, couscous, and cafés offering *le Sandwich tunisien* vie with more traditional French eating places.

For centuries Paris has attracted regional chefs with their specialities. As Edna St Vincent Millay learned, the sauerkraut of Alsace reached the capital of France long before she did. *Choucroute* is usually a hearty dish, served with slab bacon, sausages and potatoes, to which Parisians add pepper, cloves, garlic and bay leaves. Sometimes the *choucroute* is surrounded by pork chops. Different sorts of mustard will be on offer. Usually the wine will be an Alsatian Riesling, and the waiters and waitresses may well be wearing traditional Alsatian dress.

Savoyards have also moved to Paris, bringing the food of their own region. The stuffed cabbages of the Auvergne are not hard to find. There are some celebrated restaurants serving the dishes of the Dordogne. The *cassoulet* of the Languedoc and the fish stews of Normandy are both readily available in Paris, often cooked by immigrants from these regions.

So is fast food. The word *frites* indicates its presence. *Steak-frites* or *poulet-frites* — often referred to as $\frac{1}{4}$ *poulet-frites* — are among the dishes advertised outside restaurants that in no way claim gastronomic excellence but can provide value for money. In short, if you add the Turkish, Jewish and Chinese establishments, the 10,000 Paris restaurants and 40,000 cafés in the city offer a profusion of dishes unequalled elsewhere in Europe.

The street café is quintessentially Parisian. As Oscar Hammerstein II put it:

The last time I saw Paris,
Her heart was warm and gay;
I heard the laughter of her heart
In every street café.

Here each morning the French take their croissants and *café au lait*. Later, people call for a drink, a wine or draught beer (*bière pression*). They pay less if they stand drinking at the counter (*le zinc*) than if they sit at a table or outside on the *terrasse*.

French law requires every restaurant to post menus outside the establishment. These often include set menus (of several courses) at exceedingly reasonable prices. The cheapest will include the *plat du jour*, a main course which the chef is anxious to serve, perhaps because he has too much of it left over from the previous day.

Parisian meals can be leisurely affairs. Restaurants start to fill up soon after noon and may have no more places by one o'clock. In the evenings Parisians do not start to eat much before eight-thirty or nine o'clock. To expect a welcome after ten o'clock is unreasonable. Only the cheap, lively *brasseries* stay open and welcoming outside these hours.

As for drink, the cheapest bottle on the list will be the owner's *réserve du patron* or *cuvée de la maison*: an excellent straightforward wine chosen by the patron for his customers. Next will follow the decent wines of the Loire and the Languedoc. Then prices rise sharply for fine vintages.

Most Frenchmen and women end their meal with a coffee (which will not be included in the price of a set menu); not the breakfast *café au lait* nor the coffee with heated milk (*café crème*) which many drink in bars during the day, but black coffee, served with a couple of lumps of sugar in the saucer.

Night life

The area south of Montmartre is famed for its night life. Arnold Bennett observed in 1913 that, 'Nobody who has not lived intimately in and with Paris can appreciate the unique savour of that word *femmes*.' No doubt he was thinking partly of Montmartre, of the Boulevard de Clichy and of the Place Pigalle. In September 1925 the American novelist William Faulkner spent an evening at the 'Moulin Rouge' on the Boulevard de Clichy. He wrote home to his mother:

Anyone in America will tell you it is the last word in sin and iniquity. It is a music hall, a vaudeville, where ladies come out clothed principally in lipstick. Lots of bare beef, but that is only secondary. Their songs and dances are set to real music – there was one with not a rag on except a coat of gold paint who danced a ballet of Rimsky-Korsakoff's, a Persian thing; and two others, a man stained brown like a faun and a lady who had on at least 20 beads, I'll bet money, performed a short tone poem of the Scandinavian composer Sibelius. It was beautiful.

The 'Moulin Rouge' is but one of many nude or near-nude cabarets in the region around Montmartre. The best ones are extremely glamorous and equally expensive. The American dancer Loïe Fuller is generally credited with bringing this tradition to the 'Théatre des Folies-Bergère' in rue Richer, where she first began to perform in 1897. Her techniques (huge fluttering veils, mirrors, coloured lights, dazzling theatrical displays) spread to and remain essential to the repertoire of other cabarets such as the 'Moulin Rouge' and the 'Crazy Horse'. Cabaret artists of the calibre of Joséphine Baker added to the reputation of these risqué spectacles. Joséphine opened her own club, 'Chez Joséphine', in rue Fontaine in 1926. The magazine *Vogue* declared 'The woman is like a living drawing by Aubrey Beardsley or Picasso.'

Rue Fontaine can also claim credit for another development in Parisian night-clubs. In the Place Blanche (where rue Fontaine joins rue Blanche) is an all-night pharmaceutical chemist which in the years after World War II shared the premises of the first transvestite cabaret, predecessor of many such 'specialist' establishments.

But night life in Paris is not merely a matter of night-clubs. The two leading theatres of France, the Comédie Française (at no.2, rue de Richelieu) and the Théâtre National de l'Odéon (in the Place de l'Odéon) lead a long string of others. In addition the Opéra (in the Place de l'Opéra) and the Opéra Comique (at no.5 rue Favart) offer spectacles almost unrivalled elsewhere in the world. Between

October and March you can enjoy circus at the Cirque d'Hiver (at no.110 rue Amelot). The Orchestra de Paris has its home in the Salle Pleyel (at no.252 rue du Faubourg-Saint-Honoré), and other concert halls include the Théâtre des Champs-Élysées (whose official address is no.15 Avénue Montaigne) and the Palais de Congrès (at Porte Maillot). There are also a good number of clubs to satisfy jazz fans. Finally Parisians love cinema enough to enjoy watching undubbed foreign films (announced as *version originale* or simply *v.o.*).

Evening cruises on the *vedettes* of the Pont-Neuf take place between May and October, leaving at 21.00, 21.30 and 22.20. In summer, you can take an illuminated *bâteau-mouche* along the Seine from Pont de l'Alma at either 20.30 or 21.00 (and meals are served on the earlier of the two trips).

Up-to-date information on every kind of Parisian entertainment can be found in two magazines: *L'Officiel des Spectacles* and *Pariscope*. In addition, helpful cultural information is available from the Maison de la France, at no.8 Avénue de l'Opéra, open daily from 10.00 to 20.00.

Important information

French banks open from Monday to Friday from 09.00 to 16.30 (except on the day before a public holiday when they close at noon). At weekends you can change money at the *bureaux de change* at the Gare du Lyon and the airports. On Saturdays the *bureau* of the Crédit Commercial de France (CCF) is also open at no.103 Champs-Elysées.

Main public holidays in France are 1 January, Easter Day and Easter Monday, the Monday of Pentecost, 1 May, the feasts of the Ascension and the Assumption (15 August), 1 November, 11 November, and Christmas Day.

Finally a word about transport in Paris. By air the city is easily reached, especially by way of Charles de Gaulle airport, which was designed with Gallic clarity and whose direction signs ought to be a model for other international airports. The swiftest way from here to the centre of the city is by the airport bus that leaves from outside terminal 2B roughly every ten minutes. In just over half an hour you should reach the central airport terminal at Porte Maillot, close by the Métro station of the same name. Alternatively a train leaves every quarter of an hour during the day from Roissy Rail, reaching the Gare du Nord in approximately 45 minutes.

The underground in Paris, the Métro, occasionally surfaces to proffer superb views of the city. It is cheapest to buy a book of ten tickets (known as a *carnet*). Each line is known by its *direction*, that is by the name of its terminus. You change from one line to another at a *correspondance*. The Métro starts at 05.30 and closes down shortly after midnight.

Buses in Paris accept Métro tickets. Otherwise you can buy a slightly dearer ticket from the driver. In either case you are required to cancel the ticket by sticking it into a punch behind the driver's seat. The driver tells you how many tickets each journey costs. The buses tell you where they are going by means of plans inside and outside. (You can obtain your own plan of all the routes from RATP (the Parisian bus service), no.53, Quai des Grands-Augustins or from the RATP bureau at the Place de la Madeleine.) Paris buses stop running around 21.00, and most do not run on Sundays and public holidays (as indicated on the bus stops).

In the 1960s and 1970s Paris improved its transport yet more by creating a speedy network of trains known as the *Réseau Express Régional* (the RER). There are also taxis (though the author of the *Benn Blue Guide to Paris* so distrusts their drivers that he recommends the tourist to be always ready to seek the help of the nearest *gendarme* in case of a dispute over a fare). Drivers expect a tip of about 15 per cent. Fares rise alarmingly at night. And it is frequently forgotten that a taxi is required to take you to Paris airports without the addition of a return fare.

Lastly there are *bâteaux-mouches,* plying the River Seine from ten o'clock in the morning, and leaving from Pont de l'Alma on the left bank. From these you will get entrancing views of, for instance, the Ile de la Cité and Notre-Dame, to a recorded commentary in French, German, English and Italian.

Venice

When I grew tired I left the narrow alleyways and took my place in a gondola. I wanted to enjoy the view from the opposite side, so we passed the northern end of the Grand Canal, around the island of Santa Chiara, into the lagoons and next into the Giudecca Canal before continuing as far as the Piazza San Marco. Lying back in my gondola, I suddenly imagined myself, as every Venetian does, a lord of the Adriatic.

Johann Wolfgang Goethe, 1786

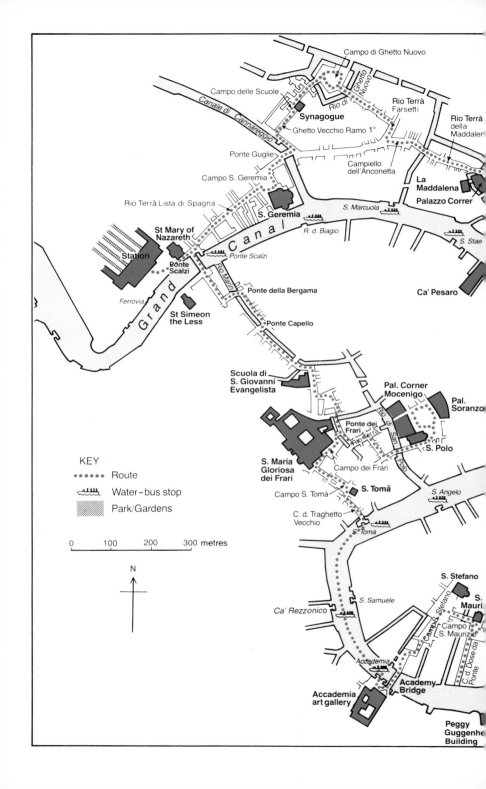

Venice

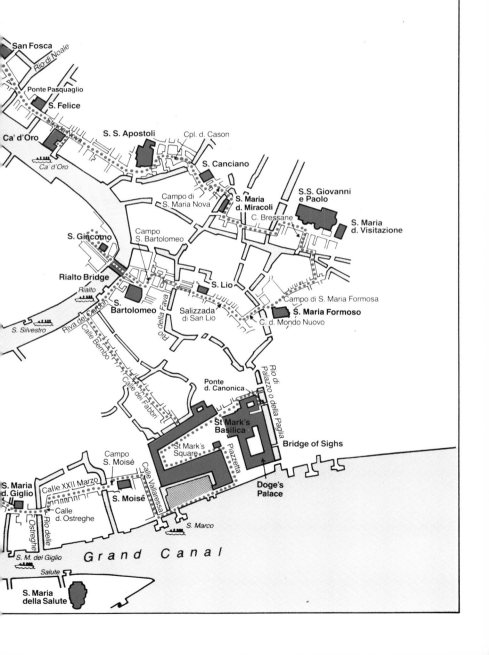

San Fosca

Rio di Noale

Ponte Pasquaglio

S. Felice

Ca' d'Oro

Ca' d'Oro

S. S. Apostoli

Cpl. d. Cason

S. Canciano

Campo di S. Maria Nova

S. Maria d. Miracoli

S.S. Giovanni e Paolo

C. Bressane

S. Maria d. Visitazione

S. Giacomo

Campo S. Bartolomeo

Rialto Bridge

Rialto

S. Silvestro

Riva del Carbon

Calle Bembo

Calle de' Fabbri

S. Bartolomeo

Rio della Fava

S. Lio

Salizzada di San Lio

Campo di S. Maria Formosa

S. Maria Formoso

C. d. Mondo Nuovo

Ponte d. Canonica

Rio di Palazzo o della Paglia

St Mark's Basilica

Campo S. Moisé

St Mark's Square

Piazzetta

Bridge of Sighs

S. Maria d. Giglio

Calle XXII Marzo

Calle Valaressa

Doge's Palace

S. Moisé

Calle d. Ostreghe

Rio delle Ostreghe

S. Marco

S. M. del Giglio

Grand Canal

Salute

S. Maria della Salute

Venice is a good place to wake up in. The dawn chorus of the birds can be magnificent. Then, somewhere nearby, a clock strikes seven, and you can turn over in bed confident that a second clock will chime seven a few minutes later. And then the church bells start to ring.

Venice is also a lovely spot to arrive at. The aeroplane usually flies over the floating city before landing at Marco Polo or San Nicolò airport. To arrive by train is almost as entrancing (and Italian railway fares are extraordinarily cheap). As you roll along the long causeway to the railway station, you see water on either side and, in the mornings, an endless train of barges bringing in provisions for the waterlocked city.

The railway station opens directly out on to the Grand Canal down a massive flight of steps. Here tourists sit in summer, looking across at the eighteenth-century church of St Simeon the Less, its green copper dome and Corinthian portico a modest version of the Pantheon in Rome. This is indeed a place that exceeds expectations, as Dickens knew:

Nothing in the world that you ever heard of Venice, is equal to the magnificent and stupendous reality. The wildest visions of the Arabian nights are nothing to the piazza of St Mark, and the first impression of the inside of the church. The gorgeous and wonderful reality of Venice is beyond the fancy of the wildest dreamer. Opium couldn't build such a place.

A city tour

The railway station is as good a place as any to begin a tour of the city, but those who would like to amble gently or are short of time may prefer to start from St Mark's (p. 172). Turn left past the church of the Scalzi, opposite one of the three bridges that span the Grand Canal. This church is dedicated to St Mary of Nazareth, but it once belonged to Carmelite friars. These holy men went about barefoot, hence its name (*Scalzi*), which means unshod. The lovely baroque façade was designed by Giuseppe Sardi in the 1670s, though the basic plan of the building is by Baldassare Longhena and the statues are by Bartolomeo Falcone. The church is rarely open, so should you manage to get in don't miss the chance of seeing Giovanni Domenico Tiepolo's fresco of St Teresa in Glory, in the second chapel on the right.

Until 1915 an even greater Tiepolo painting graced this church: the ceiling fresco of the Transfer of the Holy House of Loretto. When the Austrians shelled Venice in World War I this masterpiece was destroyed. Somehow the 1934 imitation seems to me a shady fake.

Go on past the church along the bustling Rio Terrà Lista di Spagna, crammed with shops selling jewellery and Venetian glass, salami and ham, clothing and masks, shoes and leather goods, wine and fruit. Here are inexpensive hotels and slightly more expensive restaurants, some of them up charming alleyways. The street opens out into the square in front of the church of San Geremia, whose eighteenth-century dome stands alongside an ancient thirteenth-century brick campanile. As well as its two pizzerias, the square has two medieval wells, where most Venice piazzas have only one.

The uncorrupted body of St Lucia lies inside the church, martyred at Syracuse and brought here as a precious relic. A notice declares that she can not only cure ailing eyes but also is continually interceding for the peace of the world – and of Italy in particular.

Go on through the square and almost immediately you are upon one of Venice's surprises: the old Jewish ghetto. Once over the canal, bridged by the Ponte Guglie, turn left along its bank. Don't forget to look back at the faces carved on the bridge. Fifty or so paces along the canal bank there is a notice on the wall (in Hebrew and Italian), pointing to the *SINAGOGH*, and an exhibition of Hebrew art. An alleyway leads to the ghetto. Here are shops selling Jewish delicacies (*dolci ebraici*), as well as a Jewish bakery. Suddenly you reach a tiny square with the Jewish school and synagogue directly in front of you and (on the wall opposite) a monument to the 200 Venetian Jews, 800 Italian Jews and six million Europeans slaughtered by the Nazis between 1939 and 1945. On the school wall another plaque commemorates twenty-four Venetian Jews who died fighting for Italy in World War I.

Jews suffered many atrocities, and not surprisingly the Venice ghetto remembers them. Continue on over another little canal bridge and you find the beautifully quiet Campo di Ghetto Nuovo. Against a wall here are seven bronzes by A. Blates, depicting Jewish sufferings in concentration camps between 1943 and 1945, with the inscription:

Our memories are your only grave.

This square also houses the sixteenth-century synagogue and a Jewish museum (which opens daily from 10.30 to 13.00 and from 14.30 to 17.00, except on Saturday and Sunday afternoons).

To the left of the synagogue another quiet passage leads over a canal and down Calle Ghetto Novissimo to join Rio Terrà Farsetti, where you turn right and then left along Calle de Pistor. Venice's bustle has reappeared, but not yet its tourist snares. Fruit, vegetable and flower shops spill out onto the street. In the Campiello dell' Anconetta is the Italian Theatre (Teatro Italia) – very Venetian gothic, with a winged lion at the top of the façade.

Pass along the narrow Calle dell'Anconetta, over the canal bridge, down Rio Terrà de la Maddalena, and into Strada Nova, a relatively wide shopping street in Venetian terms. Notice the hexagonal church of the Maddalena just before the Ponte San Antonio and the sixteenth-century well in the same street. Venice is littered with fine churches and many that would be visited eagerly elsewhere are here given scarcely a glance. Such a building is the church of San Fosca, at the end of the Strada Nova. Rebuilt in the seventeenth century, it was embellished with a new façade in 1741, but preserves its fifteenth-century bell-tower. Opposite is the fifteenth-century Palazzo Corner.

Crossing the bridge dedicated to Niccolò Pasquaglio, look right, across the Grand Canal, for a glimpse of a yet more splendid palace, the Ca' Pesaro, the finest baroque building on the canal. This masterpiece was created by Baldassare Longhena on behalf of Giovanni Pesaro, Doge of Venice, in 1658. Today it serves as the city's museum of modern art.

Strada Nova runs on past the sixteenth-century church of San Felice and over another canal bridge. Now keep an eye open for an alleyway on the right and an insignificant notice announcing what by all accounts is the second greatest gothic building in Venice: the

Ca' d'Oro. Matteo Raverti built it between 1422 and 1440, and others enriched it. It is called Ca' d'Oro because its carvings were once enhanced with gold leaf. Rightly, this lovely house is now a magnificent art gallery. (It opens from 09.00 to 14.00, closing an hour earlier at weekends, and the entrance is half-way down the alleyway.)

Retrace your steps along the little alleyway and continue along Strada Nova, at the end of which are another couple of lovely churches. Unless you are an addict, however, I would recommend giving them only a glance, as you are now close to two that should on no account be missed. On the wall of SS Apostoli (which contains a fine Tieopolo, dates from the sixteenth and eighteenth centuries and boasts a campanile of 1672) a notice points in the direction of one of them: SS Giovanni e Paolo. Obey this sign, turn left around the end of SS Apostoli, take the narrow turning right and cross the Campiello della Cason into the Calle de la Malvasca. Cross the canal, walk past the early eighteenth-century church of San Canciano (with its brick campanile) and turn left when you reach a well.

The alley opens out into the Campo di Santa Maria Nova and to your right is that exquisite oddity, the marble-clad church of Santa Maria dei Miracoli (which is also called Santa Maria Nova). This piece of Tuscan architecture, which would look more at home in Florence, was introduced into the Veneto by Pietro Lombardo in the 1480s. The raised chancel approached by a flight of steps harbours the venerated miracle-working portrait of the Blessed Virgin Mary and her Son (by Niccolò di Pietro Paradisi). The barrel-vaulted roof is splendidly carved, and in 1528 was decorated by Pier Maria Pennacchi with paintings of the saints and Old Testament prophets.

A helpful sign outside points the way to the church of SS Giovanni e Paolo. The route runs to the left over a canal bridge, along the narrow Calle delle Erbe, over another canal bridge and left into the great Campo di SS Giovanni e Paolo. What immediately hits the eye is not the church but the celebrated, arrogant, renaissance statue of Bartolomeo Colleoni on his stallion, which Andrea Verrocchio of Florence created in 1481. It was unfinished on Verrocchio's death in 1488, and Alessandro Leopardi completed the masterpiece in 1496. The mercenary commander Colleoni had died in 1475 and paid for the memorial himself. The Venetians took his money and promised to raise the statue in St Mark's Square. Once Bartolomeo was safely dead, they changed their minds.

The huge gothic barn of a church, which the Venetians nickname Zanipolo, was begun a century and a half earlier by the Dominicans and finished in the 1450s. Its splendid doorway, by Antonio Gambello, marks a turning point between the gothic and renaissance in Venetian architecture, but although it has a foot in both camps it is still a masterpiece. Inside, no fewer than twenty-five Venetian doges are buried, most of them commemorated with superb monuments (above all that of Doge Michele Morosini on the right of the high altar, just where the apse begins). On the last wall pillar on the right you can see the grisly foot of St Catherine of Siena, venerated as a holy relic. Close by in the right transept is a famous stained-glass window, dated 1473 and created by the Murano glass-maker Antonio Licino da Lodi. I cannot quite understand why it is considered such great glass. The colours are undeniably magnificent, but the faces of those portrayed here have disappointingly faded.

The church of SS Giovanni e Paolo is flanked by the marble-fronted civic hospital, once the Scuola Grande di San Marco. These schools were charitable foundations and there were once six of them (one in each quarter of the city). Happily the confraternities that ran them were as keen on artistic excellence as they were on charity. At the Scuola Grande di San Marco they employed Pietro Lombardo and his sons in the fifteenth century to create a magical marble façade, brilliantly conceived to suggest three-dimensional pictures by the use of perspective. The present hospital chapel was built two centuries later by Scamozzi and boasts a Veronese crucifixion and a painting of St Ursula by Tintoretto.

On the wall opposite the church of SS Giovanni e Paolo a notice points east to Santa Maria Formosa and San Marco. The route runs by way of Calle Bressane (to the right of the notice). Cross a canal and continue south to a T-junction, where a right turn takes you into the delightful square of Santa Maria Formosa, surrounded by palaces and housing a little morning market.

The church itself, founded by Saint Magnus in the seventh century, was transformed into a marble renaissance treat by the architect Mauro Coducci in 1492. The campanile was finished in

1688. The name Santa Maria Formosa is delightful, for *formosa* means 'ample', and the church is dedicated to a vision of the Blessed Virgin Mary, vouchsafed to Saint Magnus, in which she appeared in an exceedingly buxom form.

Walk straight across the square down the side of the church and cross a canal bridge into Calle del Mondo Nuovo. Turn right at the end of this street and keep going. On the way you skirt the seventeenth-century church of San Lio (Tiepolo decorated its ceiling, and its beautiful Giusoni chapel was designed by Pietro Lombardo). Cross another canal bridge and a couple of passageways crammed with shops lead to Campo San Bartolomeo.

In the middle of this busy square stands a nineteenth-century statue of Carlo Goldoni (by Antonio del Zotto), Venice's most celebrated dramatist, complete with periwig and walking-stick. Non-Venetians have never quite appreciated Goldoni to the full. The Englishman Thomas Babington Macaulay judged Macchiavelli's play *Mandragola* 'superior to the best of Goldoni'. In 1873 while on his Italian journey the American Henry James watched one of Goldoni's comedies performed in Rome in the Venetian dialect. 'I could but half follow it,' he admitted, but added, 'enough, however, to be sure that, for all its humanity and irony, it wasn't so good as Molière.' What he did admire was the Venetian style of acting. The players possessed, he wrote, 'a marvellous *entrain* [spirited liveliness] of their own; they seem even less than the French to recite.'

Goldoni has his back to the street you need to take to reach the celebrated Rialto Bridge. At the end of the sixteenth century Antonio da Ponte designed its span of 48 metres, a single arch crossing the Grand Canal. For centuries the only way of crossing the canal, other than by boat, was at this point, originally by a bridge of boats, then by the wooden structure which da Ponte replaced. No one thought to build another bridge across the Grand Canal for over two and a half centuries. And since this point was the heart of Venetian market-trading, da Ponte decided to divide his bridge into three passages, with a couple of rows of shops on the outer ones.

On the other side of the bridge is the oldest church in Venice (the eleventh-century San Giacomo), a remarkable survival since a fire virtually destroyed the old market surrounding it in 1514.

Underneath arcades designed a few decades later by Jacopo Sansovino you can buy clothes, wine, leather goods, fruit, vegetables, masks and cheap trinkets.

Cross back over the Rialto and turn right along the Grand Canal, one of the few stretches where it is possible to walk alongside the water. Most people look outwards, towards the canal, but if you look at the buildings as you go by you will see a portrait relief of the statesman and Italian patriot Mazzini, carrying a copy of his own book *Doveri Del Uomo*, at the head of an arcade. Past two magnificent Venetian palaces and across another bridge, turn first left along the narrow Calle Bembo which becomes Calle Fabbri on the way to the superb Piazza San Marco.

St Mark's Square is large enough for three sets of musicians under awnings to regale those customers who can afford the drinks and food on offer. A thousand years ago St Mark's Basilica was fronted by a mere vegetable garden. The bell-tower was a lighthouse and was raised to its present pre-eminence only in the sixteenth century. This campanile lasted until 14 July 1902, when it suddenly collapsed. The architects Luca Beltrami and Gaetano Moretti rebuilt an exact copy (albeit slightly strengthened, one hopes), nearly 99 metres high, which was opened on 15 April 1912. The 'Loggetta', Jacopo Sansovino's exquisite former meeting-place for the Venetian patricians at the base of the campanile, also perished in the disaster and was also meticulously restored. Over its three arches are statues of Pallas, Mercury, Apollo and Peace, all designed by Sansovino between 1537 and 1540, all restored early in our own century.

The bells of the tower are almost as famous as the campanile itself: the 'Marangona', rung to call guild members to work and to signal the end of their labours; the 'Trottiera', rung to call the great ones to the Doge's Palace; the 'Pregadi', whose toll proclaimed that the senate was in session; the 'Maleficio', announcing an execution; the 'Nona', which tolled at noon. Only one survived the 1902 collapse. Pope Pius X paid the cost of replacing the others in the new tower.

In the centre of the huge square, paved with trachyte and marble from the Euganean hills, tourists endlessly feed the pigeons. To the east rises the façade of St Mark's, fronted by flagstaffs on bronze pedestals which Alessandro Leopardi created in 1505. Here too stands the bishop's palace, much younger than the church next door, for during the thousand years of the Venetian Republic St Mark's was not the bishop's cathedral. His seat was the cathedral of San Pietro di Castello, on its own island to the east, and now scarcely visited in spite of its entertaining, marble-covered leaning bell-tower and its Palladian façade.

To the left again stands the bizarre clock-tower of the Piazza San Marco, which Mauro Coducci designed at the very end of the fifteenth century. On top two bronze statues of Moors strike the hours by hammering a great bell. Below them on the face of the tower is the winged lion of St Mark, symbol of the city of Venice as well as of the Christian evangelist, set here on a blue sky with stars. Below is the clock itself, accompanied by the signs of the zodiac.

Mauro Coducci also designed the imposing Procuratie Vecchie, whose arches run along the north side of the piazza. Here lived the procurators whose task was to administrate and care for St Mark's itself. Opposite, the south side of the square is flanked by the Procuratie Nuove, which Vincente Scamozzi and Baldassare Longhena created just over a century later. Their ingenious design picks up all the characteristics of the Procuratie Vecchie (two storeys over an arcaded gallery) and transforms them into a strict but delicious classicism, sporting Doric, Ionic and Corinthian columns. Napoleon Bonaparte rightly decided that this complex building was worthy of transformation into a royal palace.

As you face the basilica the square behind you is closed with the Fabbrica Nuova, which is frequently called the Napoleon wing, since Bonaparte built it in 1810 (replacing the church of San Gimignano). The astounding basilica beckons across the great square, architecture famously matched in prose by John Ruskin:

a multitude of pillars and white domes, clustered into a long low pyramid of coloured light; a treasure-heap, it seems, partly of gold, and partly of opal and mother of pearl, hollowed beneath into five great vaulted porches, ceiled with fair mosaic, and beset with sculpture of alabaster, clear as amber and delicate as ivory, – sculpture fantastic and involved of palm leaves and lilies, and grapes and pomegranates, and birds clinging and fluttering among the branches, all twined together into an endless network of buds and plumes; and in the midst of it, the solemn forms of angels, sceptred, and robed to the feet, and leaning to each other across the gates, their figures indistinct among the gleaming of the golden ground through the leaves beside them, interrupted and dim, like the morning light as it faded back among the branches of Eden, when first its gates were angel-guarded long ago.

Ruskin's phrase a 'treasure-heap' is brilliant. Basically the basilica dates from the eleventh century; but nothing here is so simple as that. Take the reliefs on the façade. The first, on the left, was created by the Romans. The fourth is Byzantine, dating from the twelfth century. The rest were sculpted in the next century. The interior was covered with mosaics in 1204. The gothic statues on the façade were added in the late fourteenth century. And what Ruskin supposed were Greek horses are bronze copies of four splendid Roman imperial statues which had reached Constantinople in the fourth century and were brought to Venice at the beginning of the fourteenth.

Another treasure, shipped here in 828 from Alexandria, is the supposed corpse of St Mark. Before that date the basilica was dedicated to St Theodore. Inside, a mosaic of 1660 (over the Capella Zen, the sixteenth-century funerary chapel of Cardinal Giambattista Zeno) illustrates the momentous journey made by the apostle's bones.

St Mark's Basilica remains a house of God as well as a museum of the richest eastern art. If you arrive around 11.30 am on a Sunday, you will be fortunate enough to receive the episcopal blessing of the Patriarch of the city, as he sits enthroned. Above him Christ Pantocrator, also enthroned, is depicted in gold and mosaic over the apse of the basilica. A splendid rood screen guards the apse from worshippers and profane alike. On it all twelve Apostles flank their crucified Lord.

Before walking on to the Doge's Palace, an essential diversion is to view the celebrated Bridge of Sighs. At the far end of the little square to the left of the basilica the Calle della Canonica reaches the Ponte della Canonica. From here there is an excellent view of the chunky bridge which Antonio Contino designed at the beginning of the seventeenth century for the purpose of bringing prisoners to be examined by the state inquisitors (hence the sighs).

The Doge's Palace in the Piazzetta to the right of San Marco was built between 1309 and 1442 as the magnificent residence of the rulers of Venice. Here is Venetian gothic at its peak: exquisite arches seemingly scarcely capable of supporting the pink and white marble wall and six gothic windows above. (The pink is marble from Verona, the white from Istria.) On the façade are delicious carvings of Adam (drunk), the archangel Gabriel, and Adam and Eve (almost naked). Here too the brilliant Jacopo della Quercia carved a judgment of Solomon, topped again by the avenging archangel Gabriel. The interior is equally sumptuous. Antonio Rizzo created the superb east wing of the courtyard. He also designed the great staircase (the *Scala dei Giganti*), which Jacopo Sansovino adorned with massive statues of Neptune and Mars. The huge main hall (built in 1340) once housed the deliberations of all 1700 Venetian patricians. Fittingly, the oil painting of paradise at the entrance by Jacopo Tintoretto is the biggest oil painting in the world. Ruskin wrote that Tintoretto painted it because he believed in paradise, 'But he did not paint it to make any one think of heaven; but to form a beautiful termination for the hall of the Greater Council.'

The interior is covered with superb paintings including Domenico Tintoretto's frieze of 76 doges. One of them is blacked out: Marin Falier, who was put to death for treason in 1355. You can visit the Doge's Palace in summer from 08.30 to 18.00, apart from Sundays, when it closes at 13.00; from mid October to March it closes on weekdays at 14.30.

On the other side of the Piazzetta from the Doge's Palace stands the Old Library (also known as the Libraria Sansovino from the name of its architect Jacopo Sansovino, who designed it in the mid sixteenth century). This was the very first piece of renaissance architecture in Venice. Today it houses the city's main library and its archaeological museum.

Walk to the quayside and turn right for a stroll along the water. This is the start of the Grand Canal. Opposite across the lagoon are two famous churches, both with domes, both fronted with classical white marble façades. They are San Giorgio Maggiore and (to the right and further away) the Redentore. San Giorgio Maggiore is built on its own island on the site of a Benedictine monastery. From 1565 to 1576 the brilliant Andrea Palladio oversaw its construction to his own designs. Simone Sorella completed Palladio's majestic façade forty-five years later.

The Redentore was built in honour of Jesus the Redeemer, again to the designs of Andrea Palladio, as a thank-offering after Venice had survived the savage plague of 1577. Its façade is lovely, its interior sublime. You can visit San Giorgio Maggiore and the church of the Redentore by taking water bus no.5.

Go as far as you can along the quayside that leads from the Piazzetta of San Marco, and then turn right down Calle Vallaressa, which boasts the little Teatro del Ridotto, standing next to a stupendous fish restaurant. Here are expensive glass shops, selling not so much art as Venetian kitsch. Once renowned throughout the Western world for its craftsmen and artists, to my mind much of the artistic impulse of the city has stultified. There is nothing now to rank with the associations of craftsmen who specialized in ceramics, printing, cabinet-making, and stucco-work. (You can see their work and their history set out in the Corner Museum in the Piazzetta near San Marco.) Once gold- and silversmiths were lavishly patronized, while bronze founders created some of the superb church doors of the city. Today the shops of the Calle Vallaressa, spilling over from those in St Mark's Square, sell the glass and leather goods that represent the decadent end of this great tradition.

Turn left past the church of San Moisè the Prophet into the church square, the Campo San Moisè, and look back at its magnificent (if, at present, dusty and pigeon-stained) façade, built by Alessandro Tremignon in 1668. Inside, behind the high altar, Moses is depicted receiving the tablets bearing the ten commandments of God. The view from the bridge over the canal on the far side of the square reveals how the rich baroque façade of the church contrasts with its lovely fourteenth-century bell-tower, a beautiful, understated campanile, with simple arches, not a hint of flamboyance and just a modest balustrade.

The route continues along the wide Calle XXII Marzo, with its banks and antique shops and narrow streets running off at either side. At the end turn left into the Calle delle Ostreghe and cross over the canal. This is a favourite haunt of gondolas and you can, if you wish, pick up one for a trip here. In summer the narrow streets are cool, and the squares often seem like blazing deserts of sunshine. The next piazza, the Campo del Traghetto, contains a memorial to human pride. In the early 1680s Giuseppe Sardi designed a baroque church that glorifies not God but a mere mortal (though a rich one), Antonio Barbaro, who had left the money for Santa Maria del Giglio in his will. His statue dominates the entrance, flanked by statues of virtues which he fondly supposed he possessed.

Past this church two bridges, the Ponte Dudo e Barbarigo and the Ponte Zaguri, lead into Campo San Maurizio. A plaque records that Alessandro Manzoni, undoubtedly the greatest of all Italian romantic novelists, lived here in 1803 and 1804. Unfortunately these were not the years of his greatest fecundity, for Manzoni's masterpieces (*Il Conte di Carmagnola*, *Adelchi* and *I Promessi Sposi*) were all written in the 1820s.

The church of San Maurizio (a nineteenth-century neo-classical reconstruction) stands on the right at the end of the square, and a narrow passage (the Calle del Piovan) leads on over the Ponte Santo Stefano into the Campo Santo Stefano. Here there is an infinitely more delightful church, boasting three paintings by Tintoretto and a fantastic roof designed in the form of a ship's keel. But before taking this route, a small diversion offers a couple of entertaining sights. On the left opposite the church of San Maurizio the Calle del Dose da Ponte leads as far as the Grand Canal, across which you can see the unfinished Peggy Guggenheim building (*non finito*, as the Venetians call it, though it is packed with Kandinskys, Picassos, Magrittes and Chiricos). Walking back you get a bizarre view of Santo Stefano's precariously leaning bell-tower, by far the most alarming in the whole of Venice.

The statue in the middle of the Campo Santo Stefano is of a brooding Niccolo Tommaseo (erected in 1882). Who was he? Turn left across the square and on the wall is the bust of another long forgotten Venetian genius, Felice Cavalotti ('soldier, legislator and poet', as the inscription declares). A few paces more take you to the wooden span across the Grand Canal, the Academy Bridge. This bridge has remained in its temporary state since the 1930s, when it was constructed to replace its faulty nineteenth-century prede-cessor. I like to pause on it and look left along the Grand Canal as far as the double domes and golden globe of the church of Santa Maria della Salute. Like the church of the Redentore, this was built as a thank-offering after Venice was delivered from the plague (this time in 1630). Baldassare Longhena, its architect, designed it in the shape of a crown, to signify the heavenly coronation of Jesus's mother, the Blessed Virgin Mary.

On the other side of the Academy Bridge is the Accademia art gallery, which opens daily from 09.00 to 14.00 (closing one hour earlier on Sundays). The greatest collection of Venetian painting in the world, including works by Titian and Tintoretto, is housed here.

From the Accademia take the water bus no.1 for two stops to San Tomà, in order to visit a church that no one should miss on the briefest visit to Venice. Walk from San Tomà along Calle del Traghetto Vecchio. Turn right into Campo San Tomà, where there is an extraordinary phenomenon for Venice: a restaurant that caters for vegetarians. I have eaten in the evening in this small, charming place, with its awning spreading out into the square, whilst a couple of teenage lovers kissed and an elegant lady reclined against the well-head, waiting for her assignation. The brick buildings, the red and yellow plastered houses, the church with its Corinthian capitals and five statues, illuminated at night and yet looking as if the builders had forgotten to finish the top half of the façade, add their own graciousness to the scene. As I looked up from my fillet of sole, the long-awaited friend of the elegant lady arrived, a slightly balding gallant, and she smiled radiantly.

Cross Campo San Tomà diagonally, passing the elegant lady's renaissance well-head in the middle, and take the right-hand alley. Turn left and then almost immediately right into the Campo dei Frari with its magnificent huge brick gothic church. Curiously enough, this is an unfashionable part of this most fashionable city, and you can eat or drink here surprisingly cheaply.

The Frari was created by the followers of St Francis of Assisi, who had brought a new understanding of its founder's simplicity to the Christian Church. These friars reached Venice in the early thirteenth century and built a modest church here. More and more believers flocked to their sanctuary, and in the 1330s they decided to build a much greater building to serve these supplicants. It was finished a century or so later.

On the outside of the church of the Frari delicate, spare marble enhances the decor. Above the doorway is a statue of Jesus risen from the dead, sculpted in 1581 by Alessandro Vittoria. In the previous century Bartolomeo Bon sculpted the statues of the Virgin Mary and St Francis which stand on the two other columns. Inside, Franciscan simplicity is enriched by the grandeur of later tombs.

The most astounding of these tombs to my mind is set just inside the entrance: the tomb of Doge Giovanni Pesaro, supported by four straining negroes in tattered clothing. Giovanni Pesaro was doge for only two years, from 1658 to 1659. Ten years later he died and Baldassare Longhena created this megalomaniac monument. Melchior Barthel of Dresden sculpted the negroes. Bernardo Falcone of Lugano added two grisly black bronze skeletons holding up inscriptions. The doge is represented as he liked to remember himself, dominating a great Venetian throng with his oratory, and seated beneath a canopy of red marble.

Over the high altar is the greatest masterpiece of the Frari church, Titian's *Assumption*, created when the artist was 41 years old. Titian had already collaborated with his master Giovanni Bellini in creating the triptych of the *Virgin and Child* in the sacristy of this church. Here you can discern Bellini's signature (Joannes Bellinus) and the date (1488) in the artist's own hand. Titian's *Assumption* also carries a signature: Ticianus. Here St Peter kneels, overwhelmed by the Virgin's apotheosis. St Thomas points wonderingly at her. Since Titian loved to paint in rich reds, the Virgin's traditionally blue clothing is represented simply by her cloak, while her robe is a gleaming crimson. Cherubs around her hail the mother of Jesus. Above everyone, God the Father welcomes her into heaven.

On the way to the sacristy, do not miss what is said to be a masterpiece by Donatello, in the chapel to the right of the high altar. In truth I regard it as an extremely unprepossessing statue of an angry St John the Baptist, painted in gold and brown. This is the only one of Donatello's statues left in Venice. Then marvel at the Bellini triptych in its gilded *trompe l'oeil* frame, the Madonna flanked by St Mark (who looks out at us with his open Gospel in his hand), while the pot-bellied infant Jesus stands erect on his mother's knee.

Amongst the other masterpieces of this church do not neglect to stroke the sumptuously carved choir-stalls, made by the Cozzi family of woodworkers and finished in 1468. The pyramid monument to Antonio Canova (matched by one in Vienna, see p.196) is bizarre enough, since it was designed in 1794 by Canova not for himself but for Titian. Those who commissioned it ran out of money and the project was abandoned. When Canova died in 1822, a fund was raised to finish the memorial to contain his own embalmed heart. The genius of Canova is represented on the left with his torch extinguished. Next to him reclines the winged lion of Venice. Above is his relief bust, surrounded by the symbol of immortality (a snake). Mourners on the left make their melancholy way into the dread darkness of the tomb.

Here too is the first equestrian monument in Venice, to the right of the high altar and left of the sacristy door: a monument to Benedetto Pesaro by Lorenzo and Giambattista Bregno. Titian's own monument is one created in 1853 (though he died in 1576). Since Canova's projected memorial was never dedicated to the great painter, it is fitting that this overwrought tomb should have been designed by two of Canova's most talented pupils, Luigi and Pietro Zandomeneghi. They sculpted semblances of the master's works around him, one of which we now know he never painted.

Opposite the west door of the church of the Frari the Ponte dei Frari crosses a canal, where you turn right, then left into the Rio Terra and second right. A bridge over a canal to the left leads into the Campo di San Polo. This is another lovely, virtually unknown square, with a renaissance well in the centre, flanked by intimate jettied houses and by fine palaces: the fifteenth-century gothic Palazzo Soranzo; the sixteenth-century Palazzo Corner Mocenigo; and the eighteenth-century Palazzo Tiepolo-Maffetti. The church of San Polo itself, though much restored in the nineteenth century, boasts a fourteenth-century bell-tower and a fifteenth-century doorway which some claim was designed by Bartolomeo Bon. Inside are paintings by Tintoretto and Tiepolo.

Retrace your steps to Campo dei Frari, turning left instead of right over the bridge opposite the west door. Over another bridge take the Calle della Chiesa into a little square, turning left and then right at the far side. Hidden away in this street is the Scuola Grande di San Giovanni Evangelista (whose courtyard is faced by a splendid marble screen designed by Pietro Lombardi in 1481). From here a leisurely five minutes' walk takes you back to the railway station. Continue past the Scuola to the bank of the canal Rio Marin and follow it left. Cross the canal at Ponte Capello and continue along the other side. Cross the next canal bridge (Ponte della Bergama), where a notice at the end of a little alleyway directs you right, *Alla Ferrovia*, over the Grand Canal by the Ponte dei Scalzi (named after the nearby Scalzi church and built by Eugenio Miozzi in 1934). The station square is on your left.

Further delights

The Grand Canal

A ride in a water bus along the Grand Canal is one of the treats of Venice that should not be missed. On either side are superb palaces, gilded and decorated, painted with the rich reds discovered by the great Venetian artists. As John Ruskin wrote of these palaces,

while the burghers and barons of the North were building their dark streets and grisly castles of oak and sandstone, the merchants of Venice were covering their palaces with porphyry and gold; and at last, when her mighty painters had created for her a colour more priceless than gold or porphyry, even this, the richest of the treasures, she lavished upon walls whose foundations were beaten by the sea: and the strong tide, as it runs beneath the Rialto, is reddened to this day by the frescoes of Giorgione.

These palaces were built by one family and enriched by another, inhabited by a third family and taken over by a fourth. The greatest, the Ca' d'Oro (where the water bus happily stops to pick up passengers), with its superb tracery, was adapted from a twelfth-century Byzantine palace by the Contarini family. There are many more palaces in the city named after and built by this rich merchant family.

Other rich Venetian merchants built equally sumptuously. Four of the five surviving sons of Giorgio Corner, who died in 1527, inherited his stupendous fortune and proceeded to build outrageously expensive palaces, of which one of the greatest is the Palazzo Corner della Ca' Grande. You see it immediately after the fourth canal on your right, if you take the water bus up the Grand Canal from St Mark's Square (or just before the third canal on your left after the Academy Bridge, if you are travelling along the Grand Canal the other way, in the direction of San Marco).

Jacopo Sansovino was the architect of this perfectly proportioned building. He had trained as a sculptor in Florence under Andrea Sansovino, whom he admired enough to borrow his surname, and here for the first time the Tuscan and Roman high renaissance made its debut in Venice. The powerful rustication of the first storey is essentially Tuscan. The brackets framing the mezzanine windows derive directly from Michelangelo's brilliant Palazzo Medici in Florence.

Descendants of the Corner family lived in this palace until 1812. Then Andrea Corner sold it to the Austrians, whose imperial delegates to Venice relished its splendour (though for some reason they transferred its lovely well-head to the square of SS Giovanni e Paolo, where it remains to this day). After the unification of Italy the Austrians departed and the palazzo is now the residence of the prefect of Venice.

At every turn along the Grand Canal a new delight appears. Several of the buildings have fascinating histories, such as the stunning Ca' Rezzonico which stands just three canals up from the Academy Bridge on the left bank. The baroque genius Baldassare Longhena began building it in 1667. His patrons ran out of money, and the building remained incomplete until 1745, when Giorgio Masari was commissioned by the rich Rezzonico family to finish it. It took him eleven years and the result is a masterpiece. Two years later Carlo Rezzonico became Pope Clement XIII. He is remembered both for his shameless nepotism and for his remarkable prudery. He created two of his nephews cardinals and made another a Roman senator. And he had fig leaves placed on every naked statue in the Vatican.

Beyond the Ca' Rezzonico the water bus turns right and ahead you see the onion-domed tower of the church of San Bartolomeo with the great dome of San Salvatore beyond it to the right. On the same side of the canal the bus passes the renaissance Palazzo Corner-Spinelli, which Mauro Coducci designed in 1485. Then the Rialto Bridge comes into sight. Soon after the bridge, there is a stop at the legendary Ca' d'Oro. Across the water is the finest baroque palace in Venice, Longhena's Ca' Pesaro. Today it houses the city's oriental museum and gallery of modern art. The elegant church of San Stae a little further on boasts a neo-Palladian façade. Then the thirteenth-century bell-tower and eighteenth-century dome of San Geremia appear ahead.

The bus stops at San Marcuola, a church which Masari designed around 1730 and which still lacks its marble façade. On the opposite bank stands a thirteenth-century palace (largely rebuilt in 1869), which is now the city's natural history museum but for centuries was the home of Turkish merchants, hence its name, the Fondaco dei Turchi. Finally the bus reaches the Scalzi bridge and Venice's splendid railway station.

Gondolas

Reminiscing about Venice, Henry James remembered best of all not the great squares or churches or even the basilica of St Mark and the Piazzetta. 'I simply see a narrow canal in the heart of the city — a patch of green water and a surface of pink wall,' he wrote. 'The gondola moves slowly; it gives a great smooth swerve, passes under a bridge, and the gondolier's cry, carried over the quiet water, makes a kind of splash in the stillness.' Floating about in a gondola gave him the delightful feeling of being part of Venice itself.

Exactly this sensation can be enjoyed today, though at an exorbitant cost. The gondola is an extraordinary craft, its comb-like prow (known to the Venetians as *il ferro*) representing in its shape the six divisions of the city and the crescent-shaped island of Giudecca (the limit of the lagoon opposite St Mark's Square). Each craft is 10.87 metres long, a mere 1.42 metres at its maximum width, and rises no more than 0.62 metres from the water. The boat bulges on the left-hand side, where the gondolier stands, by exactly 24 centimetres. Eight different woods are used in constructing a gondola: larch, cherry, fir, walnut, elm, oak, lime and mahogany.

A ride after dark is extremely romantic. With a little light flickering at either end, the gondolas seem in a world apart. Often a little group sails together, with a singer in one boat to entertain the passengers. I have found it infinitely cheaper and almost as romantic to stand on a bridge over the Rio Marin in the evening. Here you can watch packs of gondolas pass by, with an accordion playing in one and a singer in another.

Murano and glass-blowing

In 1291 Venetian glass-blowers settled on the island of Murano (in fact five islands linked by bridges) and have been there ever since. Take water bus no.5 (from Piazzale Roma or San Marco) to reach Murano. At Fondamenta dei Vetrai and at Fondamenta Manin you can buy elaborately designed glassware. In the Palazzo Giustinian is the Museo della Arte Vetraria, which opens from 10.00 to 16.00

except Wednesdays (closing at 12.30 on Sundays and holidays). And of course you can watch glass being blown.

Murano also boasts two fine churches, San Pietro Martire with its splendid glass chandeliers (as you might expect), and the much older SS Mario e Donato, which oddly enough has none. San Pietro Martire also houses two fine altarpieces by Giovanni Bellini. Mario e Donato, which dates from the twelfth century, has a lovely apse and a magical mosaic floor of 1140.

On a short visit to Venice you can save time and still see glass-blowing on weekdays without a trip to Murano by crossing the Guard Canal to Santa Maria della Saulte and walking over the Ponte del Abazia on the right. In the street ahead is a glass shop with a resident master glass-blower (and several apprentices). It takes fifteen to twenty years for an apprentice to become a master, and most of them come from old glass-blowing families. Each piece they make is baked in a kiln for at least twenty-four hours. There is always some eight per cent of breakages in the kiln, sometimes more. All this skill produces both supremely tasteful objects and remarkable kitsch.

Excursion to Vicenza

Vicenza is less than an hour from Venice by the faster trains and offers a completely different experience from the water-locked islands, for Vicenza is supremely the city of the great architect Andrea Palladio, a man, as Goethe put it, 'so strongly imbued with the instincts of the ancients that he acutely felt the petty, narrow spirit of his own times and, instead of conforming to it, set about transforming it to fit his own high ideals.' His success is seen above all in Vicenza.

Born in 1508 at Padua, Palladio was a friend of Tintoretto and Veronese. Apprenticed to a Paduan stone-carver at the age of thirteen, he so chafed at his irksome duties that in 1524 he broke his contract and ran away to Vicenza. He found himself in a city already brimming with exquisite palaces, and he found himself at home. To his adopted city he bequeathed some of his own greatest works.

Walk from Vicenza railway station up Viale Roma and turn right through the city walls and past the medieval citadel. Here you immediately come upon three massive columns, almost certainly by Palladio, or perhaps by his pupil and devoted disciple Vincenzo Scamozzi. Turn right into the Piazza Castello. The building turned sideways on is the Palazzo Porto-Breganze, which Scamozzi built at the end of the sixteenth century, faithfully following his master's designs. Here some of Palladio's favourite themes are immediately apparent, particularly the three columns on the façade. Walk on down the hill past the cathedral, which was savagely bombed in 1944, to reach first a piazzetta with a statue of Palladio (put here in 1859) and then his masterpiece, the splendid basilica.

Its name signifies not a great church but the city's meeting-place and hall of justice. In the mid fifteenth century Domenico da Venezia built a gothic hall with lovely brick vaults here, known as the Palazzo della Ragione. In 1549 Palladio began its transformation, wrapping it in a huge classical envelope. He gave it two colonnaded galleries, one Doric in style, the other Ionic, and a golden copper roof. The ground floor is filled with shops and banks and a restaurant. On Saturday mornings a fruit and flower market flourishes in the Piazza delle Erbe to the south. On the opposite side you look from the galleries over the Piazza dei Signori at the lovely (though unfinished) Loggia del Capitano, which Palladio designed in pink and white stone for the Venetian governor in 1571. The basilica opens on weekdays, except Monday, from 09.30 to 12.00 and from 14.00 to 17.00. It closes on Sunday afternoons. At its north corner rises the Torre di Piazza, begun in the twelfth century and raised twice, in 1311 and 1444. A good place to admire Palladio's basilica is while having a drink in the Gran Caffè Garibaldi on the corner of the square.

Walk towards the two free-standing pillars at the end of the square (one bearing the lion of St Mark, the other a statue of the Saviour) and up the pedestrianized Contrà Daniele Manin. At the end of this street stands the fourteenth-century Palazzo da Schio — very Venetian gothic with sweet chimneys, and housing a collection of local antiquities amassed by the Schio family.

Here turn left into Corso Palladio and then right along Contra Porti, a street of exceedingly fine palaces. On the right at no.8 is the fifteenth-century Palazzo Thiene-Cavalloni. A few paces further, at no.11, stands the massive façade of Palazzo Porto-Barbarano, built by Palladio in 1578. Opposite this palazzo the Banco Popolare is housed in the renaissance Palazzo Thiene which Lorenzo da Bologna built in the late fifteenth century. Next door to it stands the gothic Palazzo Tirissino-Sperotti. And at no.17 is the delightful Palazzo Portó-Breganze, all Venetian gothic save for Lorenzo da Bologna's renaissance doorway.

On the other side of the street a plaque declares that Luigi da Porto, who wrote the tale of Romeo and Juliet, died here in May 1529 aged only 43. This is undoubtedly Romeo and Juliet territory. Palazzo Colleoni-Porto at no.19 boasts two delightful balconies, matching those on no.17 (but not copying them, for these are in brick, those in plaster). Next door, no.21, is Palladio's unfinished Palazzo Iseppo da Porto, its façade dating from 1552.

Shortly the walk reaches the river, where you turn right along the street called Giuseppe Apolloni and first right again into Contrà Giacomo Zanella, another street of architectural delights, with its gothic palaces and delicious double balconies. To these gothic treats Palazzo Negri de Salvi offers a fifteenth-century renaissance contrast and the church of Santo Stefano an admixture of the baroque. A little further on is the Palladian façade of Palazzo Thiene.

Contrà San Gaetano Thienne leads back to Corso Palladio. Turn left along the arcaded street to find Palladio in his religious vein, for he enriched the thirteenth-century church of Santa Corona (which is closed on Monday mornings and every day from 12.00 to 15.30) with its Capella Valmarene. Palladio was buried in Santa Corona in 1580. Here too is a splendid *Baptism of Christ* by Giovanni Bellini as well as an *Adoration of the Magi* by Paolo Veronese.

The dullish Palazzo de Palladio at no.165 is attributed to Palladio. You would never guess the fact, but further on in Piazza Matteoti are two of his masterpieces: the Palazzo Chiericati and the Teatro Olimpico. The first, built in 1551, is now the city's art gallery and museum, open except Mondays and Sunday afternoons from 09.00 to 12.00 and 14.30 to 17.00. The Teatro Olimpico must be one of the most unusual masterpieces in Italy, Palladio's last creation (and finished by Scamozzi after his death). Here the two architects created a remarkable three-dimensional stage out of wood and stucco, and scenery representing a piazza with streets set out in magical perspective. The Teatro Olimpico opens at the same hours as the Palazzo Chiericati, though on weekdays it closes one hour earlier.

Outside the theatre is a statue of Fedele Lampertico, a public-spirited man who lived from 1833 to 1906. If you have time to visit the thirteenth-century church of San Lòrenzo (on Corso Fogazzaro, which runs north from Corso Palladio), you will find a notice declaring that he bought and demolished a house that leaned against and obscured the view of this lovely basilica. Inside this church is a new monument, a bronze bust of St Maximilian Kolbe, the Polish Catholic priest who chose to die in a Nazi concentration camp in place of a married man who had, as the bronze records, 'a wife and children'.

Food and drink

Venice can be an expensive city, but very many restaurants offer a fixed price menu, usually of three courses with a considerable amount of choice – though the price rises and the choice diminishes as you approach San Marco.

Curiously these menus rarely offer Venetian specialities (except for *fegato alla veneziana*, thin slices of liver cooked on sweet fried onions). Rather you will be eating straightforward Italian dishes: vegetable soup, pasta, veal and the like. As for wine, you are likely to be offered Valpolicella, Merlot, Tocai, Pinot, Sauvignon, or of course the cheapest available, i.e. the *vino della casa*. White wines, which the Venetians drink young, include Tocai Friulano and Grigio. They happily drink the red Bardolinos from Verona.

Venetian gastronomy can do better than this. Once, after all, the city was the main source of spices for the rest of Europe. The Arab world added its own traditions of cooking to those of the Veneto (including the habit of mingling sultanas with almost anything). Then the Austrians brought their own distinctive flavours: goulash and delicious cakes.

Another liver dish worth searching out is *fegato in tortiera*, in which thin liver slices are covered in breadcrumbs and fried in butter before being sprinkled with lemon and sugar. Venetians like offal: brains, hearts, lungs and sweetbreads. The doges are said to have loved *risi e bisi* (rice with peas, plus chopped ham). And fish is served in abundance, as *frittura mista*, as *calamari fritti*, as *baccalà alla vicentina* (cod, Vicenza style), as an hors d'oeuvre (*antipasto di pesce*), as *saor* (sardines and onions fried in oil) and simply as stockfish (*stoccafisso*).

Night life

Take care not to be looking for anywhere to eat late in the evening. Venice tends to close down early. Its night life is thus fairly restricted. But there are exceptions. One is the famous Casino on the Lido, where you can gamble from three in the afternoon till three in the morning. The Lido also boasts two night-clubs, the Casanova Club and La Perla, both open until 03.00.

You can reach the Lido in 45 minutes by boat from Piazzale Roma or in 25 minutes from San Marco.

Important information

Banks in Venice do not open for very long: just from 08.30 to 13.20 on weekdays. Bureaux de change stay open longer, and are often still open as late as 19.00.

Watch out for public holidays (when banks and shops close), which include 25 April, 1 May, 15 August, 1 November, 21 November and 8 December as well as the ones you would expect.

As for getting around the city, Mark Twain once joked that the city 'must be a paradise for cripples, for verily a man has no use for legs here'. Far from it: Venice makes no provisions at all for anyone confined to a wheelchair (or otherwise handicapped in moving about physically) to get across its many bridges.

Apart from this major fault, it is a city easy to travel around in. Venice is small, and you can quickly walk virtually anywhere. The system of water buses is cheap and good (the price depending on whether you take the fastest, the *motoscafo*, the next fastest, the *diretto*, or the one that stops at every picking-up point, the *accelerato*). You can buy a 24-hour ticket (a *biglietto turistico*) at any boat stage and travel on any water bus except the no.2.

Buses from Marco Polo airport to Piazzale Roma take twenty minutes, run from 06.10 to 12.20, and are infinitely less expensive than motor launches or the still dearer water taxis. The cheapest way to reach the city centre from San Nicolò airport on the Lido is by water bus.

Vienna

This is one of the most perplexing cities that I ever was in. . . . It has immense palaces, superb galleries of paintings, several theatres, public walks, and drives crowded with equipages. In short, everything bears the stamp of luxury and ostentation; for here is assembled and concentrated all the wealth, fashion and nobility of the Austrian empire.

Washington Irving, 1822

Playing the Viennese singing master in Noël Coward's *Bitter Sweet* and pining for his home, Nelson Eddy observes nostalgically, 'We have festivals in the spring. Young boys and girls dance. Their clothes are brightly coloured, blending in the sun. The old people sit around under the trees, watching, tapping their sticks on the ground, remembering when they too were young and in love.' And so they do today in Vienna, especially in the pedestrianized streets around the great gothic cathedral.

Fittingly, as the singing master spoke those words he was seated at a grand piano. Vienna, the city of Franz Léhar and the Strauss family, is a city of grand pianos. Sit in the Café Schwarzenberg (at no.17 on the monumental Kärntnerring), which has been serving cream cakes, coffee, wine and beer since 1861. A concert pianist will regale you with the seductive strains of Strauss, and around seven o'clock in the evening some of those expensive, charming horse-drawn carriages that tour the streets draw up at the traffic lights outside on their way home. Outside too a street sign points to Budapest. On mild evenings you can drink coffee in the open air and watch the colours change on the huge fountain in front of the Soviet war memorial.

These links with Russia and Budapest recall Vienna's romantic, powerful, sometimes tragic past. This city, far smaller than London or Paris, was once capital of the mighty Austro-Hungarian empire until its collapse at the end of World War I. As a result, much of the architecture is imperial — often rococo or baroque, always regal and princely — yet a delightfully unspoiled medieval centre lies at the heart of the city. Its grandeur is allied to intimacy. Today Vienna is actually shrinking: the 2 million inhabitants of 1913 are now a mere 1.5 million.

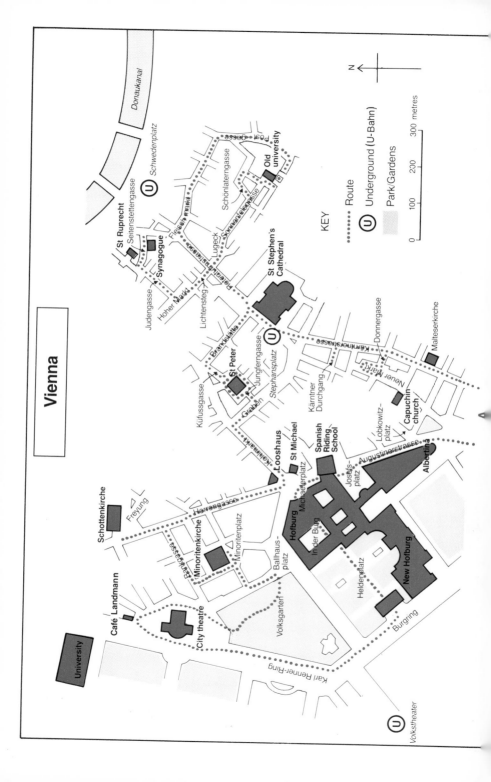

Vienna

KEY

••••• Route

Ⓤ Underground (U-Bahn)

░░░ Park/Gardens

|0 | 100 | 200 | 300 metres|

N

Donaukanal

Schwedenplatz Ⓤ

St Ruprecht
Seitenstettengasse

Synagogue

Judengasse

Hoher Markt

Lichtensteg

Brandstätte

Fleischmarkt

Rotenturmstrasse

Lugeck

Wollzeile

Schönlaterngasse

Post gasse

Old university

St Stephen's Cathedral

Stephansplatz Ⓤ

Kärntnerstrasse

Donnergasse

Neuer Markt

Kärntner Durchgang

Lobkowitz-platz

Capuchin church

Malteserkirche

Kufussgasse

Graben

St Peter

Jungferngasse

Kohlmarkt

Looshaus

St Michael

Michaelerplatz

Spanish Riding School

Josefs-platz

Augustinerstrasse

Albertina

Schottenkirche

Freyung

Bankgasse

Herrengasse

Minoritenkirche

Minoritenplatz

Ballhaus-platz

Hofburg

In der Burg

Heldenplatz

New Hofburg

Burgring

Café Landmann

University

City theatre

Volksgarten

Karl Renner-Ring

Volkstheater Ⓤ

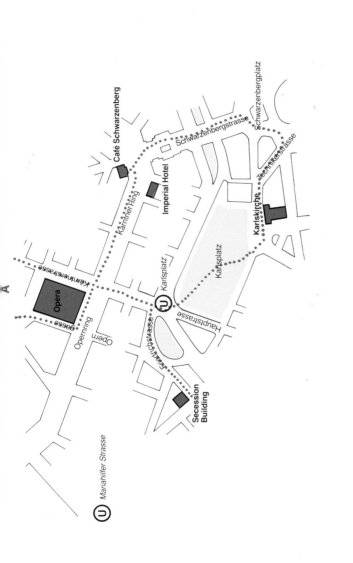

A city tour

The Café Schwarzenberg is a good place to start a tour of Vienna. Almost opposite is the Imperial Hotel. Built in 1867 as a palace for the Duke of Württemberg and transformed into a hotel in 1873, the Imperial housed the Wagner family two years later while he worked on *Tannhäuser* and *Lohengrin*. When it opened as a hotel its chef created a remarkable delicacy, the 'Imperial Torte', which became Kaiser Franz Josef's favourite cake. After his death in 1916 no more were made for fifty years. Then the recipe was rediscovered, and today you can eat a slice with your *tee* (sic) or coffee, or even send one home in a wooden box, suitably sealed. The recipe is still considered a secret, though it is not difficult to discern five layers of chocolate cake interspersed with five thin layers of almond paste — the whole topped with marzipan.

Naturally the Imperial has always employed superb pianists, though (on request) they are willing to descend to playing the 'Harry Lime Theme' from Orson Welles' film *The Third Man*. They are capable of much better. When the famous international pianist Horowitz reached Vienna on his European tour in 1987, he stayed at the Imperial. He came into the Maria Theresa bar, greeted the pianist and with a bow presented him with complimentary tickets for his own concert that evening.

Turn left along Kärntnerring from the Imperial Hotel and you soon reach Opernring and the Opera. Vienna's state opera house was built as the court opera house in the 1860s by the architects August von Siccardsburg and Eduard van der Nüll. Initially it was so hated and so much criticized that van der Nüll committed suicide and (coincidentally or not) von Siccardsburg died a couple of months later. Today it is beloved, ranked amongst the leading opera houses of the world. Gustav Mahler, Richard Strauss and Herbert von Karajan have been its directors. Much of it was destroyed by air raids in World War II, but the opera house has been totally restored.

Three hundred performances a year are invariably packed. And in February the President of Austria opens the famous Opera Ball, the highpoint of Vienna's fashionable pre-Lent carnival. I have merely watched it on television from my hotel bedroom, although I sat beforehand in the Imperial Hotel whilst handsome men in tails and ribbons and beautiful (or faded) ladies in fabulous dresses took an apéritif before gliding for scarcely a hundred metres in their limousines to the ball. The whole affair is as spectacular as grand opera, with a hundred debutantes in white escorted by slim young men, and languorous Viennese waltzes opening the exceedingly expensive evening.

Far homelier and equally typically Viennese is the nearby 'Stadtheuriger' in the Augustiner Keller. Walk along Operngasse at the far side of the opera house and then turn left along Augustinerstrasse. The Augustiner Keller opens daily from ten in the morning, and after 18.30 in the evening there is music — of a special kind. A 'Schrammel' quartet, made up of two violins, a guitar and an accordion, will break into traditional 'Heuriger' songs. The Heurigers are places that serve wine remarkably cheaply by Viennese standards. Usually a wreath of evergreens is hung on a pole outside to show that you can buy the new vintage.

The food served at the Augustiner Keller is typically Viennese and is chalked on a board outside. Inside, there are delicious smells of cooked meats and chickens roasting on spits and you can see the original brick arches of the cellars of the former Augustinian monastery. People sit chatting at tables in little green and black cubicles. Here you can quaff glasses of Augustiner, or a dry Veltliner, a mild Domkaiptel, a richly scented Gumpoldskirchner, a sharp, refreshing Traminer, or what the Viennese call 'G'spritzer' and 'Glühwein' (both red and white).

The Albertina itself (no.1 Augustinerstrasse) is a palace built in 1781 for a Portuguese count. It takes its name from the son-in-law of the dominating eighteenth-century Empress Maria Theresa, Duke Albert von Sachsen-Teschen, who employed Louis de Montoyer to enlarge the building in the early years of the nineteenth century. De Montoyer incorporated part of the monastery next door into the new Albertina. And Duke Albert, a discriminating art lover, formed the basis of the astounding collection which can still be seen here. It includes, for instance, over 40,000 Old Master drawings, the greatest such collection in the world. There are 140 drawings by Albrecht Dürer alone, as well as lovely works by Leonardo da Vinci and Rubens. The equestrian statue of Archduke Albert (which looks out on to the back of the opera house) was made by Kaspar von Zumbusch in 1898, in honour of the field marshal who led Austrian troops to victory at the battle of Custozza in 1866.

You are now suddenly in the midst of Viennese high society, or at least amid architectural reminders of the great princes who used to serve as courtiers of the Holy Roman Emperor. On the right of the Albertina is the Palais Lobkowitz, built in the early baroque style between 1685 and 1687 by Giovanni Pietro Tencala – one of the many Italians brought to Vienna by these rich aristocrats. Its façade was later embellished by an even greater architect who had imbibed Italian baroque and brought it back to Vienna: Johann Bernhard Fischer von Erlach. Today the Palais Lobkowitz is the French cultural institute. It once hosted glittering receptions and fabulous concerts. The first performance of Beethoven's Eroica Symphony was given here in 1803, dedicated to the hero (some said the scourge) of Europe, Napoleon Bonaparte.

A little way up the Augustinerstrasse is the Augustinian church, a stupendous mixture of gothic and baroque architecture. Duke Frederick the Fair paid for its construction in 1327 and building took place between 1330 and 1339. Three centuries later this magnificent building became the court chapel, and the Habsburgs set about embellishing it. The tower was finished in 1652. Baroque stucco-work was added (though Kaiser Josef II decided to turn the clock back and regothicize parts of the building).

Here lie the hearts of the Habsburgs – 54 of them are preserved in urns in the Heart Crypt (or *Herzgrüftelkammer*). Here Napoleon married his second wife, Marie Louise, in 1810, the daughter of Kaiser Franz I whose Holy Roman Empire the upstart Frenchman had just smashed into oblivion. Here is a bizarre, frightening pyramid tomb by Canova (there is virtually an exact replica in Venice), made for the earthly remains of Maria Theresa's daughter the Archduchess Maria Christine. Here and there on the walls you can still make out ancient wall-paintings. Do not miss stroking the beautifully carved pews or admiring the baroque organ-case. The music in this church is still splendid. (A list of services, with the accompanying music, is posted at the door.) I have heard a superb performance of Mozart's *Missa Brevis* in C Major at an

Organsolomesse on a Sunday.

A plaque on the wall outside records another Mass, held on 13 September 1683 in the presence of Jan III Sobieski, King of Poland, after he had saved Vienna from the destructive savagery of the Turks. In the peaceful years that followed the city was reconstructed, many of the nobility building splendid palaces. Go on to Josefsplatz immediately beyond the church with the renaissance Palais Palffy on the right, its façade dating from 1575. Here Mozart's *Marriage of Figaro* was first performed, and a 'Figaro room' inside commemorates the occasion. Today the aristocrats have departed and the Palais Palffy is an exhibition gallery. But the shades of the great ones remain in the architecture of Josefsplatz. Josefsplatz was once the Augustinian cemetery, which an enterprising Kaiser transformed into a pleasure garden. Today it is dominated by an equestrian statue of Kaiser Josef II, modelled in 1807 by the sculptor Franz Anton Zauer who based it on that of Marcus Aurelius in Rome. The baroque façades of the Hofburg overlook the statue. And next to the Palais Palffy stands the classical Palais Pallavicini, which a banker and count named Moritz Fries commissioned from the architect Ferdinand von Hohenbirg in 1784. The architect designed four massive caryatid women, shamelessly displaying bare legs and breasts, to hold up the portico of the main façade.

At the far end of the square the route passes between the imperial stables and the celebrated Spanish riding school, which Kaiser Ferdinand founded in 1572. Its horses, bred from Andalusian mares mated with Arab and Berber stallions, are known as Lipizzaner because the original imperial stud farm was at Lipizza in Trieste. In their black boots, white breeches, brown jackets and black two-cornered hats, the horsemen exercise their stallions (without stirrups) in the unique skills of classical dressage, once common throughout Europe but now known only here. Tickets are hard to come by, and performances take place on Sunday mornings (and Wednesday evenings) apart from the months of January, February, July, August and the second half of December. Naturally the winter riding school is an architectural masterpiece, designed by Fischer von Erlach and built between 1729 and 1735.

Go on to Michaelerplatz, a square dignified by three famous buildings: the Looshaus, St Michael's church and the imperial palace (the Hofburg). The Looshaus has always seemed to me absurdly overrated. Architecturally it is of singular importance. Designed by Adolf Loos in 1910 (after he had won a competition for the commission), it is virtually without ornamentation apart from the pleasing green marble. Avant-garde, a 'building without eyebrows' as its critics maliciously observed, I find it boring. Others have dubbed it 'cigarette lighter', 'silo', 'dustbin', 'marble coalshed', 'prison'. These critics were all right.

Not so the church of St Michael opposite. It was begun in the thirteenth century, embellished several times, and finally partly rebuilt in the late eighteenth century. In consequence it is an architectural melange. It has a nave, crypt and transept built in the late romanesque style; a choir and tower in the gothic style; a neo-classical façade of 1792; the largest baroque organ in Vienna, built by Johann David Sieber in 1714 and richly gilded; twentieth-century monuments to vanished Habsburgs; and a stunning baroque decoration added to the chancel by the architect d'Avrange in 1781. In 1782 the stuccoist Karl Merville further embellished the chancel with a wildly ornate depiction of the fall of the angels, with cherubs flying giddily about heaven and avenging angels slashing at the damned. As almost always in Viennese churches, there are special boxes in which the upper-crust worshipped so as to keep themselves apart from the lower orders. To the left of the organ as you go in, the flames of hell are busily devouring the damned.

Across the square is the arch of the Michaelertor, with its magnificent wrought ironwork (and its two fountain statues, representing naval and military power, set up in 1897, a couple of decades before Austria's might finally collapsed). This pierces the first of the great façades of the Hofburg, Vienna's imperial palace. This is an extraordinarily complex building unlike, say, Buckingham Palace in London, and yet it still offers a strange unity, a blend of different courtyards and wings (called *Trakte* by the Viennese). Kaiser Franz Josef I helped to create this unity in the second half of the nineteenth century by opening up the way from Michaelerplatz across the great Heldenplatz to the Ring. Fischer von Erlach certainly helped by designing the splendid semi-circular Michaeler-trakt fronting Michaelplatz, which was begun to his plans in 1723, though not completed (and inevitably slightly altered) until the 1890s. The superb dome is 54 metres high.

Through the Michaelertrakt archway lies the square known as In der Burg, an altogether delightful courtyard flanked by the oldest part of the palace, the thirteenth-century Schweizerhof or Swiss Court, rebuilt by Ferdinand I in the first half of the sixteenth century. It is called the Schweizerhof because in the eighteenth century it was guarded by Maria Theresa's Swiss mercenaries. The Schweizertor is a provocative blue and red renaissance gateway, leading to the gothic royal chapel (1447–9) which you can visit only if you go to Mass on Sunday mornings. Facing you across In der Burg is the Leopoldinische Trakt, a late sixteenth-century building added to a hundred years later, and the favourite home of Empress Maria Theresa and her husband Joseph II. Opposite the Schweizerhof is the renaissance Amalientrakt, named after Amalia, the widow of Kaiser Josef I, who lived here. The fourth side of the square contains the official home of the Austrian president, the imperial chancery trakt (Reichskanzleitrakt), a gracefully arrogant baroque building created by Lukas von Hildebrandt in 1723. And in the middle of the square is a statue of Kaiser Franz, the last Holy Roman Emperor (known as Franz II) and Emperor of Austria (in which capacity he was known as Franz I) till 1835.

Franz was one of the weakest rulers imaginable, no match whatsoever for Napoleon Bonaparte and singularly ungenerous to his servants. Ironically, the Milanese sculptor Pompeo Marchesi, who created the statue in the 1840s, has surrounded this unprepossessing man with the four virtues of peace, strength, faith and justice.

Walk on through the Hofburg and into the huge Heldenplatz. Its south-east side is flanked by the great bulk of the New Hofburg, now housing museums and part of the Austrian national library, a massive pile built by Gottfried Semper and Karl Haesenauer in the 1880s and 1890s. The square itself contains two superb equestrian statues, both by Anton Fernkorn. One, sculpted in 1865 at the expense of Kaiser Franz Josef, is of Prince Eugene of Savoy, the soldier-courtier rebuffed by Louis XIV of France who became one of Austria's finest warriors. The other is to my mind a brilliant technical achievement, again paid for by Franz Josef, and this time sculpted five years earlier. It represents the Archduke Charles, Austrian commander at the battle of Aspern (the sole occasion when Napoleon was rebuffed by Austria). The archduke is represented raising the imperial standard, his stallion supporting itself solely on its hind legs, balanced by a magnificent flowing tail. The archduke was once asked whether he had ever performed such a feat, and answered that he was far too small and feeble to have ever lifted such a heavy battle-flag.

On the other side of Heldenplatz is another war memorial: the outer gateway with its twelve Doric pillars, which Peter Nobile designed in the 1820s in the classical style to commemorate the battle of Leipzig. In 1934 its interior was redesigned by Rudolf Wondracek as a memorial to the fallen of the imperial army from 1618 to 1918, and inside is the tomb of an unknown soldier.

We have now reached the Burgring, and a reasonable plan would be to turn right along it and call in at the Café Landmann on the corner of Karl Renner-Ring, opposite the University and beside the city theatre. This was for many years the favourite café of President Bruno Kreisky, Austria's most distinguished president in the years after World War II, and is now the haunt of students, politicians and actresses. The Café Landmann is not cheap. On the other hand, you can read several of the world's newspapers and magazines here while you drink or eat. The Café serves Gösser beer, one of the two most popular kinds drunk in Vienna. As the Viennese say: *Gut, besser, Gösser* (i.e. 'good, better, but Gösser is best'); and *Schwach, schwacher, Schwechater* (i.e. 'weak, weaker, and flat out from too much Schwechater'!)

In the Café Landmann you can order goulash and dumplings. Frankfurter sausages, gherkins and fried eggs, different sorts of fillets, with onions, potatoes and other vegetables smothered in herbs, spices and cheese. If you want to enrich your diet further, finish off your meal with a *Kaffee Maria Theresa*: a black mokka, with orange liqueur and masses of cream on top.

Then walk back through the Volksgarten to Ballhaus Platz. The Volksgarten is filled with enchantments: a bronze fountain of 1875 depicting fauns and nymphs; Peter von Nobile's Theseus temple of 1823; a statue of 1889 commemorating the Austrian dramatist Franz Grillparzer, with scenes from six of his plays; and Nobile's coffee house. Ballhaus Platz contains the splendid Austrian foreign office, which Lukas von Hildebrandt built between 1716 and 1721. It housed the Congress of Vienna which redrew the map of Europe after the Napoleonic wars. In Minoritenplatz to the north is the church of the minor friars (Minoritenkirche), whose hexagonal tower once had a steeple until the Turks blasted it to pieces in 1683. The interior (and most of the building) dates from the fourteenth century and contains an entertainingly bizarre feature: a mosaic copy of Leonardo da Vinci's *Last Supper*, made in 1814 by Giacomo Raffaelli on behalf of Napoleon.

North of this church at no.9 Bankgasse stands one of the three Viennese palaces owned by the fabulous Princes of Liechtenstein. This, their baroque town palace, was designed by Domenico Martinelli in the last years of the seventeenth century. Prince Hans Adam von Liechtenstein (known as Hans Adam the Rich, for so wealthy was he that many supposed he had discovered the secret of turning base metals into gold) called upon another Italian, Gabriel de Gabrieli, to modify and finish it. It has some remarkable treasures inside, including the fantastic baroque staircase which Antonio Bellucci frescoed, Santino Bussi stuccoed and Giovanni Giuliani embellished with sculptures, but the palace is not open. It is some compensation that the 1705 doorway and the main façade are almost as magnificent.

Architecture buffs find this region of Vienna particularly fascinating. For instance, if you wish to see what a nineteenth-century classical architect like Joseph Kornhäusel could add to Vienna's ecclesiastical treasures, turn right down Bankgasse and then left along Herrengasse to see the Schottenkirche (a church originally built for Irish Benedictine monks): curling leaves on the ceiling, a massive reredos behind the high altar, great swags and cherubs and chandeliers. Opposite is the Palais Kinsky, a contortedly elaborate example of early eighteenth-century baroque, designed by Lukas von Hildebrandt for Count Daun. Next to the Schottenkirche is the Schottenhof, once the monastery building and rebuilt in the 1820s. Close by, at no.3 Freyung (so called because fugitives who fled to this square were once given sanctuary), is the Palais Harrach, which Domenico Martinelli began in 1702 (though the façade is basically mid nineteenth-century).

Walk back along Herrengasse past Bankgasse to another magical treat, the Palais Ferstel, formerly the Austro-Hungarian bank and built by the architect Heinrich Ferstel between 1856 and 1859. Its Freyung passage is now a superb shopping arcade, decorated with delicate plasterwork. At its heart lies a fountain displaying three sportive mermaids (each with two tails) holding hands and supporting three medieval workmen. Crowning them all is a damsel with a fish. Glassware, stationery, pottery, clothing, leather goods, and antiques are sold amidst the splendid ironwork. A little further down the street (at no.14) is the Café Central, also by Heinrich Ferstel. This masterpiece of nineteenth-century gothic was savagely damaged in World War II, but now its marble, its delicate plasterwork flowers, its multi-coloured arcading, its arches picked out in green and blue and pink with sweetly repeated flowers and curly brass chandeliers have all been superbly restored. At the doorway is a model of an old Viennese codger drinking coffee. Join him at least in a coffee, especially if the weekend manages to begin on a Thursday lunchtime, when one of those decadent Viennese orchestras composed of teenage girls dressed in blue blouses, black dresses and white boaters plays Strauss and Léhar with the utmost seriousness.

Herrengasse leaves behind the nymphet musicians and continues with shops down one side and palaces on the other in the direction of Michaelerplatz. Here you might pause for a moment at the shop called Loden-Plankl, which has been selling traditional Viennese clothing since 1830. (It is delightful, from the feathered hats for men to the ladies' dirndls; even in winter, wrapped up in furs like Eskimos, Viennese women remain stylish.)

Kohlmarkt now leads north-east into Graben, which was the city moat in Roman times. Duke Leopold VI filled it in in the late twelfth century, and soon it became a busy market square. Its present form is basically nineteenth-century, with two remarkable exceptions.

The first is Lukas von Hildebrandt's Palais Bartollotti-Partenfeld (no.11, Graben), built in 1720. And Graben houses the famous and grisly Viennese plague column, set up in memory of those who died of the plague in 1679. The plague is sculpted as a grotesquely ugly woman with withered breasts, being cast down by faith. Although Fischer von Erlach had a hand in the design, Matthias Rauchmiller was responsible for the overall conception of this baroque masterpiece, though most of the statues (including that of the kneeling donor, Kaiser Leopold I) are by Paul Strudel.

In Graben walk resolutely *away* from the cathedral (saving it for later) and into Jungferngasse to see the church of St Peter — yet another baroque masterpiece by Lukas von Hildebrandt, though incorporating Vienna's second oldest church. Inside, the frescoed dome by J. M. Rottmayr is matched in flamboyance only by M. Steinl's outrageously ornate carving of the martyrdom of St John Nepomuk (who was thrown into the River Moldau). To the right under an altar lies the corpse of St Benedict, happily more or less fully dressed.

Behind the church of St Peter take Küfussgasse into Brandstätte and walk along it to the cathedral. You can still delay the high point of the tour by turning left down Rotenturmstrasse, past the archbishop's palace on the right (instantly recognizable by his carved coat of arms incorporating a cardinal's hat). The palace was designed by an Italian, Giovanni Coccapani, and built between 1630 and 1640.

Rotenturmstrasse houses dress shops, and leads to Vienna's oldest street, the Fleischmarkt, which the Romans called Via Carnorum. This is the site of the city's first meat market, and the butchers' guild established itself here in 1330. Turn right along Fleischmarkt. Past the Greek Orthodox church on the left (designed by Theophil von Hansen and built in the 1780s) appears the jettied medieval inn where 'Ach Du Lieber Augustin' was first sung (a ditty about the charismatic medieval Viennese preacher Abraham a Santa Clara). Then turn right again at the post office into Postgasse where there is a splendid Dominican church of 1634. Even more splendid is the square reached through the archway on the right. The lovely former university, finished in 1755 by the French architect Jean Nicolas Jalot de Ville-Issay, stands beside the Jesuit university church which Kaiser Ferdinand II paid for in the early seventeenth century (in thanksgiving for the Catholic victory over the Protestants during the Thirty Years War at the Battle of the White Mountain).

Another delight of this area is Schönlaterngasse, a winding street lined with splendid houses – part palaces, part medieval homeliness. Turn right at the end into Sonnenfelsgasse and you will emerge into Lugeck, with its welcome Café Gutenberg (opposite a statue of Gutenberg, the inventor of printing). And Lugeck leads back to Rotenturmstrasse.

Cross Rotenturmstrasse and follow Lichtensteg to explore the Hoher Markt, the oldest square in the city. This is where the Roman praetorian Marcus Aurelius once lived. At no.3 you can visit excavated Roman ruins (between 10.00 and 16.00 on weekdays, between 14.00 and 18.00 on Saturdays and between 09.00 and 13.00 on Sundays). The lovely marriage fountain depicting the wedding of the Virgin Mary was designed by Fischer von Erlach around 1730. And here is the magical art nouveau (*Jugendstil*) Anker Clock, made by Franz von Matsch in 1911. It plays tunes on the hour like a quaint fairground organ, while marionettes depicting figures from Viennese history, 2.7 metres high, trundle quaintly across a flying buttress.

Vienna's synagogue is nearby, down Judengasse and then right along Seitenstettengasse – an oddly classical building for a synagogue, built by Josef Kornhäusel in 1826. Opposite, through the arch, is Vienna's oldest church, the Ruprechtskirche. To visit the most spectacular, return to Rotenturmstrasse from Hoher Markt, turn right, and there it is.

The famous fretted spire of St Stephen's cathedral is 136.7 metres high. What the English visitor Frances Trollope wrote about it in the 1830s remains true today. 'This church of St Stephen's is so very beautiful, with its dark mellow tone of colouring, its rich carvings, its graceful proportions, and the indescribable air of dim religious sanctity which seems to envelop every part of it, that I suspect it is not easy to form a fair unprejudiced opinion on [its] merits,' she wrote. 'The interior of this beautiful church is as fine as the exterior,' Mrs Trollope added. 'The pillars which support the nave are the most richly ornamented that I remember; and the extraordinary profusion of stone carving in pillars, pulpit, altars, and monuments, gives to the whole building the air of a holy museum.' Much of the building had to be restored after the bombs of World War II but this has been done splendidly. Of the many delights in this building, notice the lifelike figures carved on the pulpit, representing the four doctors of the Church.

Friedrich III, the first Habsburg crowned as Holy Roman Emperor, has his tomb here. But a far grislier and fascinating spot for those who wish to meditate on the death of kings is the imperial crypt (the *Kaisergruft*) under the Capuchin church in Neuer Markt. On the way there, take a drink in Adolf Loos' American Bar, not far from the cathedral, a building I find much more congenial than his Looshaus in Michaelerplatz. Find it by walking a few hundred metres along Kärntner Strasse from the cathedral and taking the first right into little Kärntner Durchgang. This 1908 building is a tiny masterpiece, sensationally crammed into a space 4.6 by 2.4 metres.

A few paces further on along Kärntner Strasse, turn right into Donnergasse which leads into the Neuer Markt. The magnificent fountain playing in the square is the most famous creation of the architect Georg Raphael Donner and the finest in Vienna. Known as the Donnerbrunnen, it was set up in 1739 and depicts Providence surrounded by four rivers (the March, Enns, Traun and Ybbs).

At the far corner of the Neuer Markt stands the Capuchin church, whose burial vault is the imperial mausoleum. Its opening times are fairly inconvenient (from May to September daily from 09.30 to 16.30; from October to April daily from 09.30 to 12.00), but a visit is richly rewarded. Ring the doorbell to the right of the church's main entrance and a custodian lets you in.

Kaiser Mathias and his wife Anna (who died in 1619 and 1618 respectively) left money to found a Capuchin monastery here, and instructed that they were to be buried in the crypt of the church. Twelve Kaisers and fifteen of their consorts lie in the crypt today (though their hearts are in the Augustiner church and their intestines in the cathedral). The Empress Marie Louise, second wife of Napoleon Bonaparte, was brought here after her death in 1847 and lies next to the sarcophagus of her father Kaiser Franz. Napoleon's son (the Duke of Reichstadt) also lay here for 108 years until Hitler took his corpse back to Paris. The last person to be buried in the crypt was the wife of Karl, the last Austrian emperor (she died in 1944). The only non-Habsburg here is Countess Fuchs, the beloved governess of Maria Theresa. All of them rest in sarcophagi, the oldest simple lead or pewter ones, the later ornate, masterly (and frequently grisly) copper ones.

The crypt is one of the most horrible places I know. The tone is set immediately right of the entrance by a grinning bronze skull, wearing the imperial crown, one of four crowned death-heads decorating the sarcophagus of Kaiser Carl VI who died in 1740. But the masterpiece among these tombs is undoubtedly the double sarcophagus which, twenty-six years before her death, Maria Theresa had constructed for herself and her husband Franz Stephan I of Lorraine. It was designed by the brilliant Viennese master of the rococo, Balthasar Ferdinand Moll, and Maria Theresa had to have the crypt extended to fit it in. In front of them is the sarcophagus of the enlightened despot Joseph II, who died in 1790.

There is tragedy here too. One sarcophagus contains Archduke Maximilian of Austria, who misguidedly agreed to set himself up as Emperor of Mexico and was executed by Mexican revolutionaries in 1867. And his brother, old Kaiser Franz Josef, had the crypt further enlarged to accommodate his own massive sarcophagus, which is flanked (on a lower level, of course) by those of his wife Elisabeth, who was assassinated at Geneva in 1898, and his son Crown Prince Rudolf, who shot himself at Mayerling in 1889.

Leave the crypt and retrace your steps to Kärntner Strasse. This is Vienna's busiest pedestrianized shopping street, lined with banks and noisy with one-man bands. Street artists too frequently offer free entertainment. I once watched a brilliant white-faced mimic, who cunningly walked behind unsuspecting visitors, perfectly imitating their every gesture, while they wondered what other people were laughing at.

As you walk right along Kärntner Strasse, you will see the church of the Knights of Malta (the Malteserkirche), built in 1809, on the east side. Here too is Vienna's casino, where people play blackjack, roulette and baccarat in the former Esterhazy palace.

Pass by the opera on your right, cross the Ring with care and continue along Hauptstrasse to Karlsplatz. Here are both art nouveau and baroque treasures. To the right (by way of Friedrichstrasse) you reach Josef Maria Olbrich's stunning *Jugendstil* Secession Building of 1898. Built for avant-garde artists (led by Gustav Klimt) who wished to distinguish themselves sharply from contemporary academic art, it is topped by a golden cupola of intertwining leaves (which contemporary enemies of the Secession dubbed 'the golden cabbage'). Over the entrance is set the legend, 'TO EACH AGE ITS ART, TO ART ITS FREEDOM'.

To the left, on Karlsplatz itself, are two exquisite art nouveau railway stations designed by Olbrich's teacher Otto Wagner. Only one serves its original function (housing an underground station); the other is a most elegant coffee-house.

The stupendous Karlskirche surpasses even these lovely works of architecture. Kaiser Karl VI vowed to build this church should the plague of 1713 pass harmlessly by and he dedicated it to St Charles Borromeo. The inscription over the church recalls its desperate origins: *Vota mea reddam in conspectu timentium Deum* ('My vow is fulfilled in the sight of those who fear God'). A galaxy of baroque masters competed to design it, and Johann Bernhard Fischer von Erlach won, defeating among others such geniuses as Lukas von Hildebrandt and Ferdinando Galli-Bibiena. When he died in 1723 his son Josef Emmanuel Fischer von Erlach finished the work. Outside are two monumental columns, modelled on Trajan's column in Rome, with spiral reliefs depicting the life of St Charles Borromeo. Imperial eagles crown them. Inside, Michael Rottmayr frescoed the dome to the glory of Charles Borromeo, and (in a moment of Counter-Reformation arrogance) depicted Luther's translation of the Bible being consigned to the flames of hell.

Leave the church, turn right and walk along Symphonikerstrasse into Technikerstrasse. On the left of Technikerstrasse is the French embassy built in 1909 to the designs of Chédanne, a building that would lack interest save for the singular fact that it was intended not for Vienna but for Constantinople. The plans for two embassies were mixed up, and that destined for Turkey ended up here.

Technikerstrasse leads on to Schwarzenbergplatz, with its impressive Soviet war memorial, built in 1945 to honour the Russian dead of World War II. To the left is an equally impressive statue of Prince Schwarzenberg, generalissimo of the Austrian, Prussian and Russian armies when the coalition of three nations took on Napoleon in 1813 and 1814. And so Schwarzenbergstrasse leads back to the Café Schwarzenberg, where we began our tour.

Further delights

The Belvedere
The delights of Vienna are by no means exhausted by this tour. On no account should a weekend visitor miss seeing the Belvedere. The Belvedere is a 10-minute walk from the Café Schwarzenberg or is reached by tram no.71 in the direction Zentralfriedhof (alight at Unteres Belvedere).

Prince Eugene of Savoy commissioned the Belvedere after he had repulsed the Turks in 1693. The Bavarian landscape gardener,

Dominique Girard, designed the splendid tiered gardens. With fountains and pools and shady corners, this is a wonderful place to sit, and from the top you have a view out over the city. Johann Lukas von Hildebrandt built the Lower Belvedere from 1714 to 1716 and the Upper Belvedere from 1721 to 1722. The Lower Belvedere is a magical museum of baroque art. The Upper Belvedere is even more astounding (reached by the D tram in the direction Südbahnhof), housing amongst many other treasures Austria's museum of nineteenth- and twentieth-century art. Here is a Hans Makarat room, with his massive *Triumph of Ariadne*. Here you can see the wan figure of Kaiser Franz Josef's wife Elisabeth, painted in pensive mood by Anton Romakos in 1883. Here is a whole room of wild works by Oskar Kokoschka. It is hard to know what to single out, but I was particularly drawn to Egon Schiele's anguished paintings of his tormented women (in *Die Familie*, painted in 1918, even the baby looks pensive, while the parents are deeply sad), and above all to the room full of paintings by Gustav Klimt.

Here you can see Klimt's bejewelled *Kiss* of 1908, a sumptuous portrait of Frau Fritza Riedler which Klimt painted in 1906, and an even richer portrait of Frau Adele Bloch-Bauer done the following year. Here too is Klimt's unfinished, delicious painting of Eve nestling against Adam, dated 1917. There is also a fascinating work entitled *The Bride*, which was unfinished when Klimt died of influenza in 1918. This reveals that, before adding dresses to his portraits of women, the artist first painted them nude.

The Belvedere is open every day except Mondays from 10.00 to 16.00.

Schönbrunn

Do not miss, either, a trip to Schönbrunn (take the U2 underground railway to Schottentor), the Versailles of the Habsburgs, though designed to surpass Louis XIV's creation and unlike Versailles built on a hill-top site. Fischer von Erlach began it, commissioned by Kaiser Leopold I in the late eighteenth century. Maria Theresa completed it, employing Italian architects to transform baroque into rococo. The treasures it contains include a Viennese hall of mirrors, the celebrated peacock room and the tapestry hall. It is surrounded by glorious gardens crowned by Fischer von Erlach's megalomaniac triumphal monument set on top of the hill above the palace. The

grounds are open daily from 06.00 to dusk. The palace is open from
09.00–12.00 and from 13.00–17.00 (closing an hour earlier in
winter).

The Liechtenstein Palace

Another Sunday treat is to visit the Liechtenstein Garden Palace,
which opens every day except Thursdays from 10.00 to 18.00, and
is reached by the D Tram (direction Nussdorf; alight at
Fürstengasse, when you see a sign saying *Museum Moderner Kunst*
on the left). Domenico Martinelli designed this baroque delight for
Prince Hans Adam von Liechtenstein, and it was built from 1688 to
1711. Today it houses the Austrian museum of modern art (Andy
Warhol, Schmidt-Rottluff, a fat, half-dressed lady painted by Max
Beckmann, pop art by Roy Liechtenstein). But to my mind it should
be visited above all to have the experience of walking through a
magnificent baroque palace. Notice the superb ceilings, painted by
the prince's Italian agent Franceschini.

The tram ride from the centre of Vienna to the Liechtenstein
Garden Palace follows the monumental boulevards known as the
Ring. Buildings along the route to look out for are the Votivskirche
with its twin gothic towers, paid for by the family of Kaiser Franz
Josef after he had survived an assassination attempt in 1853 and
designed by Heinrich Ferstel; the splendid City Hall, designed by
Friedrich Schmidt in 1872; Heinrich Ferstel's university building,
constructed from 1873 to 1883; Theophil von Hansen's 'Greek-
antique' parliament building of the same date; and the City Theatre,
designed by Gottfried Semper (who built the celebrated Dresden
Opera House), opened in the presence of Kaiser Franz Josef in 1888
and the scene of some of the greatest triumphs of his friend the
actress Katharina Schratt.

The imperial apartments in the Hofburg

The imperial apartments in the Hofburg (see the city map) can be
visited every day from 08.30 to 16.30 (13.00 on Sundays). The
Kaiser's winter palace has 3600 rooms in all but happily the guided
tour takes in only the finest. Here you are shown three portraits of
Kaiser Franz Josef, the last painted when he was a weary man of 85,
a year before his death. Here are his simple soldier's bed and his
smoking room (Franz Josef loved cigars). Here are portraits and

statues of his wife, with her tiny waist. Most bizarrely, here are the hanging wall-bars and gymnastic rings of this barely sane woman, who dieted with anorexic fanaticism, anxiously seeking signs of the slightest wrinkle on her exquisite features.

The Prater

The Prater today is far more than the great wheel of *The Third Man*. If that is frightening enough, I should never dream of personally experiencing the convoluted Big Dippers and the terrifyingly spinning fun-fair entertainment, not to speak of the ghost trains. Children love them. You can eat in restaurants or cycle under the trees while they enjoy the fright of their lives.

The speediest way to the Prater is by the underground railway from Karlsplatz (line U1, direction Zentrum Kagran), and you can have a more leisurely ride back by tram from outside the main gates.

Excursion to
Baden and Mayerling

This excellent day's excursion needs a hired car but the total distance involved is scarcely 100 kilometres. Take the road from the Café Schwarzenberg to Schwarzenberg Platz and bear right into Prinz Eugen Strasse. Now follow the signs to Laxenburg (which take you along Laxenburger Strasse). The parish church of Laxenburg is astoundingly beautiful, and homely too, a lovely baroque building, begun in 1693 and finished in 1726. Inside, a carved St Michael spiritedly downs Lucifer, the battle depicted in stucco-work below the organ. The nearby town hall is decorated with paintings of Duke Albrecht III in 1388 giving Laxenburg the right to hold its market, and Maria Theresa directing the building of the *Schloss* in 1753. In the Rathaus Stübe nearby you can peacefully drink a quiet glass of beer, before taking a walk in the park which surrounds the *Schloss*.

Leave Laxenburg by following the signs for Münchendorf and then Guntramsdorf and find your way to the delightful wine village of Gumpoldskirchen. Pine branches and lamps tell you that here the *Heuriger* are functioning in full swing. All around are vineyards, and in the middle of the hamlet stands the ancient church of the Teutonic knights. From Gumpoldskirchen follow the road to the enchanting spa town of Baden, and park by the parish church. Here the pedestrianized centre resembles a charming village, with shops selling books, leather goods, fashionable clothing and food. The town hall is a splendid classical affair, built by Josef Kornhäusel in 1815, resembling a well-proportioned piece of Wedgwood pottery, painted yellow and white. In the centre of the town-hall square is a magnificent baroque column built as a thank-offering for deliverance from one of the countless plagues that once troubled the people of these parts. (This one occurred in 1714.) Beyond it, opposite the town hall, is the humble Kaiser house of 1792, summer residence of Kaiser Franz I between 1813 and 1834 and of Kaiser Karl IV between 1916 and 1918.

Find the little Magdalenenhof, at no.10 Frauengasse, opposite the former Augustinian monastery, where monks flourished from 1285 until 1811 and which now serves as a school. Beethoven spent the autumn of 1822 here and the dramatist Grillparzer stayed each summer from 1848 to 1850, and again in 1860. Turning right at the bottom of this street will bring you to the classical Leopold's spa (behind the market) and then to the majestic domed casino. (The market sells vegetables, fruit and chickens, closing on Saturdays at noon and all day Sunday.)

Old Kaiser Franz Josef, virtually deserted by his wife, would bring his friend the actress Katharina Schratt to Baden. It is now not easy to determine precisely how close these two were, though there were periods when they breakfasted together every day; and once, overwhelmed with jealousy that she continued to visit her former lover Count Hans Wilczek, the Kaiser begged Katharina never to see the count again. Franz Josef knew that the request was unreasonable. 'My only excuse is my jealousy and that I love you very much,' he wrote, begging Katharina to tear up the letter. (Naturally, she did not.)

From Baden drive along the route signposted Helenental, past ancient ruined castles to left and right. The road to Mayerling, which lies a mere 14 kilometres from Baden, appears quite suddenly on the left. Here stood the hunting lodge in which, one fateful day in 1889, Crown Prince Rudolf shot his mistress Mary Vetsera and then himself. He lies in the imperial crypt in Vienna. She was smuggled in a coach, a dressed-up corpse, to the monastery of Heiligenkreuz; in an attempt to hush up the scandal.

At Mayerling all that remains of those scandal-defaced buildings is a little hunting-lodge. Rudolf's mother was of the orthodox faith, and an orthodox nunnery was set up here to care for the spot where her son died. The nuns will still take you round the more or less obliterated scene of his suicide. Then drive on past the convent up over the hill for four more kilometres to the sensational monastery of Heiligenkreuz, founded by Duke Leopold the Saint in 1135. You can wander freely around much of the entrancing pink and white irregular cloister. Tours of the romanesque chapel, library and some of the richly decorated monks' quarters take place on the hour from 09.00 to 11.00 and from 13.30 to 16.30 on weekdays, and from 13.30 to 16.30 on Sundays.

The earthly remains of Mary Vetsera are not in the monks' cemetery (where little lights are kept burning by the living to remember the dead), but just outside the village of Heiligenkreuz. Just where the road to Mödling leaves the village a sign *Zum Friedhof* points the way. Drive up between the trees to the little parking place. Directly inside the cemetery gate turn left and walk up for a few short paces to her grave, with its marble cross and its inscription:

MARY
FREIIN V. VETSERA
GEB 19 MARZ 1871
GEST 30 JÄNNER 1889
Wie eine Blume sprosst der
Mensch auf und wird gebrochen.
Job 14.2.

[Mary
Fräulein V. Vetsera
born 19 March 1871
died 30 January 1889
'We bloom like a flower
and then are cut down.'
Job 14.2.]

Drive on to Mödling, noticing Schloss Liechtenstein, which was founded in 1165, high on its hill to the left. In the middle of Mödling is a memorial to the doughty mayor, Josef Schöfell, who stopped the destruction and sale of the Vienna woods. Beethoven loved this spot. He spent the summers of 1818 and 1820 here. 'God Almighty, I am happy in the woods,' he wrote. 'You speak to me through every tree.' Wagner lived and composed here. The musician Hugo Wolf found inspiration in the neighbourhood. And Schubert composed lullabies at Mödling.

To climb to the late gothic parish church of St Othmar is quite a stiff undertaking, but well worthwhile. A plaque on its wall marks the spot where virtually the whole population of Mödling was slaughtered by the Turks in 1683. The church itself was destroyed by the infidel and rebuilt in 1690 with a splendid baroque roof, pulpit and organ. Next to it is the lovely little chapel of St Pantaleon, built in the second half of the twelfth century, with contemporary wall-paintings inside and a baroque dome. On its romanesque doorway carved huntsmen and dogs pursue a stag. Now walk down Pfarrgasse, with its renaissance town hall and two ancient buildings (one dated 1564, the other late fifteenth-century), as far as Kornmarkt. Everywhere are elegant boutiques, ancient houses, cafés and tea shops. Kaiserin Elisabeth-Strasse boasts shoe shops spilling out on to the street and leads to the Spitalkirche. Just across the main road from here is a rolling countryside of grass and trees, running alongside the Mödling brook whose ripples Schubert tried to match in music. And then Trieste Strasse leads you back to the Wiedner Hauptstrasse, which in turn leads to Vienna.

Food and drink

Don't suppose because of their apparently common language that Germans and Austrians share similar food and drink. Viennese food is richer, far more sensual than German, enriched by the traditions of

Hungarian and Serbian cooking. It can, however, be quite as heavy and filling as any German dish. If you try escalopes of pork in cheese dough with spinach dumplings (*Schweinspiccata in Käseteig gebacken mit Spinatspätzln*), you will probably wish you hadn't started the meal with, say, beef broth with semolina dumplings (*Giessknockerl-suppe*). Heavier still is a Viennese favourite: boiled rump of beef served with creamed spinach and hashed potatoes (*Tafelspitz mit den klassischen Beilagen*).

But the dishes on Viennese menus can be as appetizing as these, without being quite so heavy and rich. Typical first courses (*Vorspeisen*) are baked mushrooms (*Gebackene Champignons*), or *Heringsalat*, finely sliced pickled herrings with diced cucumber and apples. Favourite soups (*Suppen*) include a broth with liver dumplings (*Leberknödelsuppe*), *Markknödelsuppe*, a clear soup with bone marrow dumplings, *Tropfteigsuppe*, a soup with Swabian dumplings, and goulash soup (*Gulyassuppe*).

As for the main course, leaving aside the celebrated *Wiener Schnitzel* in its various forms (*Holsteiner Schnitzel, Champion Schnitzel* and the like), Viennese specialities include chicken in paprika sauce (*Paprikahuhn*); the simple and delicious *Wiener Zwiebelrostbraten*, an entrecôte steak served with roast onions; the yet simpler, slightly more piquant *Bauernschmaus*, varieties of pork on a bed of sauerkraut; and the powerful veal knuckle with sour cream (*Kalbsvögerl mit Rahm*). Boiled short ribs (*Beinfleisch*) is another country dish come to town.

Slightly more up-market dishes (but not much more so) are tender *Gespickten Rindsbraten*, a sirloin larded with bacon and dressed in a red wine sauce; and pork cutlets served in Serbian fashion (*Schweinkoteletten 'Serbische Art'*), that is garnished with onions, tomatoes and pimentoes enriched with a spicy sauce.

As for drink, the Viennese relish a delightful group of white wines (particularly Grüner Veltliner and Riesling Kabinett), red wines (predominantly Blauer Burgunder and Blaufränkisch) and the splendidly refreshing Sekt.

The Viennese also drink endless cups of coffee, one of which they entertainingly name after the garb of monastic orders: a *Kapuziner* is a black mokka with copious dollops of cream. For my own part I always order a *mélange*, a reasonably milky compound without the usually obligatory rich thick cream.

Probably the best place to enjoy Viennese food and wine at remarkably inexpensive prices is in one of the *Heuriger* in the Grinzing district, where proprietors sell their own family cultivated wine. Along with the wine you can eat mayonnaise potato salad or Austrian dumplings, bouillon with liver dumplings, veal or pork cutlets and skewers of pork, finishing off with cottage cheese curd pie or apple strudel crammed with cream.

Night life

Vienna means music, with an annual Haydn festival in March, waltz and operetta concerts from April until October, the 'Viennese summer of Music' throughout July and August and the famous New Year's Day concert of the Vienna Philharmonic, as well as the performances at the Staatsoper (at no. 2 Opernring) and the Volksoper (at no.28 Währinger Strasse). Jazz fans should sample the delights of 'Jazz-Galarie Casablanca' (at no.2 Goldschlagstrasse), 'Jazzland' (at no.29 Franz-Josefs-Kai), 'Papa's Tapas' (at no.10 Schwarzenbergplatz) or 'Opus One' (at no.11 Mahlerstrasse). Remember too that the Burgtheater is only one of five major Viennese theatres.

Night life in Vienna does exist, but fitfully and not as super-abundantly as that of Paris. The Casanova Revue-Theater at no.1 Dorotheergasse offers 'internationale Erotikshows'; Eve, a night-club at no.3 Führichgasse (on the corner with Kärntnerstrasse), promises patrons an 'elegantes Striptease-Lokal'; the Mona Lisa club at no.21 Reinprechtsdorfer Strasse claims to be Vienna's most intimate bar; the Moulin Rouge at no.11 Walfischgasse describes itself as the city's premier night-club; the advertisements for the Opium-Höhle at no.4 Habsburgergasse simply proclaim 'girls, girls, girls'.

A useful monthly guide-book, *Hallo Wien*, is a compendium of information on sightseeing, culture, wining and dining and entertainment, published by the Vienna Chamber of Commerce,

Tourist Board and Cultural Office. Most hotels and the Tourist Office at no.5 Kinderspitalgasse offer information about opera and concerts. In addition to *Hallo Wien*, the tourist board publishes a monthly leaflet (called simply *Programm*), setting out virtually every cultural event in the city.

Gamblers can play roulette, baccarat and blackjack at the Casino Wien (at no.41 Kärntnerstrasse) daily from 16.00.

Important information

Vienna's international airport, Wien Schwechat, is 19 kilometres from the centre of the city. The airport bus runs from here to the Vienna Hilton, every thirty minutes from 06.00 to 08.00 and then every twenty minutes until 19.20. Aeroplanes arriving after 19.20 are also met by buses, and a regular train service connects Schwechat with Vienna's south and west railway stations.

Transport within Vienna is beautifully integrated, with trams, buses and the new underground railway all accepting 3-day Vienna rover tickets, which can be bought at tourist information offices, at the south and west railway stations, at tobacconists and at travel agents, as well as in the U-Bahn information offices of Karlsplatz, Stephansplatz, Praterstern and Zentrum-Kagran. Buying blocks of five, eight or more tickets (which can also be obtained from vending machines) presents considerable savings. When boarding a tram, bus or train, a ticket should be stamped in the little machines at the stations or on the vehicles. Many trams and trains are *Schaffnerlos*, i.e. running without conductors, though from time to time ticket inspectors appear, with powers to fine those travelling without tickets.

Viennese banks close at weekends, opening on weekdays from 08.00 to 15.00, with an extension on Thursdays until 17.30. The exchange agencies on the west and south railway stations operate daily from 07.00 to 22.00. Notice too that Austrians love holidays, when nearly everything closes down. A few are on 1 and 6 January,

Easter Monday, May Day, Ascension Day, Whit Monday, Corpus Christi, 15 August, 26 October, 1 November, Christmas Day and Boxing Day.

Index